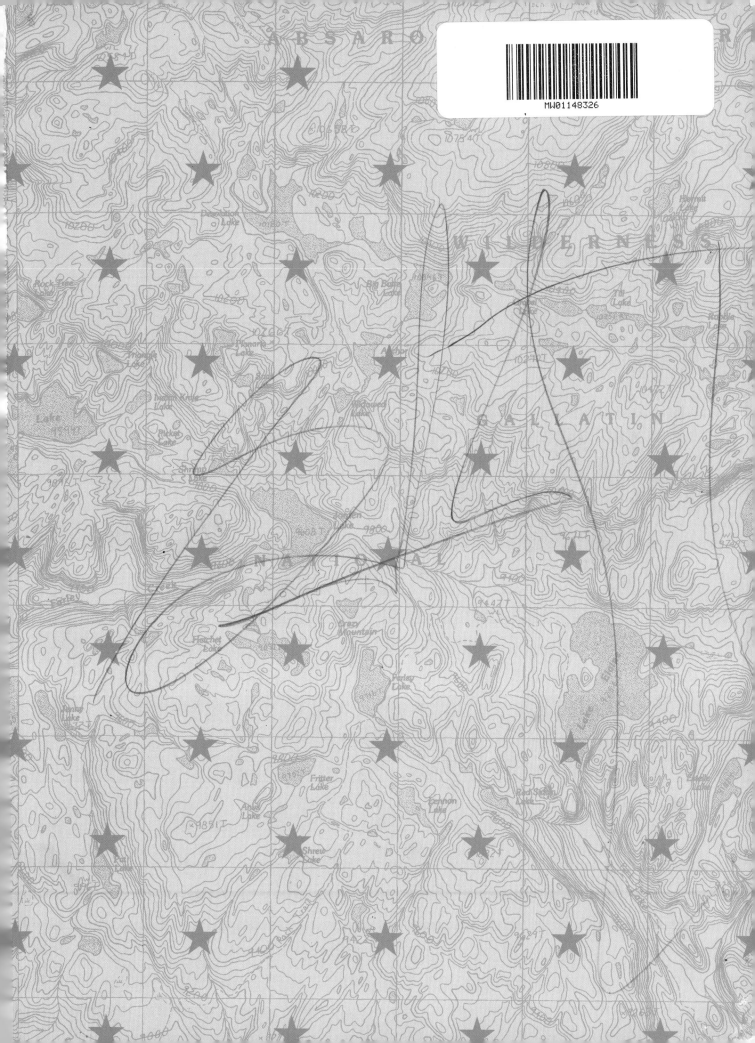

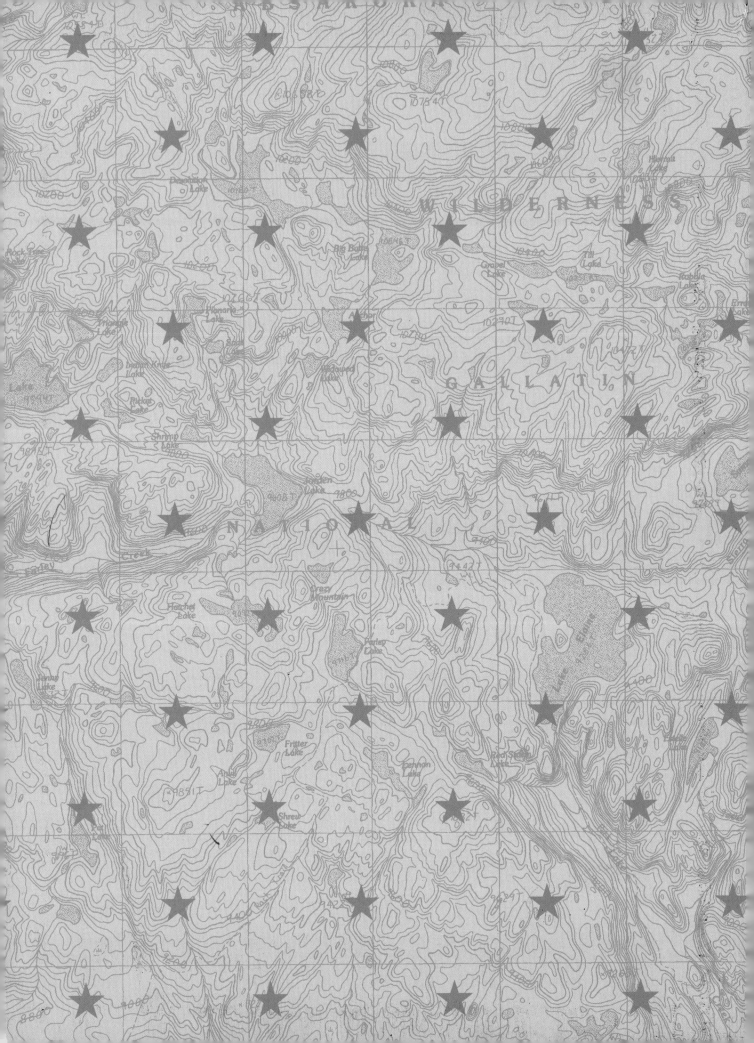

HOUGHTON MIFFLIN

SOCIAL STUDIES

★ ILLINOIS STUDIES ★

Visit **Education Place**®
www.eduplace.com/kids

HOUGHTON MIFFLIN   BOSTON

ILLINOIS

★ AUTHORS ★

Senior Author
Dr. Herman J. Viola
Curator Emeritus
Smithsonian Institution

Dr. Cheryl Jennings
Project Director
Florida Institute of
    Education
University of North Florida

Dr. Sarah Witham
Bednarz
Associate Professor,
    Geography
Texas A&M University

Dr. Mark C. Schug
Professor and Director
Center for Economic
    Education
University of Wisconsin,
    Milwaukee

Dr. Carlos E. Cortés
Professor Emeritus, History
University of California,
Riverside

Dr. Charles S. White
Associate Professor
School of Education
Boston University

Consulting Authors
Dr. Dolores Beltran
Assistant Professor
Curriculum Instruction
California State University, Los Angeles
(Support for English Language Learners)

Dr. MaryEllen Vogt
Co-Director
California State University Center
for the Advancement of Reading
(Reading in the Content Area)

HOUGHTON MIFFLIN
SOCIAL STUDIES

★ ILLINOIS STUDIES ★

 HOUGHTON MIFFLIN   BOSTON

ILLINOIS

Consultants

Philip J. Deloria
Associate Professor
Department of History
  and Program in
  American Studies
University of Michigan

Lucien Ellington
UC Professor of Education
  and Asia Program
  Co-Director
University of Tennessee,
Chattanooga

Thelma Wills Foote
Associate Professor
University of California,
Irvine

Stephen J. Fugita
Distinguished Professor
Psychology and Ethnic
  Studies
Santa Clara University

Charles C. Haynes
Senior Scholar
First Amendment Center

Ted Hemmingway
Professor of History
The Florida Agricultural &
  Mechanical University

Douglas Monroy
Professor of History
The Colorado College

Lynette K. Oshima
Assistant Professor
Department of Language,
  Literacy and Sociocultural
  Studies and Social Studies
  Program Coordinator
University of New Mexico

Jeffrey Strickland
Assistant Professor, History
University of Texas Pan
  American

Clifford E. Trafzer
Professor of History and
  American Indian Studies
University of California,
Riverside

Teacher Reviewers

Barbara Carson
Robert Crown School
Wauconda, IL

Susan Maki
Cotton Creek Elementary
Wauconda, IL

Printed in the U.S.A.

ISBN: 0-618-42377-X

123456789-WC-12 11 10 09 08 07 06 05

Contents

Contents . . . . vi–xvii

▶ About Your Textbook xviii

▶ Reading Social Studies xxii

▶ Social Studies: Why It Matters xxiv

Bringing the world to your classroom!

UNIT 1 The Land and the People

🌐 **Unit Almanac** — Connect to Today 2

CHAPTER 1 Illinois's Land and Early People   4

Vocabulary Preview Reading Strategy: Predict and Infer 4

Lesson 1 | Core   **Land and Water** 6
         | Extend Geography — Lost Kaskaskia 10

Lesson 2 | Core   **Early People** 12
         | Extend History — Cahokia: The Great City 16

Map and Globe Skills Review Map Skills 18

Lesson 3 | Core   **The Illinois** 20
         | Extend Economics — Canoe Traders 26

Chapter 1 Review and Test Prep 28

Unit 1 Review 🅦 Current Events Project 30

UNIT 2   Exploration and Colonization   32

🌐 **Unit Almanac** — Connect to Today 34

CHAPTER 2   Exploring Illinois   36

Vocabulary Preview   Reading Strategy: Question 36

Lesson 1 | Core   **Early Exploration** 38
          | Extend   Primary Source — Mapping the Land 42

Lesson 2 | Core   **The French and British in Illinois** 44
          | Extend   Technology — Fort de Chartres 48

Graph and Chart Skills   Make a Timeline 50

Chapter 2 Review and Test Prep 52

CHAPTER 3   Conflict in Illinois   54

Vocabulary Preview   Reading Strategy: Summarize 54

Lesson 1 | Core   **Controlling the Land** 56
          | Extend   Geography — Looking West 60

Reading and Thinking Skills   Identify Cause and Effect 62

Lesson 2 | Core   **The American Revolution** 64
          | Extend   History — Surrender at Vincennes 68

Chapter 3 Review and Test Prep 70

Unit 2 Review   (WR)   Current Events Project 72

UNIT 3

Growth and Expansion   74

🌐 **Unit Almanac** — Connect to the Nation 76

CHAPTER 4   The Illinois Territory   78

Vocabulary Preview   Reading Strategy: Question 78

Lesson 1   Core   **A New Territory** 80
            Extend   History — Lewis and Clark 84

Graph and Chart Skills   Read a Circle Graph 86

Lesson 2   Core   **Tecumseh and the War of 1812** 88
            Extend   Biography — Ninian Edwards 92

Chapter 4 Review and Test Prep 94

CHAPTER 5   Illinois Becomes a State   96

Vocabulary Preview   Reading Strategy: Monitor and Clarify 96

Lesson 1   Core   **Statehood** 98
            Extend   Readers' Theater — The Illinois
            Constitutional Convention 102

Map and Globe Skills   Make a Map 106

Lesson 2   Core   **Western Expansion** 108
            Extend   Technology — Farming in Illinois 114

Chapter 5 Review and Test Prep 116

CHAPTER 6   **The Civil War**   **118**

Vocabulary Preview   Reading Strategy: Question 118

Lesson 1 | Core   **A Nation Divided** **120**
         | Extend   **Primary Sources** — Galena Goes to War:
                     A Memoir **124**

Citizenship Skills Understand Point of View **126**

Lesson 2 | Core   **Fighting the War** **128**
         | Extend   **Biographies** — Illinois Women
                     in the Civil War **132**

Chapter 6 Review and Test Prep **134**

Special Section Abraham Lincoln **136**

Unit 3 Review (WR) **Current Events Project**...............**144**

UNIT 4   Illinois Grows

UNIT 4   **Illinois Grows**   146

🌐 **Unit Almanac** — Connect to Today 148

CHAPTER 7   **A Time of Change**   150

Vocabulary Preview   **Reading Strategy:** Summarize 150

Lesson 1 | Core   **Illinois Industry** 152
          Extend   **Economics** — A Railroad Economy 156

Lesson 2 | Core   **Changing Times**........................158
          Extend   **Citizenship** — Hull House Reformers 162

Lesson 3 | Core   **War and Growth** 164
          Extend   **Literature** — "Your Illinois" by Kevin Stein 170

Lesson 4 | Core   **Chicago**............................172
          Extend   **Biographies** — Chicagoans Making News 176

📝 **Study Skills**   Identify Primary and Secondary Sources 178

Chapter 7 Review and Test Prep 180

| CHAPTER 8 | | Government of the People | 182 |

Vocabulary Preview   Reading Strategy: Question 182

Lesson 1 | Core | United States Government 184
         | Extend | Primary Sources — National Symbols 188

Reading and Thinking Skills Summarize 190

Lesson 2 | Core | State and Local Government 192
         | Extend | Readers' Theater — A Visit
         | | to the Capitol 196

Lesson 3 | Core | Your Role in Government 200
         | Extend | Citizenship — Let's Vote! 204

Citizenship Skills Make a Decision 206

Chapter 8 Review and Test Prep 208

Unit 4 Review WR Current Events Project 210

UNIT 5 Illinois and the World 212

🌐 **Unit Almanac** — Connect to the Nation 214

CHAPTER 9 Exploring the Midwest 216

Vocabulary Preview   Reading Strategy: Predict and Infer 216

Lesson 1 | Core   **Land and Climate** 218
         | Extend **Geography** — The Mighty Mississippi 222

Lesson 2 | Core   **Resources and Economy** 224
         | Extend **Economics** — Supply and Demand 228

Lesson 3 | Core   **The Great Lakes States** 230
         | Extend **Literature** — "Trouble at Fort La Pointe"
           by Kathleen Ernst 234

Map and Globe Skills Use a Special Purpose Map 238

Chapter 9 Review and Test Prep 240

CHAPTER 10 Neighbors in the World 242

Vocabulary Preview   Reading Strategy: Monitor and Clarify 242

Lesson 1 | Core   **Many Regions, One Nation** 244
         | Extend **Citizenship** — Volunteers at Work 248

Citizenship Skills Resolve Conflicts 250

Lesson 2 | Core   **Working Together** 252
         | Extend **Citizenship** — Universal Human Rights 256

Chapter 10 Review and Test Prep 258

Unit 5 Review (WR) **Current Events Project** 260

References

Citizenship Handbook

Pledge of Allegiance R2

Character Traits R4

Illinois Counties R6

Illinois Databank R10

Illinois Governors R12

Biographical Dictionary............. R14

Resources

Geographical Terms.................. R18

Atlas R20

Gazetteer............................ R34

Glossary R39

Index R44

Acknowledgements R50

Extend Lessons

Connect the core lessons to an important concept and dig into it. Extend your social studies knowledge!

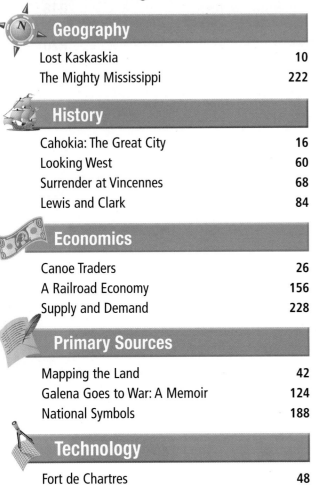

Geography

Lost Kaskaskia   10
The Mighty Mississippi   222

History

Cahokia: The Great City   16
Looking West   60
Surrender at Vincennes   68
Lewis and Clark   84

Economics

Canoe Traders   26
A Railroad Economy   156
Supply and Demand   228

Primary Sources

Mapping the Land   42
Galena Goes to War: A Memoir   124
National Symbols   188

Technology

Fort de Chartres   48
Farming in Illinois   114

Biography

Ninian Edwards   92
Mary Ann Bickerdyke   132
Jennie Hodgers   133
Mary Livermore   133
Oprah Winfrey   176
Dr. Mae Jemison   177
Marca Bristo   177
More biographies on Education Place—
www.eduplace.com/kids/hmss

Readers' Theater

The Illinois Constitutional Convention   102
A Visit to the Capitol   196

Citizenship

Hull House Reformers   162
Let's Vote!   204
Volunteers at Work   248
Universal Human Rights   256

Literature

"Your Illinois" by Kevin Stein   170
"Trouble at Fort la Pointe"
    by Kathleen Ernst   234

Skill Lessons

Take a step-by-step approach to learning and practicing key social studies skills.

Map and Globe Skills

Review Map Skills	18
Make a Map	106
Use a Special Purpose Map	238

Skill Practice: Reading Maps
8, 40, 45, 46, 58, 81, 82, 122, 225, 231

Chart and Graph Skills

Make a Timeline	50
Read a Circle Graph	86

Skill Practice: Reading Charts
220, 226

Reading and Thinking Skills

Identify Cause and Effect	62
Apply Critical Thinking	
Summarize	190
Apply Critical Thinking	

Citizenship Skills

Understand Point of View	126
Apply Critical Thinking	
Make a Decision	206
Apply Critical Thinking	
Resolve Conflicts	250
Apply Critical Thinking	

Study Skills

Identify Primary and Secondary Sources	178
Apply Critical Thinking	

Reading Skills/Graphic Organizer

Cause and Effect
6, 44, 88, 120, 158, 218

Sequence
12, 38, 64, 98, 128, 172

Categorize
20, 200, 224

Compare and Contrast
56, 192, 230

Main Idea and Details
80, 108, 152

Problem and Solution
164, 184, 252

Predict Outcomes
172

Draw Conclusions
244

Visual Learning

Become skilled at reading visuals. Graphs, maps, and timelines help you put all of the information together.

Maps

Illinois's Early People	2
Illinois Regions	8
Kaskaskia: Before 1881	10
Kaskaskia: After 1881	10
Mounds of Illinois	18
The Illinois and Neighbors	21
Trade in the late 1600s	24
Rivers of Illinois	29
Illinois Indians	30
North American Land Claims, 1720	34
Routes of Jolliet, Marquette, and LaSalle	40
North America Today	42
Illinois Settlements	45
North America in 1754	46
Land Rights in 1763	58
Looking West	60
The 13 Colonies	65
Clark's March Through Illinois	66
Free and Slave States, 1860	76
The Northwest Territory, 1787	81
Indiana Territory, 1800	82
Illinois Territory, 1809	82
Lewis and Clark	84
Migration to Illinois	109
Illinois and Michigan Canal	112
Settler's Route in Illinois	117
The Underground Railroad	121
Free and Slave States, 1860	122
Lincoln's Homes	137
Immigration to Illinois	148
A Railroad Economy	157
United States Population Density	214
The Midwest	219
Midwest Farm Belts	225
Great Lakes States: Industries	231
La Pointe Island in 1732	234
Fur Trade Route	236
Mineral Resources of the Midwest	238
Crystal Lake Beach Visitors Guide	241
United States Interstate Highways	245
Great Lakes States Industries	260

Charts and Graphs

American Indians in Illinois Today	3
Crossing the Atlantic Today	35
Illinois Population	77
United States Population	77
Population in Illinois Settlements, 1800	87
Land Size in the Northwest Territory	95
Illinois Bill of Rights	100
Population of Illinois Settlements, 1840	111
Union Soldiers	144
Illinois Population, 1900–2000	149
Top Five State Populations, 2004	149
Branches of Illinois State Government	194
Illinois Population Growth	215
U.S. Population Growth	215
Extreme Temperatures in the Midwest	220
Some Goods and Services from the Midwest	226
Supply of Popcorn	228
Demand of Popcorn	228

Diagrams and Infographics

Fort de Chartres	48
Refrigerated Train Car	153
Some Liberties Protected by the Bill of Rights	186
Lake Effect Snow	220
The Mighty Mississippi	222
Supply and Demand	229

Timelines

Events of the French and Indian War	50
Events in Colonial America	72
Major Achievements of Ninian Edwards	92
Major Events of Abraham Lincoln's Life	136

Unit Preview Timelines
1, 34, 76, 148

Chapter Preview Timelines
4, 36, 54, 78, 96, 118, 150

Lesson Timelines
12, 38, 44, 56, 64, 80, 88, 98, 108,
120, 128, 152, 158, 164, 172

Lesson Review Timelines
15, 41, 47, 59, 67, 83, 91, 101, 113,
123, 131, 155, 161, 169, 175

Chapter Review Timelines
29, 53, 71, 95, 117, 135, 181

About Your Textbook

① How It's Organized

Units The major sections of your book are units.

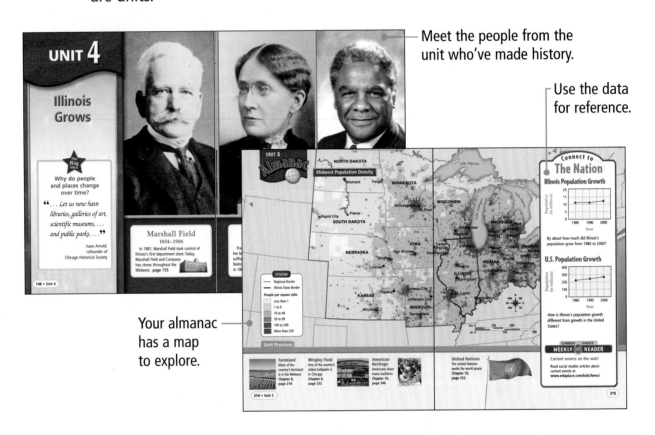

Meet the people from the unit who've made history.

Use the data for reference.

Your almanac has a map to explore.

Chapters Units are divided into chapters, and each opens with a vocabulary preview.

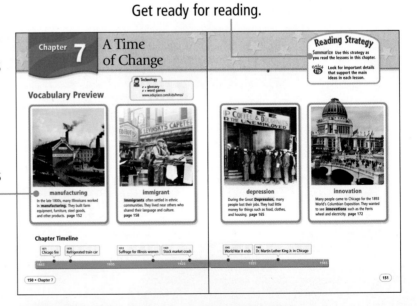

Get ready for reading.

Four important concepts get you started.

❷ Core and Extend

Lessons The lessons in your book have two parts: core and extend.

Core Lessons

Lessons bring social studies to life and help you meet your state's standards.

Core Lesson 3

Extend Lessons

Go deeper into important topics.

Extend

Primary Sources

Core Lesson

Before you read, use your prior knowledge.

Vocabulary strategies help with word meanings.

Reading skills support your understanding of the text.

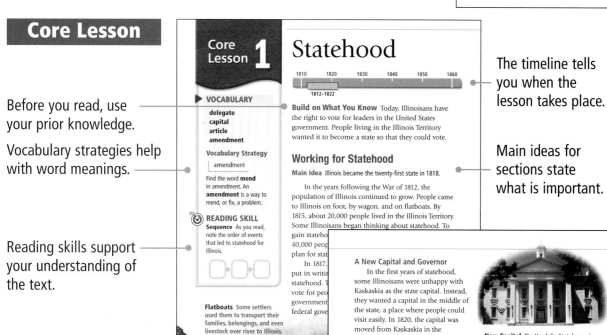

Core Lesson 1

▶ VOCABULARY

delegate
capital
article
amendment

Vocabulary Strategy

amendment

Find the word **mend** in amendment. An **amendment** is a way to mend, or fix, a problem.

📷 READING SKILL
Sequence As you read, note the order of events that led to statehood for Illinois.

Flatboats Some settlers used them to transport their families, belongings, and even livestock over river to Illinois.

98 • Chapter 5

Statehood

1810 1820 1830 1840 1850 1860
1812–1822

Build on What You Know Today, Illinoisans have the right to vote for leaders in the United States government. People living in the Illinois Territory wanted it to become a state so that they could vote.

Working for Statehood

Main Idea Illinois became the twenty-first state in 1818.

In the years following the War of 1812, the population of Illinois continued to grow. People came to Illinois on foot, by wagon, and on flatboats. By 1815, about 20,000 people lived in the Illinois Territory. Some Illinoisans began thinking about statehood. To gain statehood, 40,000 people plan for stat

In 1817, put in writing statehood. vote for peo government federal gove

A New Capital and Governor

In the first years of statehood, some Illinoisans were unhappy with Kaskaskia as the state capital. Instead, they wanted a capital in the middle of the state, a place where people could visit easily. In 1820, the capital was moved from Kaskaskia in the southwest corner of the state to Vandalia in the center.

In 1822, Illinois voters elected **Edward Coles** as the state's second governor. Over the next two years, some people asked for an amendment to the Illinois Constitution. An **amendment** is a change. These Illinoisans wanted to allow slavery throughout the state. Governor Coles, however, persuaded people to keep Illinois as a free state.

REVIEW Why did the capital move from Kaskaskia to Vandalia?

New Capitol The Vandalia Statehouse is the state's oldest surviving capitol building.

Lesson Summary

• Illinois became a state in 1818.
• The Illinois Constitution determined the state's borders, its capital, and how its government should be run.
• Illinois was a free state.

Why It Matters ...

Illinoisans continue to enjoy freedoms that were in the state's first constitution.

The timeline tells you when the lesson takes place.

Main ideas for sections state what is important.

Practice summarizing the lesson.

Studying social studies means asking why ideas are important to remember.

After you read, pull it together!

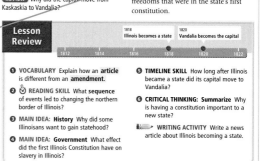

Lesson Review

1818 Illinois becomes a state   1820 Vandalia becomes the capital

1812   1814   1816   1818   1820   1822

❶ **VOCABULARY** Explain how an **article** is different from an **amendment**.

❷ **📷 READING SKILL** What **sequence** of events led to changing the northern border of Illinois?

❸ **MAIN IDEA: History** Why did some Illinoisans want to gain statehood?

❹ **MAIN IDEA: Government** What effect did the first Illinois Constitution have on slavery in Illinois?

❺ **TIMELINE SKILL** How long after Illinois became a state did its capital move to Vandalia?

❻ **CRITICAL THINKING: Summarize** Why is having a constitution important to a new state?

✏️ **WRITING ACTIVITY** Write a news article about Illinois becoming a state.

101

Extend Lesson

Learn more about an important topic from each core lesson.

Dig in and extend your knowledge.

Look closely. Learn more about history.

Look for literature, readers' theater, geography, economics— and more.

Write, talk, draw, and debate!

❸ Skills

Skill Building Learn map, graph, and study skills, as well as citizenship skills that you can use throughout life.

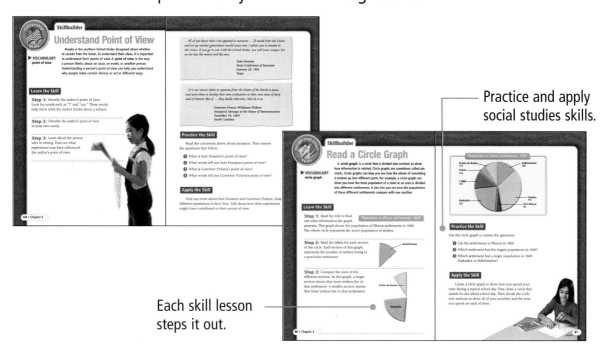

Practice and apply social studies skills.

Each skill lesson steps it out.

❹ References

Citizenship Handbook
The back of your book includes sections you will refer to again and again.

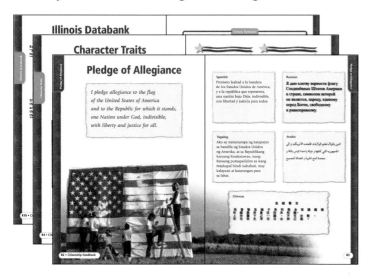

Resources
Look for atlas maps, a glossary of social studies terms, and an index.

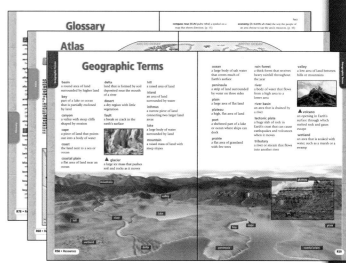

Reading Social Studies

Your book includes many features to help you be a successful reader. Here's what you will find:

VOCABULARY SUPPORT

Every chapter and lesson helps you with social studies terms. You'll build your vocabulary through strategies that you're learning in language arts.

Preview
Get a jump start on four important words from the chapter.

Vocabulary Strategies
Focus on word roots, prefixes, suffixes, or compound words, for example.

Vocabulary Practice
Reuse words in the reviews, skills, and extends. Show that you know your vocabulary.

READING STRATEGIES

Looking for the reading strategy and quick tip at the beginning of each chapter.

Predict and Infer
Before you read, think about what you'll learn.

Monitor and Clarify
Check your understanding. Could you explain what you just read to someone else?

Question
Stop and ask yourself a question. Did you understand what you just read?

Summarize
After you read, think about the most important ideas of the lesson.

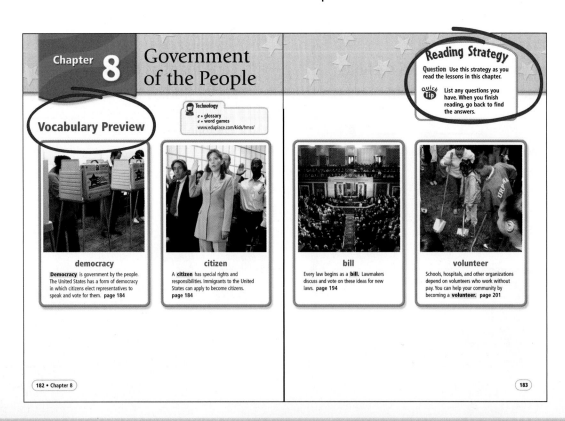

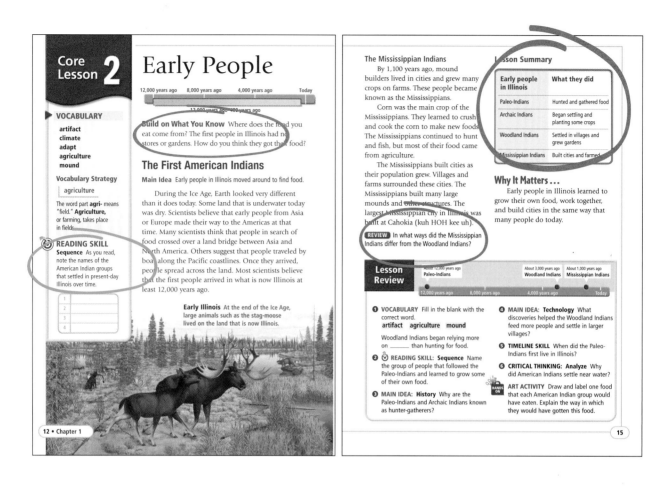

Core Lesson 2

Early People

12,000 years ago   8,000 years ago   4,000 years ago   Today

12,000 years ago—400 years ago

VOCABULARY

artifact
climate
adapt
agriculture
mound

Vocabulary Strategy

agriculture

The word part **agri-** means "field." **Agriculture,** or farming, takes place in fields.

READING SKILL

Sequence As you read, note the names of the American Indian groups that settled in present-day Illinois over time.

| 1 |
| 2 |
| 3 |
| 4 |

Build on What You Know Where does the food you eat come from? The first people in Illinois had no stores or gardens. How do you think they got their food?

The First American Indians

Main Idea Early people in Illinois moved around to find food.

During the Ice Age, Earth looked very different than it does today. Some land that is underwater today was dry. Scientists believe that early people from Asia or Europe made their way to the Americas at that time. Many scientists think that people in search of food crossed over a land bridge between Asia and North America. Others suggest that people traveled by boat along the Pacific coastlines. Once they arrived, people spread across the land. Most scientists believe that the first people arrived in what is now Illinois at least 12,000 years ago.

Early Illinois At the end of the Ice Age, large animals such as the stag-moose lived on the land that is now Illinois.

12 • Chapter 1

The Mississippian Indians

By 1,100 years ago, mound builders lived in cities and grew many crops on farms. These people became known as the Mississippians.

Corn was the main crop of the Mississippians. They learned to crush and cook the corn to make new foods. The Mississippians continued to hunt and fish, but most of their food came from agriculture.

The Mississippians built cities as their population grew. Villages and farms surrounded these cities. The Mississippians built many large mounds and other structures. The largest Mississippian city in Illinois was built at Cahokia (kuh HOH kee uh).

REVIEW In what ways did the Mississippian Indians differ from the Woodland Indians?

Lesson Summary

Early people in Illinois	What they did
Paleo-Indians	Hunted and gathered food
Archaic Indians	Began settling and planting some crops
Woodland Indians	Settled in villages and grew gardens
Mississippian Indians	Built cities and farmed

Why It Matters . . .

Early people in Illinois learned to grow their own food, work together, and build cities in the same way that many people do today.

Lesson Review

About 12,000 years ago — Paleo-Indians
About 3,000 years ago — Woodland Indians
About 1,000 years ago — Mississippian Indians

12,000 years ago   8,000 years ago   4,000 years ago   Today

❶ **VOCABULARY** Fill in the blank with the correct word.
artifact   agriculture   mound
Woodland Indians began relying more on _____ than hunting for food.

❷ **READING SKILL: Sequence** Name the group of people that followed the Paleo-Indians and learned to grow some of their own food.

❸ **MAIN IDEA: History** Why are the Paleo-Indians and Archaic Indians known as hunter-gatherers?

❹ **MAIN IDEA: Technology** What discoveries helped the Woodland Indians feed more people and settle in larger villages?

❺ **TIMELINE SKILL** When did the Paleo-Indians first live in Illinois?

❻ **CRITICAL THINKING: Analyze** Why did American Indians settle near water?

ART ACTIVITY Draw and label one food that each American Indian group would have eaten. Explain the way in which they would have gotten this food.

15

Social Studies:
Why It Matters

Learning social studies will help you know how to get along better in your everyday life, and it will give you confidence when you make important choices in your future.

WHEN I
- decide where to live
- travel
- look for places on a map—

I'll use the geography information I've learned in social studies.

WHEN I
- choose a job
- make a budget
- decide which product to buy—

I'll use economic information.

WHEN I
- ► hear the story of a person from the past
- ► read books and visit museums
- ► look closely at the world around me—

I'll use what I've learned about history.

WHEN I
- ► go to a neighborhood meeting
- ► decide who to vote for
- ► get a driver's license—

I can use what I've learned about citizenship.

Town Meeting Tonight

UNIT 1

The Land and the People

The Big Idea

Why do people like to live in Illinois?

" . . . No better soil can be found, either for corn, for vines, or for any other fruit whatever."

Louis Jolliet, French explorer, 1673

Illinois's First People

WISCONSIN

▲ Scales Mound

Rock River

KASKASKIA

Fox River

Des Plaines River

Kankakee River

Lake Michigan

IOWA

PEORIA

Illinois River

• Peoria

Dickson Mounds ▲

Sangamon River

LEGEND

PEORIA American Indians

———— Present-day border

▲ Mound site

• Modern Town

CAHOKIA

Cahokia Mounds ▲

• Cahokia

Kaskaskia River

Little Wabash River

Wabash River

MISSOURI

TAMAROA

Tamaroa •

MICHIGAMEA

• Kaskaskia

Big Muddy River

N
NW NE
W E
SW SE
S

Dogtooth Bends Mounds ▲

Ohio River

km 0   50   100
mi 0   50   100

Unit Preview

12,000 years ago   10,000 years ago   8,000 years ago   6,000 years ago

About 12,000 years ago
Paleo-Indians

First people come to what is present-day Illinois
Chapter 1, page 13

About 3,000 years ago
Early Farmers

Woodland Indians begin farming in what is present-day Illinois
Chapter 1, page 14

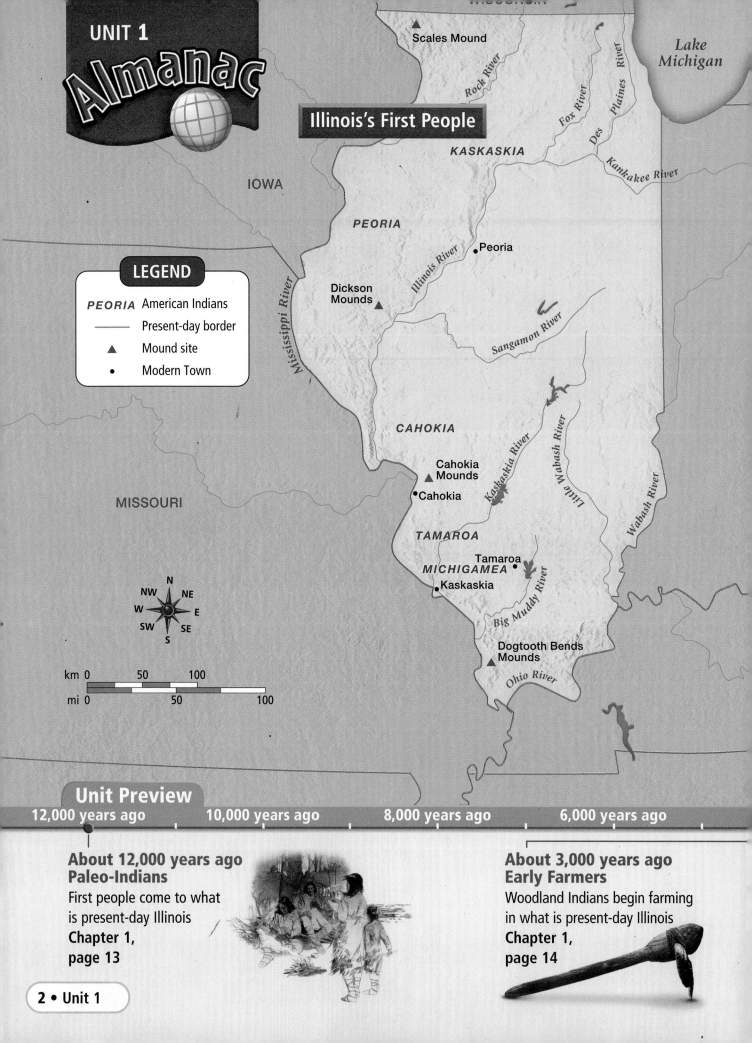

INDIANA

OHIO

KENTUCKY

1,000 years ago   2,000 years ago   Today

About 400 years ago
American Indians
Illinois Indians farm, hunt, and trade in what is present-day Illinois
Chapter 1,
page 20

Connect to Today

Illinois Indians, 1650

Major Nations	Cahokia, Kaskaskia, Michigamea, Peoria, Tamaroa

Illinois Indians Today

Major Nations	Cherokee, Chippewa, Choctaw, Haudenosaunee (Iroquois), Sioux

None of the early American Indian nations in Illinois remain in the state. By the mid-1800s, they had all moved west of the Mississippi River. Today, the Peoria live in Oklahoma.

Why do you think that the American Indian nations from 1650 left Illinois in the mid-1800s?

CURRENT   EVENTS
WEEKLY (WR) READER

Current events on the web!

Read social studies articles about current events at
www.eduplace.com/kids/hmss/

3

Illinois's Land and Early People

Technology

e • glossary
e • word games
www.eduplace.com/kids/hmss/

Vocabulary Preview

glacier

Large ice sheets once covered much of Earth. These **glaciers** helped shape many of the hills, plains, lakes, and rivers in Illinois. **page 6**

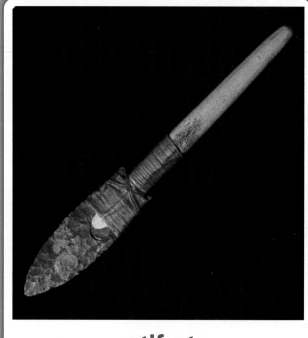

artifact

Scientists look for **artifacts** to learn more about people who lived long ago. This spear point was made by Paleo-Indians thousands of years ago. **page 13**

Chapter Timeline

About 12,000 years ago
Paleo-Indians

About 10,000 years ago
Archaic Indians

| 12,000 years ago | 10,000 years ago | 8,000 years ago | 6,000 years ago |

Reading Strategy

Predict and Infer Use this strategy as you read the lessons in this chapter.

Quick Tip Before you read, look at the lesson title and the pictures. What do you think you will read about?

agriculture

Woodland Indians learned **agriculture** to grow their own food. They used simple tools such as this hoe to prepare the earth for planting. **page 14**

trade

Trade was important to the Illinois Indians. They traveled in canoes to exchange goods they had for goods they did not have. **page 24**

About 3,000 years ago Woodland Indians	About 1,000 years ago Mississippian Indians	About 400 years ago Illinois Indians

4,000 years ago   2,000 years ago   Today

Land and Water

VOCABULARY

glacier
environment
region
prairie
erosion

Vocabulary Strategy

glacier

Glacier comes from **glacé,** the French word for "ice." A **glacier** is a large sheet of slowly moving ice.

READING SKILL

Cause and Effect Write some effects caused by glaciers forming and melting.

Cause	Effect
Glaciers form and melt. →	

Build on What You Know What can you see outside your window? Do you see city, farmland, or forest? A long time ago, you might have seen something very different from what you see today.

Ice Carves the Land

Main Idea Illinois's land and waterways have changed over time.

Thousands of years ago, temperatures were much colder than they are today. That time period is known as the Ice Age. Glaciers covered almost half of Earth. A **glacier** is a large, slow-moving sheet of ice. Glaciers crush, scrape, and change the earth as they move.

The Ice Age ended 10,000 years ago. Then the environment warmed and changed. The **environment** is the water, land, and air that surrounds living things. As the environment warmed, glaciers melted. The melting glaciers left behind deep lakes, rolling hills, and vast plains. Today, Illinois has some of these features.

Ice Sheets Glaciers can be hundreds of feet thick.

Lakes and Rivers Water flows through rivers, like the Illinois River above. Lakes, like Lake Michigan, are like giant bowls that hold water.

Rivers, Streams, and Lakes

Glaciers carved many pits and channels in Illinois. These pits and channels became rivers, streams, and lakes when filled with water from the melted glaciers.

Today, Illinois has about 900 rivers and streams and many lakes. The Mississippi River lies along Illinois's western border, or edge. Kaskaskia (kas KAS kee uh) Island rises out of the river. The Mississippi is one of the longest rivers in the nation. It runs south to the Gulf of Mexico.

The Ohio River runs along the state's southern border, or edge. The Ohio River flows all the way from Pennsylvania and joins the Mississippi River at Cairo, Illinois. The Wabash River runs along Illinois's eastern border and flows into the Ohio River.

The Illinois River cuts across the center of the state. The river connects many small towns and cities. Other rivers in the state include the Big Muddy, the Kaskaskia, the Rock, and the Chicago.

Lake Michigan forms Illinois's northeast border. It is one of the Great Lakes. The Great Lakes are some of the largest lakes in the world. They connect to other waterways in Canada that lead to the Atlantic Ocean. Other lakes within Illinois include Lake Shelbyville, Peoria Lake, and Rend Lake.

REVIEW What happened to the pits and channels carved by glaciers when the Ice Age ended?

Illinois's Land Regions

Main Idea Illinois has three main land regions.

Illinois has three main land regions, the Central Lowland, the Shawnee Hills, and the Coastal Plain. A **region** is an area that shares features such as landforms and bodies of water.

The prairies of the Central Lowland region cover most of Illinois. A **prairie** is a flat or rolling grassland. Glaciers flattened this land during the Ice Age and left behind fertile soil when they melted. Fertile means that the soil is good for growing things.

The Shawnee Hills region runs across the southern part of Illinois. Glaciers did not reach this far south during the Ice Age. Erosion has shaped the region's wooded hills, mountains, and deep valleys. **Erosion** is the wearing away of Earth's surface by water and wind.

The Coastal Plain region covers a small area at the state's southern tip. The Mississippi and Ohio rivers meet here and form a flood plain. A flood plain is the flat, low land where a river often floods. The soil here is very fertile.

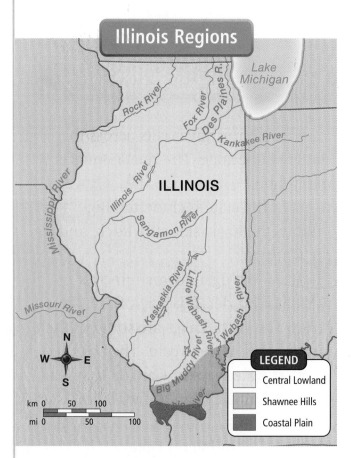

Illinois Regions

LEGEND
- Central Lowland
- Shawnee Hills
- Coastal Plain

Comparing the Land The three land regions of Illinois have different features.

SKILL **Reading Maps** What do the colors on the map show?

Central Lowland The fertile soil of Illinois's prairies is good for farming.

Erosion Wind and water have carved these rock shapes in the Shawnee Hills region.

Illinois provides people with more than just fertile farmland. Coal, lead, and oil lie beneath the ground. The woodlands provide lumber. Illinois's many lakes and rivers provide fish and water for drinking. The open prairies and many waterways make it easy to move people and products from place to place. Together, the state's land and water make Illinois a good place to live.

REVIEW Name three things that the land in Illinois provides people.

Lesson Summary

- Glaciers shaped much of the land and waterways in Illinois.
- Illinois has many rivers and lakes.
- Illinois has three main land regions.

Why It Matters...

The people of Illinois depend on the state's land and water for many of the things they need to live.

Lesson Review

1. **VOCABULARY** Name three things that make up the **environment** and affect living things.

2. **READING SKILL: Cause and Effect** What **effect** did glaciers have on the Central Lowland region?

3. **MAIN IDEA: Geography** In what ways have the land and waterways of Illinois changed over time?

4. **MAIN IDEA: Geography** Which one of Illinois's regions covers the most land?

5. **CRITICAL THINKING: Infer** What might the Shawnee Hills region look like today if glaciers had covered the land there?

WRITING ACTIVITY Write a paragraph about the land and water in your part of Illinois. What features make your area special?

Lost Kaskaskia

What could make a city disappear? The first capital of Illinois was Kaskaskia. It sat on the banks of the Mississippi and Kaskaskia rivers. French settlers first built there because it was a place that traders and settlers could get to easily. The area was at risk of floods, though.

The potential for natural disasters exists in all environments. In Illinois, rain and snow can cause the state's rivers to flood. The Mississippi River overflowed in 1881. It dug a channel through the land and joined the Kaskaskia River. Kaskaskia became an island. Over time, most of the original city fell into the river.

Mississippi River

① Friend and Foe
Rivers made it easy to travel to Kaskaskia, but their floods were a threat.

Before 1880
Floods moved the Mississippi River closer to Kaskaskia. By 1880, only about five miles of land separated the Mississippi and Kaskaskia rivers.

Today
Today, the Mississippi River flows where the Kaskaskia River was. The Old River follows the old course of the Mississippi River.

Kaskaskia in 1880
The town survived many floods before 1881.

Kaskaskia River

On the Edge
In 1899, the old state capital building sat on the edge of the Mississippi River. Two years later it had fallen into the river.

Activities

1. **MAP IT** Find out about the major rivers in Illinois and draw a map showing them. Where do they flow?

2. **DEBATE IT** Write a scene in which people debate whether to build Kaskaskia between the two rivers. Explain the arguments for and against it.

Early People

12,000 years ago   8,000 years ago   4,000 years ago   Today

12,000 years ago–400 years ago

Build on What You Know Where does the food you eat come from? The first people in Illinois had no stores or gardens. How do you think they got their food?

The First American Indians

Main Idea Early people in Illinois moved around to find food.

During the Ice Age, Earth looked very different than it does today. Some land that is underwater today was dry. Scientists believe that early people from Asia or Europe made their way to the Americas at that time. Many scientists think that people in search of food crossed over a land bridge between Asia and North America. Others suggest that people traveled by boat along the Pacific coastlines. Once they arrived, people spread across the land. Most scientists believe that the first people arrived in what is now Illinois at least 12,000 years ago.

Early Illinois At the end of the Ice Age, large animals such as the stag-moose lived on the land that is now Illinois.

Early People To find food, Paleo-Indians needed to know their surroundings well. They also learned to make spear points from stone to hunt animals.

The Paleo-Indians

The earliest people to live in the Americas are known as Paleo-Indians. Around 12,000 years ago, the first Paleo-Indians came to Illinois. Scientists called archaeologists have found artifacts such as stone spear points made by these people. An **artifact** is an object made by people long ago. Archaeologists learn about early people from artifacts.

Paleo-Indians were hunter-gatherers. They hunted large and small animals for food. They also gathered wild plants, nuts, and seeds. Paleo-Indians moved from place to place to find food. They camped near streams and lakes for water and food.

The Paleo-Indians lived at the end of the Ice Age. At that time the climate warmed. The **climate** is the usual weather of a place over time. Many of the animals and plants that the Paleo-Indians depended on died out.

The Archaic Indians

Over time, Paleo-Indians had to adapt. **Adapt** means to change in order to live in a new environment. The people who adapted became known as Archaic Indians. The Archaic Indians lived in what is present-day Illinois between 10,000 and 3,000 years ago.

Archaic Indians fished and hunted animals that adapted to the warmer climate. They continued to gather plants, nuts, and seeds. Archaic Indians used stones heated in fire to cook food. They dug pits beside their homes to store food they gathered or hunted.

The Archaic Indians began building small villages in places where they could find food and fresh water. Archaic Indians also learned to collect seeds from wild plants and grow their own plants. They grew sunflowers for seeds, and gourds for containers.

REVIEW In what ways did Archaic Indians differ from Paleo-Indians?

Woodland Village Woodland Indians lived in villages like the one above. They used hoes and other new tools to grow their own food in gardens.

The Mound Builders

Main Idea The Woodland and Mississippian Indians built long-term settlements.

Woodland Indians

Around 3,000 years ago, a new way of life spread though parts of Illinois. A people called the Woodland Indians learned that they could grow more of the plants that they once had to search for. They began using agriculture as a main source of food. **Agriculture** means farming. Woodland Indians grew squash, barley, and other plants.

Woodland Indians made tools such as hoes to help them grow their own food. They also learned to make pottery, or jars, bowls, and pots from clay. The pottery allowed them to store extra food.

When the Woodland Indians learned agriculture, they changed from hunter-gatherers to settled farmers. They built large villages as their population grew. Population means the people who live in an area. Many families began living in the same village so that they could help one another. Woodland Indians continued to gather nuts and berries. They also invented the bow and arrow to help them hunt.

Woodland Indians built mounds in their villages and became known as mound builders. A **mound** is a hill made from earth, stones, and other natural materials. Woodland Indians used some mounds as burial mounds. They held special meetings and events on mounds.

The Mississippian Indians

By 1,100 years ago, mound builders lived in cities and grew many crops on farms. These people became known as the Mississippians.

Corn was the main crop of the Mississippians. They learned to crush and cook the corn to make new foods. The Mississippians continued to hunt and fish, but most of their food came from agriculture.

The Mississippians built cities as their population grew. Villages and farms surrounded these cities. The Mississippians built many large mounds and other structures. The largest Mississippian city in Illinois was built at Cahokia (kuh HOH kee uh).

REVIEW In what ways did the Mississippian Indians differ from the Woodland Indians?

Lesson Summary

Early people in Illinois	What they did
Paleo-Indians	Hunted and gathered food
Archaic Indians	Began settling and planting some crops
Woodland Indians	Settled in villages and grew gardens
Mississippian Indians	Built cities and farmed

Why It Matters...

Early people in Illinois learned to grow their own food, work together, and build cities in the same way that many people do today.

Lesson Review

About 12,000 years ago
Paleo-Indians

About 3,000 years ago
Woodland Indians

About 1,000 years ago
Mississippian Indians

12,000 years ago   8,000 years ago   4,000 years ago   Today

❶ **VOCABULARY** Fill in the blank with the correct word.
   artifact   agriculture   mound

   Woodland Indians began relying more on _____ than hunting for food.

❷ **READING SKILL: Sequence** Name the group of people that followed the Paleo-Indians and learned to grow some of their own food.

❸ **MAIN IDEA: History** Why are the Paleo-Indians and Archaic Indians known as hunter-gatherers?

❹ **MAIN IDEA: Technology** What discoveries helped the Woodland Indians feed more people and settle in larger villages?

❺ **TIMELINE SKILL** When did the Paleo-Indians first live in Illinois?

❻ **CRITICAL THINKING: Analyze** Why did American Indians settle near water?

HANDS ON

ART ACTIVITY Draw and label one food that each American Indian group would have eaten. Explain the way in which they would have gotten this food.

CAHOKIA
THE GREAT CITY

A towering mound stands at the heart of the city. For 500 years, Cahokia was the center of a vast North American civilization. As many as 20,000 people lived there. It was the largest city on the continent. Mississippians lived much as people in cities do today. They planned their city, their buildings, and their activities.

───────────── ─────────────

1 A wooden wall surrounded the city center, where some people, such as leaders, lived.

2 Monk's Mound is the largest mound in North America. The city's ruler may have lived here.

3 The Grand Plaza in the city center was used for public activities such as markets and festivals.

4 The Twin Mounds may have been used for burials.

5 Borrow pits provided dirt and stones to build mounds.

6 Villages, where most people lived, surrounded the city center.

7 Farms provided crops such as corn to feed the people of Cahokia.

1

Activities

1. **TALK ABOUT IT** Many people lived in and around Cahokia. Discuss the ways in which people need to work together in cities.

2. **EXPLORE IT** Pick a feature discussed above. Learn more about that feature from Internet or library sources. Write a paragraph explaining what makes that feature important to Cahokia.

17

Skillbuilder

Review Map Skills

A globe is a round model of Earth. A map is a flat drawing of Earth's surface. Because maps are flat, they can appear in books and on your computer. Maps show where places are located in relation to other places. They can also show different types of information, such as the land's physical features or the borders of states, or countries.

▶ **VOCABULARY**
legend
compass rose
scale

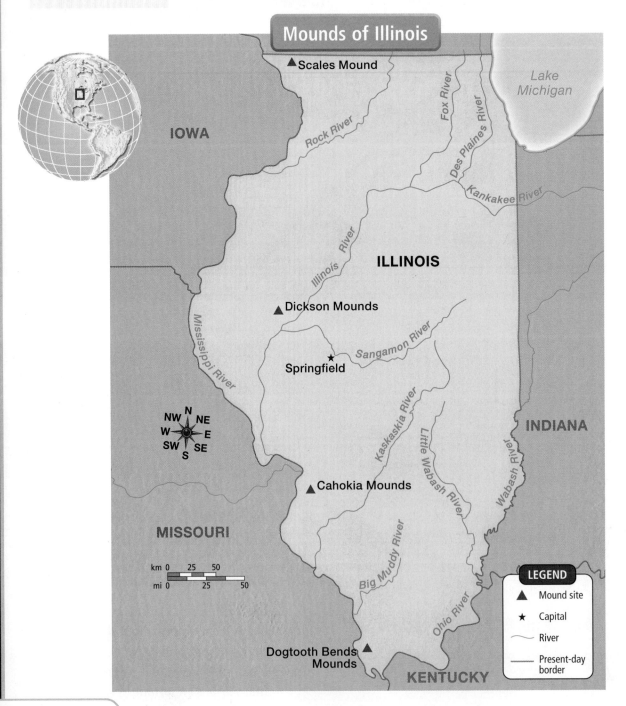

Mounds of Illinois

Scales Mound

IOWA

Rock River

Fox River

Des Plaines River

Lake Michigan

Kankakee River

Illinois River

ILLINOIS

Dickson Mounds

Sangamon River

★ Springfield

Mississippi River

NW N NE
W   E
SW S SE

Kaskaskia River

Little Wabash River

INDIANA

Wabash River

Cahokia Mounds

MISSOURI

km 0 25 50
mi 0 25 50

Big Muddy River

Ohio River

Dogtooth Bends Mounds

KENTUCKY

LEGEND
▲ Mound site
★ Capital
— River
— Present-day border

Learn the Skill

Step 1: Read the map's title. A title tells you the subject of the map. The map on page 18 is about mounds in the state of Illinois.

Mounds of Illinois

Step 2: Look at the map's legend. A **legend** explains what different symbols on the map mean.

LEGEND

▲ Mound site

★ Capital

~ River

— Present-day border

Step 3: Check directions and distances. A **compass rose** shows direction. The map **scale** allows you to measure distances on a map. Different maps have different scales.

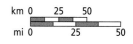

Practice the Skill

Use the map on page 18 to answer the questions.

1 What is the name of the mound site between the Mississippi River and the Kaskaskia River?

2 In what direction would a person travel to get from Cahokia Mounds to Dickson Mounds?

Apply the Skill

Use the map on page 8 and a ruler to answer the following questions.

1 What is the title of the map?

2 What is the distance represented by one inch on this map?

The Illinois

Build on What You Know Have you ever joined a club or special group? Sometimes, working in a group makes it easier to do things. In the 1600s, several American Indian groups worked together to help one another.

VOCABULARY

culture
history
resource
trade

Vocabulary Strategy

history

A **story** tells about an event, which is something that happens. **History** tells about events from the past that lead up to the present.

READING SKILL

Categorize As you read, list the plant and animal resources that the Illinois Indians depended on.

Food Resources	Other Resources

Many People Share the Land

Main Idea During the 1600s, the Illinois Indians lived in what is present-day Illinois.

No one knows exactly what happened to the Mississippian Indians. About 700 years ago, their people and culture disappeared. A **culture** is the way of life of a group of people. Smaller groups of American Indians replaced the Mississippians on the land that is now Illinois. These groups built smaller villages and continued farming.

By the 1600s, several different groups of American Indians lived in what is present-day Illinois and the surrounding area. All of these groups shared a language, but they had other differences. Sometimes they got along. Sometimes, they fought.

The Illinois The state of Illinois was named for a large group of American Indians who lived there in the 1600s. This man was an Illinois leader.

The Illinois and their Neighbors

In the 1600s, the Illinois Indians lived in what is now the state of Illinois. They lived near the rivers in central and southern Illinois. They also lived in parts of what is now Iowa and Missouri.

The Illinois included as many as twelve groups. The largest groups were the Cahokia, Kaskaskia, Michigamea (mihsh ih guh MAY uh), Peoria (peh OR ee uh), and Tamaroa (ta muh ROH uh). These groups shared a culture and history. **History** tells events of the past that lead to the present.

The Kickapoo This woman belonged to an American Indian group to the north of where the Illinois lived.

Neighbors Several groups made up the Illinois Indians. Other American Indian groups lived to the east and north.

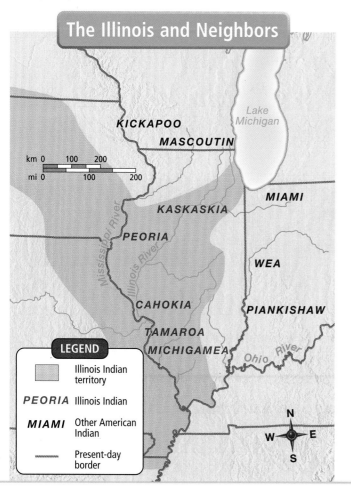

The Illinois and Neighbors

KICKAPOO

MASCOUTIN

Lake Michigan

km 0   100   200
mi 0   100   200

Mississippi River

Illinois River

KASKASKIA

MIAMI

PEORIA

WEA

CAHOKIA

PIANKISHAW

TAMAROA

MICHIGAMEA

Ohio River

LEGEND

Illinois Indian territory

PEORIA Illinois Indian

MIAMI Other American Indian

Present-day border

N W E S

Several other American Indian groups lived nearby. The Miami (meh AH mee), Wea (WAY uh), and Piankishaw (pee ahnk uh SHAW) lived in what is present-day Indiana. They also lived in Wisconsin and southern Michigan. Like the Illinois, these three groups shared a culture and history.

Groups to the north, including the Kickapoo (KIK uh poo) in what is present-day Wisconsin, wanted the Illinois's lands. They moved south and pushed the Miami out of the area. The Mascoutin (muh SKUTE ihn) also lived in Wisconsin and joined with the Kickapoo.

The Illinois fought with these northern groups. The Illinois groups worked together to protect themselves. They held onto most of their homelands until the mid-1700s.

REVIEW What did different groups of Illinois Indians share?

21

Life Among the Illinois

Main Idea The Illinois moved between settlements, depending on their food source.

The Illinois lived in ways similar to those of the earlier mound builders. They used agriculture to supply much of their food. The Illinois also relied on other food sources. These food sources were found in different places. The Illinois moved throughout the year to be near their food sources. They built settlements near each source of food.

The Illinois traveled between settlements by walking and by using canoes on rivers. They made their canoes from tree trunks. They used axes to hollow out the logs. The canoes were heavy, so the Illinois had to use poles instead of paddles to move them through the water.

Spring and Summer

In April and May, the Illinois lived in large villages. Most villages had as many as 300 longhouses. A longhouse was a long, narrow building with a door at one end. Women built the houses from poles and woven reed mats. Each longhouse had four or five fireplaces, and two families shared each fireplace.

Women planted corn, beans, squash, and other crops in these villages. They also gathered nuts and berries to eat. Illinois men fished and hunted deer and other animals. When they were not hunting, they made and repaired tools and weapons.

In June and July, most of the Illinois moved to hunting camps on the prairies. There, the men used bows and arrows to hunt bison.

Spring and Summer The Illinois lived mostly in longhouses. They built the frame of the longhouse with wood poles and covered the frame with mats woven from reeds.

At the prairie camps, women gathered wild plants. They also built small lodges, or houses, to live in during the summer. They used poles and bark from trees to make the lodges. Women also made food and clothing from the animals after the hunting was done.

The Illinois returned to their villages in late July. By then, it was time to harvest the first crop. Corn was the most important crop. The women dried and saved much of it to eat in other seasons. They also raised beans, squash, watermelon, and pumpkins.

The men continued to hunt, both near the villages and on the prairies. Women saved the meat by smoking it over small fires.

Fall and Winter

From October through March, the Illinois split into small winter villages. They built these villages beside rivers. Each village had several families.

The women brought poles and mats from their summer village to build small houses called wigwams. Each oval-shaped house was about the size of a small classroom. They had round roofs.

Food was harder to find during the winter. Men continued to hunt and fish. The Illinois also lived on corn and other foods that the women had saved earlier. At the end of the winter, the Illinois moved back to their summer villages to begin planting again. Some stopped along the way to collect sap from maple trees to make sugar and syrup.

Fall and Winter The Illinois lived in small wigwams. Like the longhouses, wigwams were made from poles and reed mats. Women often placed animal hides and furs over wigwams to keep the cold air out.

What the Illinois Made

Main Idea The Illinois made and exchanged things that they needed and liked.

The Illinois made most of the things that they needed from resources on their land. A **resource** is something that can be used. They grew their own food. They made clothes from animals that they hunted. They made tools, weapons, and containers from stone, bones, and clay.

The Illinois used trade to obtain things that they wanted but could not make for themselves. **Trade** is the exchange of goods. The Illinois traded with American Indian groups and European traders throughout the Great Lakes area. European traders came from Europe. They began to settle near the Great Lakes in the 1600s.

Goods and Trade

The Illinois exchanged hides and furs with the Osage (OH sayj) and Missouri, who lived to the south and west of them. They then traded these goods to the Ottawa (AHT uh wuh) and Potawatomi (paht uh WAHT uh mee) for useful European goods such as brass kettles, cloth, and iron tools. The Illinois kept some of the European goods for their own use and traded other items to the Osage and Missouri peoples.

The Illinois also traded with the Ottawa for porcupine quills. They used these quills to decorate things such as moccasins, or shoes. Trade helped American Indian groups across the region obtain goods that they wanted and needed.

Illinois Trade The Illinois traded with several American Indian groups and with European traders.

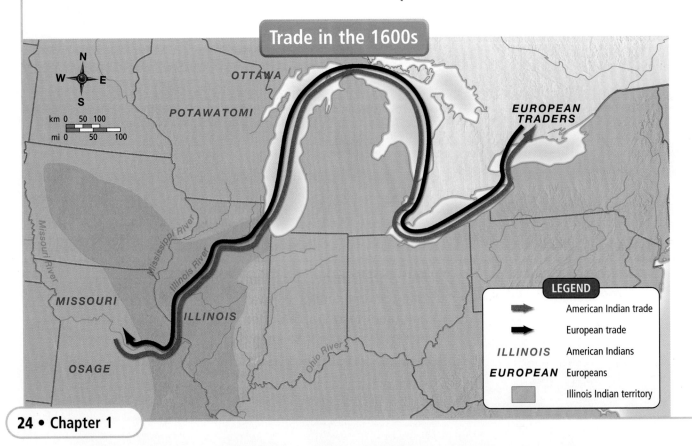

Trade in the 1600s

LEGEND
→ American Indian trade
→ European trade
ILLINOIS American Indians
EUROPEAN Europeans
⬛ Illinois Indian territory

Art and Music

The Illinois made more than the things that they needed. They also made art and other things for enjoyment. The Illinois carved many objects from wood, often in the shapes of animals. They also painted on animal hides and mats. Their art was part of their culture.

The Illinois culture also included music. People played drums, flutes, and rattles. Music was performed during gatherings and dances. The Illinois shared parts of their culture through trade, music, and art with other American Indians and the Europeans.

REVIEW What things did the Illinois trade with other American Indians?

Painted Symbols The Illinois painted symbols such as the thunderbird on animal hides. The symbols represented important beliefs and items from their lives.

Lesson Summary

- The groups that made up the Illinois Indians shared a culture and history.

- The Illinois lived in different settlements throughout the year, as their food sources changed.

- The Illinois made and traded for things they needed and wanted.

Why It Matters...

Learning how the Illinois obtained food, built settlements, and traded helps us better understand the history of the state of Illinois.

Lesson Review

❶ **VOCABULARY** Match each vocabulary word with its meaning.

culture   resource   trade

(a) something that can be used
(b) the exchange of goods
(c) the way of life of a group of people

❷ **READING SKILL: Categorize** Look at your lists of food and other resources used by the Illinois. Describe how the Illinois made shelter and gathered food from plant resources.

❸ **MAIN IDEA: Culture** Why did the Illinois live in different settlements during the year?

❹ **MAIN IDEA: Technology** Name one thing that the Illinois made for themselves and one thing for which they traded.

❺ **CRITICAL THINKING: Infer** Why do you think that the Illinois traded with other American Indians?

HANDS ON

RESEARCH ACTIVITY Learn more about one American Indian group that the Illinois fought or traded with. Explain similarities and differences between the two groups.

Extend Lesson 3

Economics

Canoe Traders

Why would an Illinois Indian load up a canoe with things he didn't need and paddle far down a river? Most people cannot produce everything they need or want. Many groups of people produce more of certain things than they can use. People learn that they can trade the extra items they don't need for things that they do need or want. The Illinois Indians used canoes to travel and trade with other American Indians and Europeans far away.

Illinois Indian Trade

What the Illinois Gave

❶ The Illinois were expert hunters. They traded animal furs and hides to other groups.

What the Illinois Received

❷ The Illinois traded animal hides and furs to other American Indian groups for porcupine quills. They used the quills to decorate their shoes and clothing.

④ Europeans also traded jewelry, such as these glass beads.

③ Europeans made metal tools and cookware, and glass beads. The Illinois traded furs and hides that the Europeans wanted to sell in Europe for these items.

Activities

1. **TALK ABOUT IT** Today, people often trade money for things, or buy them. In groups, list some things that people in your community make, and then list some things that they buy. Share your lists with the class.

2. **WRITE ABOUT IT** Many people use their skills to work for money. Write a paragraph about a skill that you have. Explain how you could use that skill in exchange for money, goods, or services.

Visual Summary

1 – 3. ✏️ ▶ Write a description about each American Indian group named below.

Paleo-Indians

_____
_____
_____
_____

Mississipian Indians

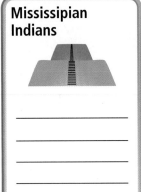

_____
_____
_____
_____

Illinois Indians

_____
_____
_____
_____

Facts and Main Ideas

✔️ **TEST PREP** Answer each question.

4. **Geography** In what ways did glaciers shape the land in Illinois?

5. **Economics** In what ways did agriculture change the lives of American Indians?

6. **Geography** Name four main waterways in Illinois.

7. **Culture** Explain where the Illinois Indians lived and what they did during spring and summer and fall and winter.

8. **Culture** In what ways did Illinois men and women share the task of providing food?

Vocabulary

✔️ **TEST PREP** Choose the correct word from the list below to complete each sentence.

environment, p. 6
adapt, p. 13
trade, p. 24

9. People must _____ in order to survive in a changing climate.

10. The exchange of goods is called _____.

11. The land, water, and air that surround living things make up the _____.

| About 12,000 years ago **Paleo-Indians** | About 10,000 years ago **Archaic Indians** | | About 3,000 years ago **Woodland Indians** | About 400 years ago **Illinois Indians** |

12,000 years ago | 10,000 years ago | 8,000 years ago | 6,000 years ago | 4,000 years ago | 2,000 years ago | Today

Apply Skills

✔ TEST PREP **Review Map Skills**
Study the Illinois map below. Then use what you have learned about map skills to answer each question.

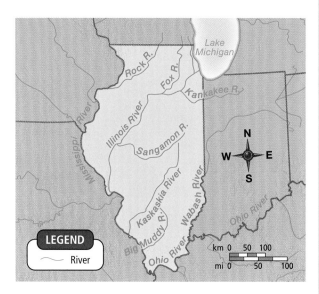

LEGEND
~ River

km 0   50   100
mi 0   50   100

12. What would you use to find out how wide the state of Illinois is?

   A. scale
   B. legend
   C. compass rose
   D. none of the above

13. Which river flows just north of the Kaskaskia River?

   A. Big Muddy
   B. Ohio
   C. Mississippi
   D. Sangamon

Critical Thinking

✔ TEST PREP Write a short paragraph to answer each question below.

14. Compare and Contrast In what ways did the lives of Paleo-Indians and Woodland Indians differ?

15. Summarize What do we know about the culture of the Illinois Indians?

Timeline

✔ TEST PREP Use the Chapter Summary timeline above to answer the question.

16. When did the Illinois Indians first live in what is present-day Illinois?

Activities

Art Activity Find out more about the art of the Illinois people. Draw an artifact that the Illinois might have made.

Writing Activity Write a story about a trading day in an Illinois Indian village.

Technology
Writing Process Tips
Get help with your description at
www.eduplace.com/kids/hmss/

Review and Test Prep

Vocabulary and Main Ideas

✔ **TEST PREP** Write a sentence to answer each question.

1. Which **region** in Illinois is largely flood plain, and which is largely **prairie?**

2. In what way has **erosion** affected the land in Illinois?

3. In what ways did the Woodland and Mississippian Indians use **mounds?**

4. In what way did the **climate** change affect people at the end of the Ice Age?

5. Name some examples of Illinois Indian **culture.**

6. Name two **resources** that the Illinois Indians used.

Critical Thinking

✔ **TEST PREP** Write a short paragraph to answer each question.

7. **Draw Conclusions** In what ways did Mississippian cities depend on agriculture?

8. **Cause and Effect** Explain the ways that the early people of Illinois depended on the region's rivers, streams, and lakes.

Apply Skills

✔ **TEST PREP** Study the Illinois map below. Then use what you have learned about map skills to answer each question.

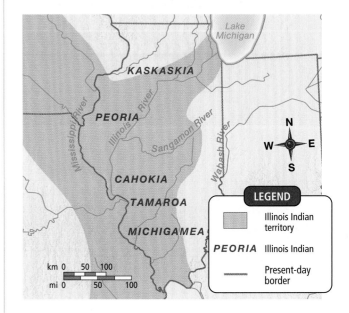

9. Which Illinois Indian group lived farthest north?

    A. Kaskaskia
    B. Cahokia
    C. Tamaroa
    D. Michigamea

10. Use the scale and a ruler to find out the distance between the Cahokia and Michigamea.

    A. about 50 miles
    B. about 100 miles
    C. about 200 miles
    D. about 400 miles

Unit Activity

Make an "Early Illinois" Poster

- Choose one thing about the early people in Illinois that you found interesting.

- Find or create pictures, photographs, or objects that show your interest.

- Make an "Early Illinois" poster, using the images that you found.

At the Library

Look for this book at your school or public library.

Journey to Cahokia: A Boy's Visit to the Great Mound City by Joy Schleh and Albert Lorenz

This fictional trip includes photographs, illustrations, and text that tell the story of the Mississippians.

CURRENT EVENTS
WEEKLY (WR) READER

Current Events Project

Create a display that shows the importance of land, climate, and resources.

- Look for an article about a harvest or seasonal festival.

- Write a description that tells what the festival celebrates.

- Find pictures to show why land, climate, and resources are important to the festival.

- Create a display with the information and pictures that you find.

 Technology
Weekly Reader online offers social studies articles. Go to **www.eduplace.com/kids/hmss/**

UNIT 2

Exploration and Colonization

The Big Idea

Why do people explore lands that are new to them?

"*We safely entered [the Mississippi] on the 17th of June, with a joy that I cannot express.*"

Jacques Marquette,
Jesuit priest and explorer, 1673

Jacques Marquette
1637–1675

Marquette spoke six American Indian languages. This allowed him to talk with American Indians on his travels. **page 39**

History Makers

Louis Jolliet
1645–1700

Louis Jolliet was an experienced explorer and mapmaker. Jolliet used his skills when he and Jacques Marquette explored the Mississippi River. **page 39**

Pontiac
1720–1769

This Ottawa chief wanted to preserve American Indian lands from European settlers. He led attacks to drive the British from what is now Illinois. **page 57**

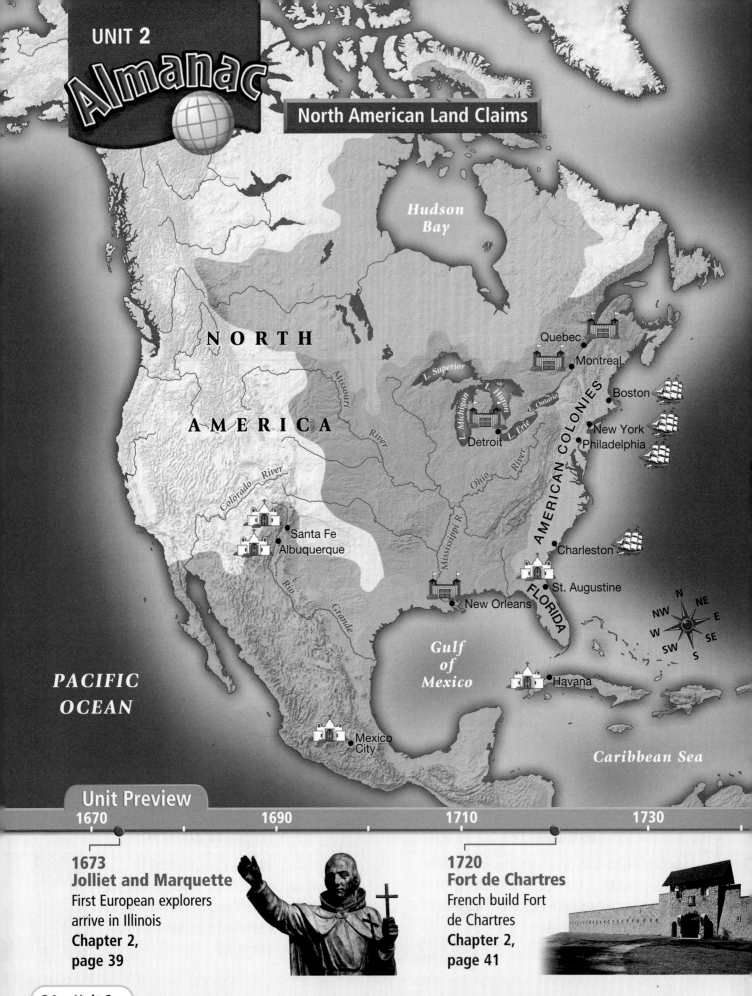

Hudson Bay

N O R T H

A M E R I C A

L. Superior

L. Michigan

L. Huron

L. Ontario

L. Erie

Quebec

Montreal

Boston

New York

Philadelphia

Detroit

Missouri River

Colorado River

Ohio River

Mississippi R.

AMERICAN COLONIES

Santa Fe

Albuquerque

Rio Grande

Charleston

New Orleans

St. Augustine

FLORIDA

N
NW NE
W   E
SW SE
S

PACIFIC OCEAN

Gulf of Mexico

Havana

Mexico City

Caribbean Sea

Unit Preview

1670   1690   1710   1730

1673
Jolliet and Marquette
First European explorers
arrive in Illinois
**Chapter 2,
page 39**

1720
Fort de Chartres
French build Fort
de Chartres
**Chapter 2,
page 41**

LEGEND

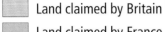 Land claimed by Britain

Land claimed by France

Land claimed by Spain

 British port

 Spanish mission

 French trading post

ATLANTIC OCEAN

km 0   300   600

mi 0   300   600

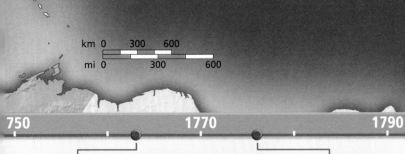

750 ——————— 1770 ——————— 1790

1763 Proclamation of 1763

Britain tries to limit western settlement

Chapter 3, page 58

1776 Liberty Declared

Colonies declare independence

Chapter 3, page 65

Connect to Today

Crossing the Atlantic, 1684

La Salle and his ships crossed the Atlantic in 58 days.

Crossing the Atlantic Today

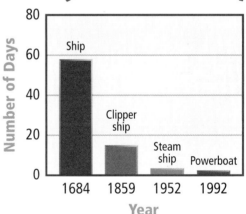

More than 300 years later, a powerboat crossed the Atlantic in 58 hours and 34 minutes.

CURRENT EVENTS

WEEKLY WR READER

Current events on the web!

Read social studies articles about current events at **www.eduplace.com/kids/hmss/**

Chapter 2 Exploring Illinois

Technology

e • glossary
e • word games
www.eduplace.com/kids/hmss/

Vocabulary Preview

missionary

Jacques Marquette was a French explorer and **missionary.** He came to teach American Indians his religion.
page 39

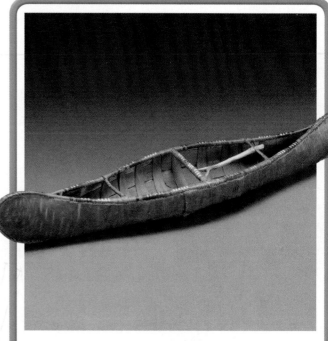

voyageur

A **voyageur** was a guide who paddled the canoes of French explorers and fur traders. In the 1700s, many French voyageurs came to work in Illinois. page 44

Chapter Timeline

1673
Marquette and Jolliet explore the Mississippi River

1720
Fort de Chartres is built

1670　　　1690　　　1710

Monitor and Clarify Use this strategy to check your understanding of the text.

Quick Tip

As you read, pause to ask yourself if you understand what you have read. If not, read the passage again.

ally

The French needed an **ally** in their fight against the British. Many American Indians were allies of the French against the British in the French and Indian War. **page 46**

treaty

France and Britain signed a **treaty** to end the French and Indian War. In the Treaty of Paris, France gave all of its lands east of the Mississippi River to Britain. **page 47**

1763
French and Indian War ends

1730   1750   1770

Early Exploration

VOCABULARY

colony
missionary
mission

Vocabulary Strategy

missionary

The suffix **-ary** means related to or connected with. A **missionary** is a person who teaches religion at a mission.

READING SKILL

Sequence Write in order the events of French exploration in Illinois.

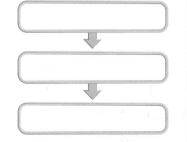

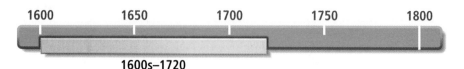

1600   1650   1700   1750   1800

1600s–1720

Build on What You Know Have you ever taken a shortcut to get somewhere? In the 1600s, Europeans looked for a water route through North America that would be a shortcut to Asia.

First Europeans in North America

Main Idea In the 1600s, French explorers explored the Mississippi River and the area that is now Illinois.

For thousands of years, many American Indian groups lived in North America. In the 1500s and 1600s people from Europe came to North America. The land was rich in resources.

England, France, and Spain started colonies in North America. A **colony** is land ruled by another country. The French were the first to start a colony in the area that includes what is present-day Illinois. They came because they wanted to control the fur trade with the American Indians living there. They were also looking for a water route through North America to the Pacific Ocean.

Explorer Ships Explorers sailed to North America from Europe.

Jolliet and Marquette As they searched for a shortcut to Asia, they strengthened France's claim to the upper part of the Mississippi River.

Jolliet and Marquette

Louis Jolliet (JOH lee eht) and **Jacques Marquette** (mahr KEHT) were the first Europeans to explore what is present-day Illinois. Jolliet and Marquette worked for France. Jolliet was an explorer. Marquette was a missionary. A **missionary** is a person who goes to another country to teach religion. Together, they tried to find a shortcut water route across North America to the Pacific Ocean. Marquette also wanted to set up a mission to teach his religion to the American Indians. A **mission** is a place where missionaries work. American Indians told Jolliet and Marquette about a river that might flow to the ocean. They decided to find this river.

In June 1673, Jolliet and Marquette reached the Mississippi River. They traveled south on the river. On the way they met Illinois and Arkansas Indians. Marquette knew six American Indian languages, so he was able to talk with the Illinois and Arkansas. Farther south they met American Indians who told them that the river flowed to the Gulf of Mexico, not to the Pacific Ocean.

Jolliet and Marquette returned back up the river. Jolliet went on to Canada. Marquette decided to start a mission in what is present-day Illinois. He built the mission at Kaskaskia.

REVIEW Why did Jolliet and Marquette explore the Mississippi River?

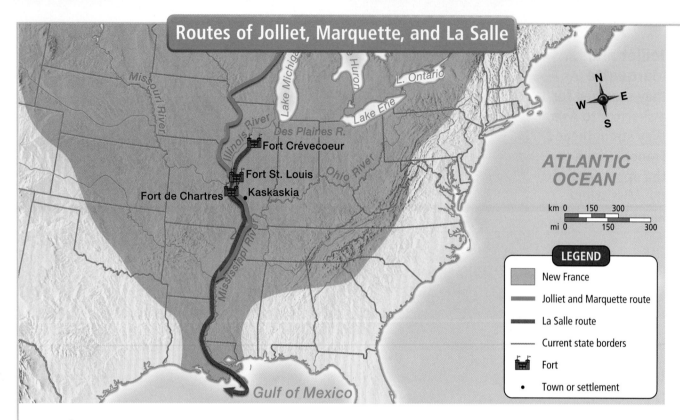

Routes of Jolliet, Marquette, and La Salle

Missouri River

Lake Michigan
Lake Huron
L. Ontario
Lake Erie

Des Plaines R.

Illinois River

Fort Crévecoeur

Fort St. Louis

Fort de Chartres

Kaskaskia

Ohio River

Mississippi River

Gulf of Mexico

ATLANTIC OCEAN

N W E S

km 0   150   300
mi 0   150   300

LEGEND

New France

Jolliet and Marquette route

La Salle route

Current state borders

Fort

Town or settlement

Explorer Routes Jolliet, Marquette, and La Salle explored parts of the Mississippi, Illinois, and Des Plaines rivers. **SKILL** **Reading Maps** Along which river did Jolliet, Marquette, and La Salle travel?

La Salle

Main Idea La Salle explored the entire Mississippi River and built two forts.

Rene Robert Cavelier, sieur de La Salle (ruh NAY roh BAIR kah vuh lee AY, SIHR duh luh SAL) was a French explorer and fur trader. He wanted France to gain more lands in North America and expand trade in furs with the American Indians. In 1680, he built the first French fort, Fort Crevecoeur (CREV uh core), near the present-day city of Peoria. The French built forts to serve as trading centers and to guard French lands. In 1681, La Salle led explorers down the Mississippi River to the Gulf of Mexico.

Fort St. Louis

La Salle's group became the first Europeans to travel the length of the river. La Salle claimed the Mississippi River and all the surrounding land and rivers for France. He named all the land he claimed "Louisiana." Present-day Illinois was part of that large Louisiana land claim. In 1682 and 1683, La Salle built Fort St. Louis near the Illinois River. It became an important trading center for fur traders and trappers. The fort sat on a cliff, letting soldiers guard the Illinois River. In time, many settlements grew around Fort St. Louis. In 1683, about 18,000 people lived near the fort.

Fort de Chartres

In 1720, the French built Fort de Chartres (duh SHAR-truh) along the Mississippi River west of Prairie du Rocher. Fort de Chartres began as a log fort. Later, the French rebuilt it using stone.

Soldiers at Fort de Chartres helped the French protect their land claims from other European countries. The soldiers also tried to keep the peace between French settlers and American Indians.

REVIEW Why did the French build forts in Illinois?

Lesson Summary

- Jolliet and Marquette were the first Europeans to explore land in what is now Illinois.

- La Salle explored all of the Mississippi River and built the first French forts in Illinois.

- Fort St. Louis became an important trading center in Illinois.

Why It Matters ...

European explorers brought new ways of life to North America, including what is present-day Illinois.

Fort de Chartres This was one of the strongest forts in North America.

Lesson Review

1673
Marquette and Jolliet explore the Mississippi River

1680
Fort Crevecoeur is built

| 1600 | 1625 | 1650 | 1675 | 1700 | 1725 |

❶ **VOCABULARY** Use the word **missionary** in a brief paragraph about Jacques Marquette.

❷ **READING SKILL** Look at your sequence chart. What was the first fort La Salle built in Illinois?

❸ **MAIN IDEA: Geography** Near which river was Fort St. Louis built?

❹ **TIMELINE SKILL** How many years after Marquette and Jolliet explored the Mississippi River was Fort Crevecoeur built?

❺ **CRITICAL THINKING: Infer** Marquette spoke the languages of several American Indian nations. Why might this be important for an explorer?

✏️ **WRITING ACTIVITY** Choose an explorer from the lesson, and write a paragraph about that person.

MAPPING *the* LAND

Can a map have a point of view? Early explorers made the first maps of the lands they saw. In 1673, Louis Jolliet and Jacques Marquette explored the Mississippi River. Jolliet's map shows the importance of the Great Lakes and the Mississippi River. He saw the waterways as the best way to increase French trade and settlement. It was easier to travel by water than by land. Jolliet's map helped open the Midwest to exploration and settlement.

North America Today

A Better Picture Mapmaking has changed since Jolliet's time. Modern maps of North America are much more accurate.

Letter
Jolliet wrote: "That great river [the Mississippi] … flows between Florida and Mexico, and on its way to the sea runs through the most beautiful country imaginable.…"

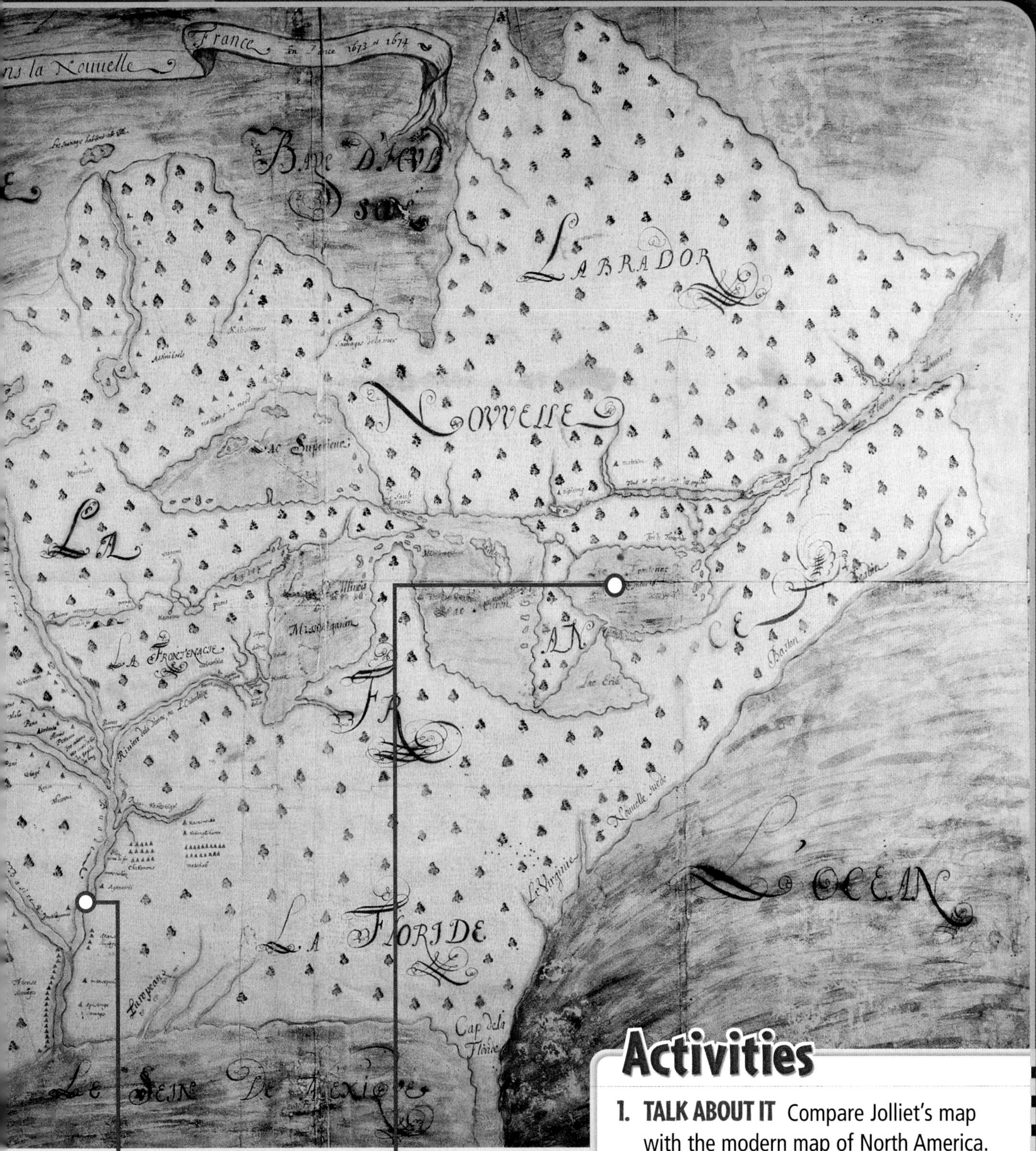

River

Jolliet drew the Mississippi and the rivers flowing into it. He saw the Gulf of Mexico, Mississippi River, Great Lakes, and Atlantic Ocean as one large waterway.

Lakes

Notice how large Jolliet drew Lake Ontario. The Great Lakes were very important to French trade and settlement.

Activities

1. **TALK ABOUT IT** Compare Jolliet's map with the modern map of North America. Discuss the ways that the maps are different and the ways that they are alike.

2. **MAP IT** Make a map of your school. Label the places that you think are important. Exchange maps with a classmate, and discuss the places that you did and did not label.

43

The French and British in Illinois

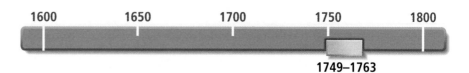

1600   1650   1700   1750   1800

1749–1763

VOCABULARY

voyageur
government
ally
treaty

Vocabulary Strategy

voyageur

Look for the word **voyage** in **voyageur**. Voyageurs were people who went on many voyages.

READING SKILL

Cause and Effect As you read, think about how certain events caused other events to happen. Write down causes and effects in a chart.

CAUSE   EFFECT

Build on What You Know What is it like to move to a new place to live? In the 1700s, the first European settlers in Illinois came to a land that was new to them.

French Settlements

Main Idea In the early 1700s, the French built many settlements in what is now Illinois.

Once people came to the Illinois country, many decided to settle there. French voyageurs were the first Europeans to settle in Illinois. A **voyageur** was someone who guided and paddled explorers' canoes. Voyageurs traded with American Indian nations, such as the Kaskaskia, Peoria, Michigamea, Tamaroa, and Cahokia. Some fur traders often lived in Indian villages and became members of the community.

Trade with American Indians was important to the French. Indians traded furs which were valuable when sold back in Europe. The French had knives, beads, blankets, and other supplies to trade for furs. Through trade, both the Indians and the French received goods that they wanted.

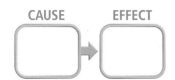

Pioneer Home Early settlers in Illinois built houses such as this one in Kaskaskia.

New French Towns

The French built missions, forts, and trading posts along the Great Lakes and in what is present-day Illinois. These places became important stops along the route between Canada and lower Louisiana.

In time, more settlers came to Illinois. They built towns around the missions and trading posts. These towns grew as more people came.

One town was Kaskaskia. It grew up around the mission that Marquette had founded. Kaskaskia was built at the place where the Kaskaskia River joins the Mississippi River. It became a busy trading center for people traveling along the Mississippi River.

Prairie du Rocher was a French town about 15 miles north of Kaskaskia. Its rich soil attracted many farmers, and a town started there.

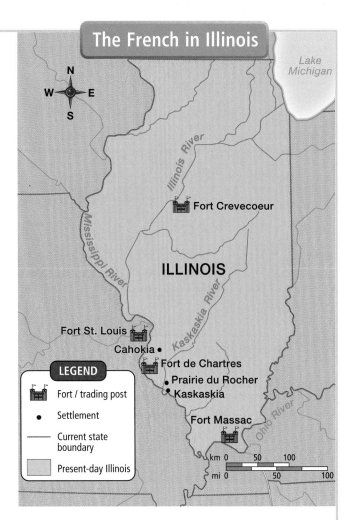

The French in Illinois

Illinois Settlements Most settlements were located in the southern part of what is present-day Illinois.

SKILL **Reading Maps** What was the southernmost settlement in Illinois?

Fort de Chartres was about five miles west of Prairie du Rocher. It was the center of French government in the area. A **government** is an organization that makes laws and keeps order. From Fort de Chartres, French officials ruled all of Illinois.

REVIEW Why was trade important to the French and American Indians in Illinois?

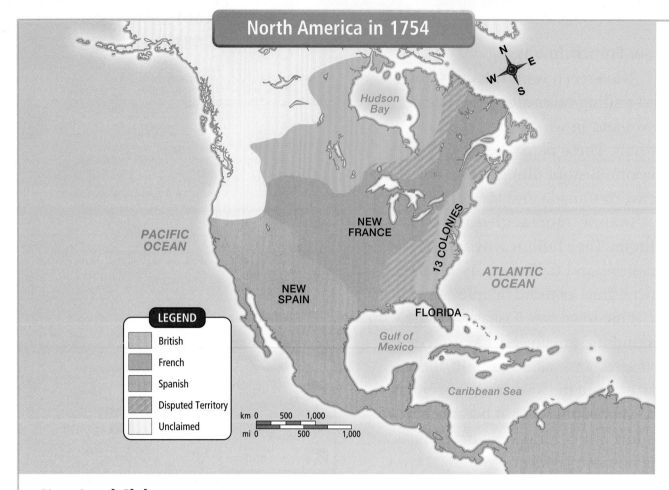

North America in 1754

New Land Claims In 1754, Spain, France and Britain claimed much of the land in North America. **SKILL** **Reading Maps** Which country claimed the land around the Great Lakes?

The French and Indian War

Main Idea Britain gained new land in the French and Indian War.

For many years, the French controlled the fur trade in North America. Great Britain also wanted to trade with the Indians. In 1749, British colonists began trading and claiming land in the Ohio Valley. France and Britain disagreed about who owned the land. France built forts to keep the British from taking over French land claims and the fur trade in North America.

The War Begins

In 1754, the French and British settlers began fighting over the land. Two years later, Britain and France declared war. This was the start of the French and Indian War.

The French had many American Indian allies. An **ally** is a person or group that joins another to work for the same goal. Most American Indians believed that if Britain won the war, British settlers would take American Indian hunting land for farms. Most American Indians, therefore, became allies of the French.

The War Ends

Most of the battles in the French and Indian War happened in Canada and in the East. British soldiers outnumbered the French and American Indian soldiers. The British took over French forts and cities in Canada. They captured the cities of Quebec and Montreal in 1759.

The French and Indian War officially ended in 1763 with the Treaty of Paris. A **treaty** is an agreement between nations. In the treaty, France agreed to give all of its land east of the Mississippi River to Britain. This included Illinois. Over the next few years, the French began moving out of their forts in Illinois and the British began moving in.

REVIEW What effect did the French and Indian War have on Illinois?

Lesson Summary

> In the early 1700s, the French controlled the fur trade in the Great Lakes area.

> In 1749, the British began claiming land in the area.

> In 1756, disagreements between France and Britain over control of the land led to war.

> The war ended in 1763 when France gave all its land east of the Mississippi River to Britain.

Why It Matters ...

The British victory over the French helped Britain strengthen its control of the eastern half of North America. Evidence of British culture still exists in Illinois today.

Lesson Review

1749	1756	1763
British settle in Ohio Valley	French and Indian War begins	French and Indian War ends

1740   1750   1760   1770

1 **VOCABULARY** Why did many American Indian nations become an **ally** of the French?

2 **READING SKILL** What happened after the French and Indian War ended in North America?

3 **MAIN IDEA: Geography** Why did Kaskaskia become a busy trading center?

4 **MAIN IDEA: Government** Which country controlled Illinois at the end of the French and Indian War?

5 **TIMELINE SKILL** How many years did the French and Indian War last?

6 **CRITICAL THINKING: Draw Conclusions** Why do you think French settlers in Illinois built towns around missions and trading posts?

WRITING ACTIVITY Write a news report for British colonists. Tell them about the end of the French and Indian War.

Extend Lesson 2

History

Fort de Chartres

From the stone walls of Fort de Chartres, French soldiers watch the Mississippi River flow past. The position of the fort near the river made it easy to get supplies to the soldiers. Forts were designed to defend against attack and support the people who lived there. Fort de Chartres was the center of French government in what is now Illinois. It was their strongest fort in North America.

Unlike most French forts, Fort de Chartres had walls made of stone instead of wood. They protected the fort from flooding and attack.

Soldiers stored weapons and supplies in the powder magazine.

Soldiers in the fort could fire muskets and cannons through holes cut in the walls.

The four corners of the fort were called bastions. Soldiers in the bastions kept watch and defended the fort.

Supplies, such as food and trade goods, were kept in the storehouse.

Activities

1. **TALK ABOUT IT** Discuss the features of Fort de Chartres. Do you think the fort is well designed? What else do you think people who lived in the fort might need or want?

2. **MAP IT** Learn more about French forts in North America. Make a map showing the location of at least three other French forts. Label waterways near the forts.

49

Skillbuilder

Make a Timeline

A timeline shows events in the order in which they happened. You can organize and remember information by making a timeline of important events and dates.

Learn the Skill

Step 1: List the important events and their dates. This list shows three events from Lesson 2.

> 1756– Britain and France declare war.
>
> 1759– The British capture Quebec and Montreal.
>
> 1763– Treaty of Paris ends the French and Indian War.

Step 2: Decide how many years you will show on the timeline. The listed events cover a time period of seven years, from 1756 to 1763. Draw the line so that each section stands for the same number of years. In this example, each section stands for one year.

1756   1757   1758   1759   1760   1761   1762   1763

Step 3: Write each event above its listed year. Add a title.

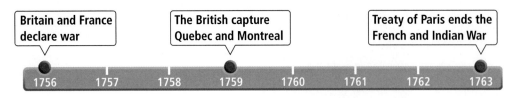

Britain and France declare war

The British capture Quebec and Montreal

Treaty of Paris ends the French and Indian War

1756   1757   1758   1759   1760   1761   1762   1763

Practice the Skill

Read the paragraph below. It tells about events that led to the French and Indian War. Answer the questions. Then make a timeline of the events.

> In 1749, British colonists began trading and claiming land in the Ohio Valley. They settled on land that the French said belonged to them. Britain and France disagreed over who owned the land. In 1754, the French and the British began fighting for control of the land. In 1756, France and Britain declared war.

1 What events and dates would you show on a timeline?

2 How many years would be covered on the timeline?

3 What title would you give the timeline?

Apply the Skill

Reread the section on page 40 about La Salle. Make a timeline to show La Salle's achievements.

Visual Summary

1 – 3. Write a description of what each person did in the area that became Illinois.

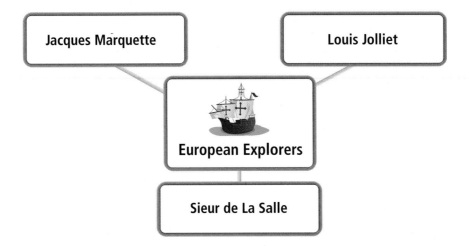

Jacques Marquette

Louis Jolliet

European Explorers

Sieur de La Salle

Facts and Main Ideas

✔ **TEST PREP** Answer each question below.

4. **Geography** What river did Jolliet, Marquette, and La Salle explore?

5. **Economics** Why did the French settle in Illinois?

6. **History** What disagreement between France and Britain led to the start of the French and Indian War?

7. **History** What happened in Illinois after the French and Indian War?

Vocabulary

✔ **TEST PREP** Choose the correct word from the list below to complete each sentence.

colony, p. 38
voyageur, p. 44
government, p. 45

8. The French began a _____ in the Great Lakes area to control fur trade in North America.

9. Fort de Chartres was the center of French _____ in Illinois.

10. Someone who guided and paddled an explorer's canoe was called a _____.

1673 Marquette and Jolliet explore the Mississippi River	1720 Fort de Chartres is built	1763 French and Indian War ends

1670   1690   1710   1730   1750   1770

Apply Skills

✔ **TEST PREP** **Timeline Skill** Apply what you learned about making a timeline. Use the information about Illinois history to answer each question.

- **1673** Jolliet and Marquette explore the Mississippi River.
- **1680** La Salle builds Fort Crevecoeur.
- **1720** French build Fort de Chartres.

11. If you marked your timeline to show every tenth year, where would Jolliet and Marquette's exploration of the Mississippi River be placed?

   A. between 1670 and 1680
   B. between 1680 and 1690
   C. between 1690 and 1700
   D. between 1700 and 1710

12. La Salle built Fort St. Louis in 1682 and 1683. Where would you place this information on the timeline?

   A. to the left of 1670
   B. to the right of 1680
   C. to the left of 1680
   D. between 1700 and 1710

Critical Thinking

✔ **TEST PREP** Write a short paragraph to answer each question below.

13. **Infer** Why do you think that the town of Kaskaskia was built at the place where the Kaskaskia River joins the Mississippi River?

14. **Summarize** Write a paragraph describing the French and Indian War.

Timeline

Use the Chapter Summary Timeline to answer the question.

15. What events took place in the 1700s?

Activities

Map Activity Explorers made maps that settlers later used. Draw a map of your school to show people how to find important places.

Writing Activity Think about life in Illinois during the 1700s. Use what you have learned to write a brief report about early towns in Illinois.

Technology
Writing Process Tips
Get help with your report at
www.eduplace.com/kids/hmss/

Chapter 3

Conflict in Illinois

Technology

e • **glossary**
e • **word games**
www.eduplace.com/kids/hmss/

Vocabulary Preview

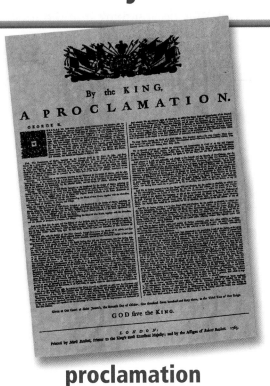

proclamation

Britain's king made a **proclamation** in 1763. It stated that colonists could not settle west of the Appalachian Mountains.
page 58

boycott

Colonists decided to **boycott** British goods. They refused to buy or use goods that came from Britain.
page 65

Chapter Timeline

1763 Pontiac's Rebellion			1773 Boston Tea Party	
1760	1765	1770		1775

Reading Strategy

Summarize As you read, use the summarize strategy to focus on important ideas.

Quick Tip Take notes as you read. Then highlight the most important information.

independence

Colonists fought for their **independence.** They wanted to be free from British rule.
page 65

constitution

In 1787, American leaders met to write a **constitution.** It explained how the government would be formed and run.
page 67

1783
United States becomes a country

1780   1785   1790

Core Lesson 1

Controlling the Land

VOCABULARY

rebellion
siege
proclamation

Vocabulary Strategy

proclamation

Proclamation comes from the word **proclaim,** which means to tell something to the public. A proclamation is a public statement.

READING SKILL

Compare and Contrast
Contrast the reactions of American Indians and settlers to the Proclamation of 1763.

American Indians	British Settlers

1760	1770	1780	1790

1763–1772

Build on What You Know Have you ever wanted to go someplace that you were not allowed? Some colonists were upset when British leaders told them that they could not settle in present-day Illinois.

British Control of Illinois

Main Idea Many American Indians tried to keep the British from settling on their land.

Britain gained control of nearly all of eastern North America after the French and Indian War. This area included present-day Illinois.

The British wanted to settle on American Indian lands. They tried to get the American Indians to sell their land. Sometimes, the British forced American Indians to leave and move farther west.

Moving West British settlers wanted to move to areas where American Indians had villages such as the one shown here.

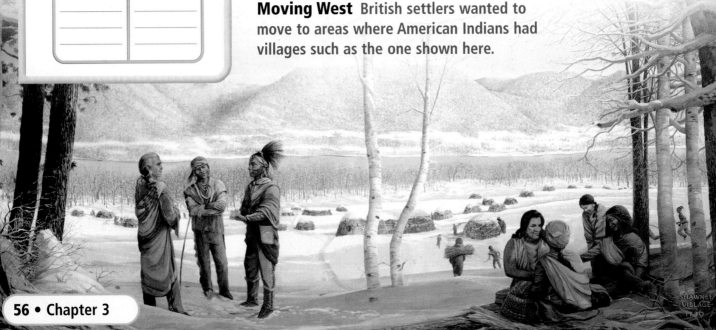

SHAWNEE VILLAGE

Pontiac and Gladwin In this picture, Pontiac meets with the commander of Fort Detroit, Major Henry Gladwin. Pontiac later laid siege to the fort.

Pontiac's Rebellion

Many American Indian leaders were angry because the British had taken their lands. They wanted the British to leave. **Pontiac** was one such leader. He was a chief of the Ottawa people. Pontiac decided to bring together several American Indian groups to plan a rebellion. A **rebellion** is a fight against a government.

Many tribes from present-day Illinois and nearby areas joined Pontiac. Pontiac and his allies wanted to capture the British forts around the Great Lakes. The battles for these forts became known as Pontiac's Rebellion.

Pontiac led a group of warriors to attack Fort Detroit in what is now Michigan. The British commander of the fort learned of Pontiac's plans, however.

Pontiac could not take the British by surprise. He had to lay siege to the fort instead. In a **siege,** a group surrounds a place and stops people and supplies from entering or leaving until the other side gives up. The siege lasted for five months. At that point, more British soldiers arrived. The British were too strong for the warriors to defeat, so Pontiac ended the siege.

Pontiac's allies had more success. They captured eight of the twelve forts that they attacked. The British fought back, though. They defeated Pontiac's forces. After three years, Pontiac realized he could not defeat the British. He signed a peace treaty that ended the rebellion.

REVIEW Why did Pontiac and other American Indians fight the British?

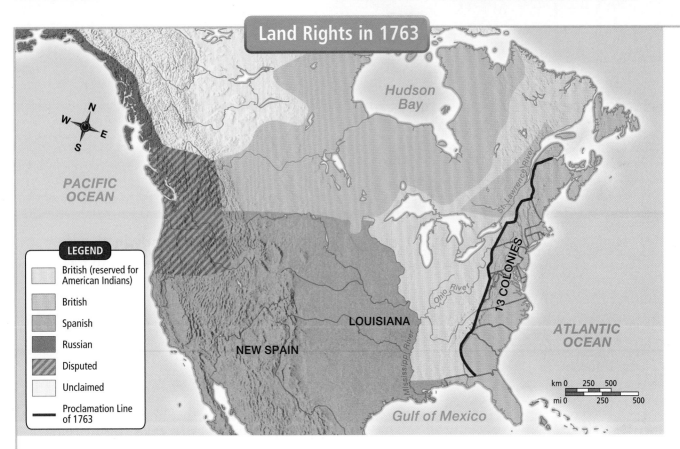

New Lands to Rule After the French and Indian War, the British had to decide what to do with the land they had gained. **SKILL** **Reading Maps** What country controlled much of the land east of the Mississippi River?

Proclamation of 1763

Main Idea King George III of Britain issued the Proclamation of 1763 to prevent further western settlement.

British leaders wanted to avoid more conflicts like Pontiac's Rebellion. So **King George III** of Britain issued the Proclamation of 1763 to keep settlers from taking more land from American Indians. A **proclamation** is an official public statement. The Proclamation said that colonists could not settle west of the Appalachian Mountains. It said that those lands belonged to American Indians.

The Proclamation was good for American Indians. They hoped it would prevent settlers from taking more land. Settlers did not agree with the Proclamation. Many believed that leaders in Britain did not have the right to tell them where they could live. Some settlers who already lived west of the Appalachian Mountains refused to leave. Others moved west.

British soldiers also lived west of the mountains. After the French and Indian War, the British began taking over French forts in present-day Illinois. In 1765, the British army took command of Fort de Chartres.

Soldiers in the West

The British army wanted to govern the West from Fort de Chartres. However, flooding from the Mississippi River damaged the fort. In 1772, the soldiers left Fort de Chartres and moved to Kaskaskia.

At that time, other disagreements were growing between British leaders and colonists in the East. The British had to send soldiers from present-day Illinois and other western lands to keep order in the colonies. As a result, the British did not have enough soldiers to stop settlers from moving farther west.

REVIEW Why did the British take over Fort de Chartres?

Lesson Summary

> Pontiac leads rebellion to stop British settlement.

> Proclamation of 1763 tries to end British settlement on American Indian lands.

> British soldiers leave western lands to restore order in eastern colonies.

> British settlers continue to push west onto American Indian lands.

Why It Matters...

After the French and Indian War, colonists began to disagree with British rule. In time, these disagreements led to conflict with Britain.

Lesson Review

1763	1765		1772
Proclamation of 1763	British take Fort de Chartres		British leave Fort de Chartres

1760   1765   1770   1775

① **VOCABULARY** Choose the word that completes the sentence.

rebellion   **proclamation**   **siege**

In 1763, Britain made a _____ to prevent further western settlement.

② **READING SKILL** **Compare** people's reactions to the Proclamation of 1763. Why were they different?

③ **MAIN IDEA: History** Why did many American Indian groups join Pontiac's Rebellion?

④ **MAIN IDEA: Government** Why did Britain issue the Proclamation of 1763?

⑤ **TIMELINE SKILL** How many years did the British occupy Fort de Chartres?

⑥ **CRITICAL THINKING: Infer** Why do you think some settlers ignored the Proclamation of 1763?

HANDS ON

MATH ACTIVITY Look at the map on page 58. Use fractions to estimate about how much of North America was set aside for American Indians.

LOOKING WEST

Land seemed to stretch forever beyond the Appalachian Mountains, but this land was closed to settlers. The Proclamation of 1763 was written to keep colonists from moving west of the Appalachian Mountains. The British decision to reserve land for the American Indians upset many colonists. They thought this was unfair because they had fought the French in order to open western lands to settlement. The colonists believed that they should be allowed to settle the land.

Poor colonists who did not own land in the East wanted to settle land across the Appalachian Mountains and start farms. Wealthy colonists also wanted to buy western lands. They wanted to divide large areas of land into smaller sections to sell to settlers.

Daniel Boone Many colonists ignored the Proclamation of 1763. In the early 1770s, Daniel Boone led a group of settlers from North Carolina across the Appalachian Mountains. This group built the Wilderness Road from what is present-day Virginia to what is present-day Kentucky. The road opened western lands to further settlement.

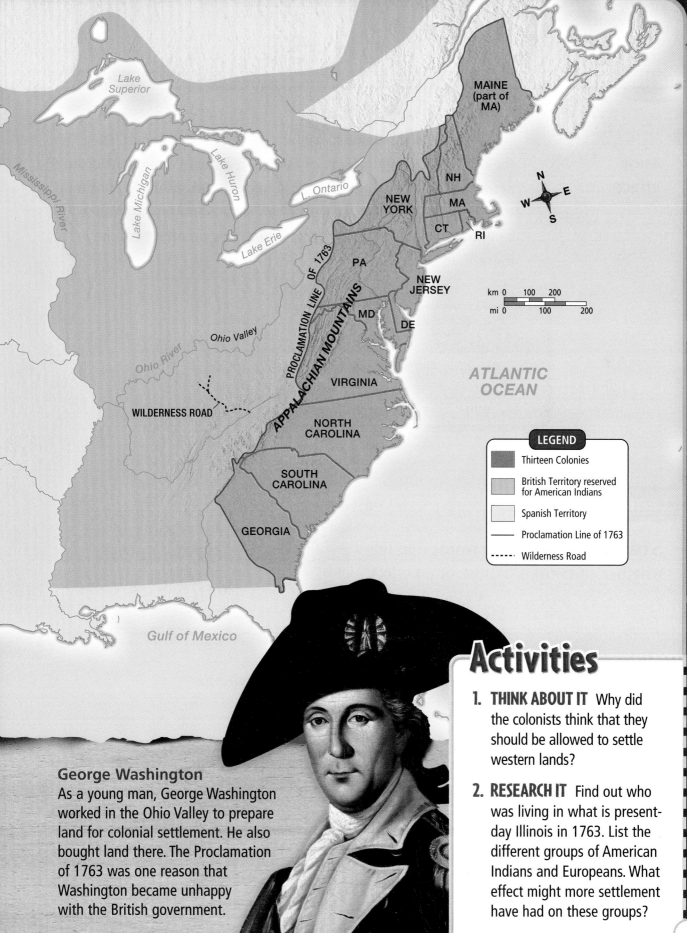

Lake Superior

Mississippi River

Lake Michigan

Lake Huron

L. Ontario

Lake Erie

MAINE (part of MA)

NH

NEW YORK

MA

CT

RI

PROCLAMATION LINE OF 1763

PA

NEW JERSEY

MD

DE

Ohio Valley

Ohio River

APPALACHIAN MOUNTAINS

VIRGINIA

WILDERNESS ROAD

NORTH CAROLINA

SOUTH CAROLINA

GEORGIA

ATLANTIC OCEAN

Gulf of Mexico

N
W E
S

km 0   100   200
mi 0   100   200

LEGEND

Thirteen Colonies

British Territory reserved for American Indians

Spanish Territory

—— Proclamation Line of 1763

----- Wilderness Road

George Washington
As a young man, George Washington worked in the Ohio Valley to prepare land for colonial settlement. He also bought land there. The Proclamation of 1763 was one reason that Washington became unhappy with the British government.

Activities

1. **THINK ABOUT IT** Why did the colonists think that they should be allowed to settle western lands?

2. **RESEARCH IT** Find out who was living in what is present-day Illinois in 1763. List the different groups of American Indians and Europeans. What effect might more settlement have had on these groups?

Skillbuilder

Identify Cause and Effect

▶ **VOCABULARY**
cause
effect

Historians often want to know why events happened. They look for causes and effects of events. A **cause** is an event or an action that makes something else happen. An **effect** is another event or action that is a result of a cause. Sometimes a cause can have more than one effect. Sometimes an effect can have more than one cause.

Cause	**Effect**
Britain defeated France in the French and Indian War.	The British took over French forts in present day Illinois.

Learn the Skill

Step 1: Look for clue words that tell whether an event is a cause or an effect.

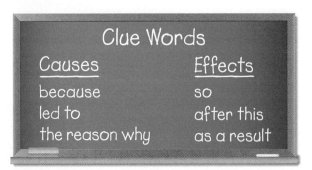

Clue Words

Causes	Effects
because	so
led to	after this
the reason why	as a result

Step 2: Identify the cause of an event. Check to see whether there is more than one cause.

Step 3: Identify the effect. Check to see whether there is more than one effect.

Practice the Skill

Reread pages 56 and 57 of Lesson 1 about British rule and Pontiac's Rebellion. Then answer the following questions and fill out a diagram like the one below.

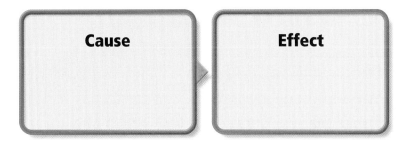

Cause	Effect

1 What caused Pontiac to rebel against the British?

2 What was the effect of more British troops coming to Fort Detroit?

3 What helped you figure out what the causes and effects were?

Apply the Skill

Pontiac's Rebellion led to other events after the French and Indian War. Reread pages 58 and 59. Then make a chart that shows causes and effects. Name some of the clue words that helped you figure out the causes and effects.

The American Revolution

1760   1770   1780   1790

1773–1788

Build on What You Know Have you ever wanted to buy a book or toy? We use money to pay for the things that we want. After the French and Indian War, Britain had to find new ways to get money.

Conflict with Britain

Main Idea Conflict between Britain and its colonies led to war.

Winning the French and Indian War cost Britain a great deal of money. To pay money it owed from the war, Britain's government had to raise money. It decided to make the colonists pay taxes. A **tax** is money that people pay a government for its services. Britain had protected the colonies during the French and Indian War. In return, the British thought that the colonists should help pay for the war.

The colonists did not agree with Britain's decision to tax them. For years, Britain had allowed the colonies to rule themselves. The colonists believed that only their local governments had the right to tax them.

Colonial Taxes Britain taxed anything printed on paper. Colonists had to pay a tax for stamps such as this one on all documents.

Colonists Take Action

Many colonists decided not to pay the new taxes. Some colonists held protests. A protest is an event at which people speak out against an idea or action. They held a boycott of British goods. A **boycott** occurs when people refuse to buy, sell, or use certain goods or services. As a result, British merchants could not sell as many goods in the colonies.

In 1773, colonists in Boston, Massachusetts, held a protest. The colonists were called Patriots. Patriots were colonists who opposed British rule. Other colonists were Loyalists. Loyalists remained loyal to Britain. The Patriots wanted to protest a British tax on tea. They dressed as American Indians and boarded British ships. They dumped tea from the ships into Boston Harbor. This protest became known as the Boston Tea Party.

The Boston Tea Party In 1773, colonists dumped tea into Boston Harbor in a protest against British taxes.

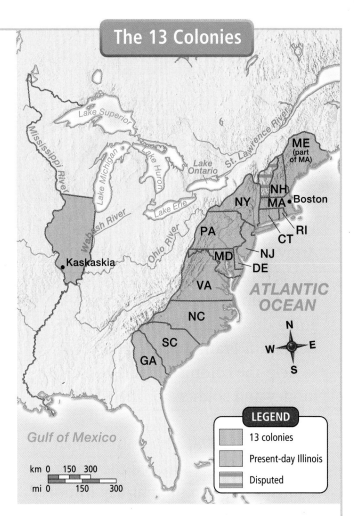

The 13 Colonies

LEGEND
- 13 colonies
- Present-day Illinois
- Disputed

km 0   150   300
mi 0   150   300

The British Colonies The colonies were located along the Atlantic coast and did not include places such as Illinois.

War Breaks Out

In the spring of 1775, Britain sent soldiers to control the colonists. The colonists organized their own army, led by **George Washington.** The American Revolution had begun. The colonies wanted independence from Britain. **Independence** is freedom. **Thomas Jefferson** helped write the Declaration of Independence, which explained why the colonies should be free. On July 4, 1776, the colonies declared themselves free from British rule.

REVIEW Why did colonists protest against paying British taxes?

The War in Illinois

Main Idea The colonies gained their independence after the American Revolution.

The war between Britain and the colonies lasted for eight years. George Washington led the colonial soldiers. They were known as the Continental Army. At first, the Continental Army lost several battles. Washington's leadership helped keep the army going during difficult times. In 1778 **Benjamin Franklin** persuaded France to help the colonies. France sent money and soldiers for the war against Britain.

Later in 1778, a colonist named **George Rogers Clark** led the war against Britain in present-day Illinois. Clark was in charge of protecting western settlers.

Clark marched to Kaskaskia with about 175 American soldiers. They arrived in the middle of the night and captured the fort without a fight. With the help of French settlers, Clark and his soldiers then marched east to Vincennes, in present-day Indiana. There, they took control of the British Fort Sackville.

Clark helped win control of lands that today make up Ohio, Indiana, Michigan, and Illinois. His victories in the West came at a time when the Continental Army also was winning battles in the East.

In 1783, the British and the colonists signed a peace treaty. In this agreement, Britain gave up control of the colonies. It also gave up all its land from the Atlantic Ocean to the Mississippi River.

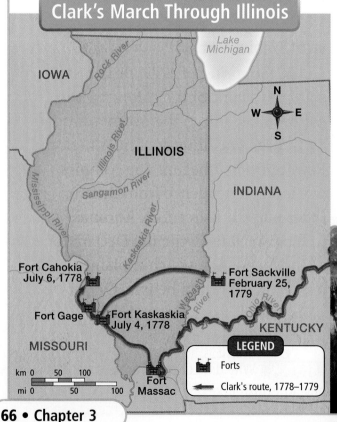

Clark's March Through Illinois

IOWA

Rock River

Lake Michigan

Illinois River

ILLINOIS

Sangamon River

Mississippi River

Kaskaskia River

INDIANA

Fort Cahokia
July 6, 1778

Fort Sackville
February 25, 1779

Fort Gage

Fort Kaskaskia
July 4, 1778

Wabash River

Ohio River

KENTUCKY

MISSOURI

km 0   50   100
mi 0   50   100

Fort Massac

LEGEND
Forts
Clark's route, 1778–1779

Clark's Route This map shows the route that George Rogers Clark took through Illinois.

Victory in Virginia At Yorktown, Virginia, colonial and French forces defeated the British in the last major battle of the war (below).

A New Country

After the American Revolution, colonists formed a new country, the United States of America. The former colonies now became states. They knew that they needed to work together as one country. They needed a plan for government.

In 1787, state leaders met to write a national constitution. A **constitution** is a plan for setting up and running a government. State leaders argued for months about what to include in the constitution. Finally, they agreed. Nine states had to accept the constitution. By 1788, nine states had done so. The United States Constitution became the country's law.

REVIEW Why did the colonies create a constitution after winning independence?

Lesson Summary

- In 1776, the British colonies declared their independence from Britain.

- During the American Revolution, troops led by George Rogers Clark took control of British forts in Illinois.

- The United States Constitution became the country's law in 1788.

Why It Matters...

The end of the American Revolution was the beginning of the United States of America.

The U.S. Constitution In 1788, it became our country's law.

Lesson Review

Timeline:
- 1773 Boston Tea Party
- 1775 American Revolution begins
- 1783 American Revolution ends
- (Timeline marks: 1770, 1775, 1780, 1785, 1790)

❶ **VOCABULARY** Write a paragraph that includes the words **tax** and **boycott.**

❷ **READING SKILL** List the **sequence** of events that took place in present-day Illinois during the American Revolution.

❸ **MAIN IDEA: Economics** Why did Britain want its colonies to pay a tax?

❹ **MAIN IDEA: History** In what way did France help the colonies during the war?

❺ **TIMELINE SKILL** How long did the American Revolution last?

❻ **CRITICAL THINKING: Draw Conclusions** Why do you think state leaders argued about what to include in the constitution?

WRITING ACTIVITY Write a news article to tell about George Rogers Clark's march through Illinois.

Surrender at Vincennes

At Vincennes, British soldiers in their red coats marched out of Fort Sackville to surrender. Colonel George Rogers Clark and his small, tired army waited for them there. Although Clark had fewer than 200 soldiers, he made the British believe he had many more. Capturing Fort Sackville helped give the colonies control of present-day Illinois and Indiana. This painting shows one artist's idea of what Lieut. Governor Henry Hamilton's surrender looked like. Frederick C. Yohn made the painting for the Indiana Historical Society in 1923.

Clark's soldiers were not as well equipped as the British soldiers. They had ragged uniforms or none at all.

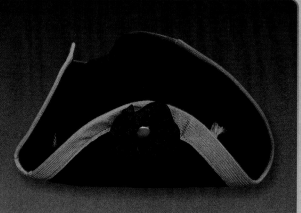

The British wore uniforms that earned them the name "Red Coats." The color of a hat's trim showed whether a man was a soldier (white) or an officer (gold).

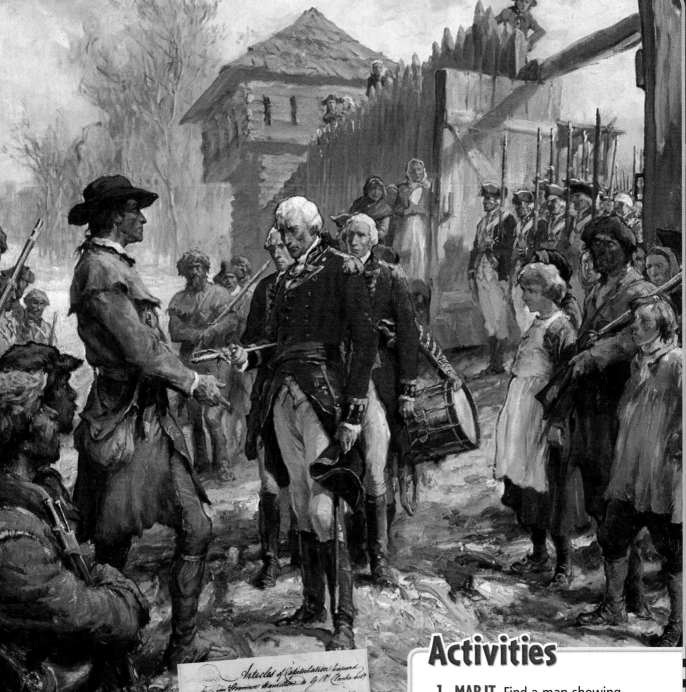

The British commander signed a document to make the surrender official. The painting shows Hamilton and his men marching out of the fort.

Activities

1. **MAP IT** Find a map showing Vincennes, Indiana. How far is it from where you live?

2. **WRITE IT** What might Hamilton and Clark be saying to each other in this painting? Write a short dialogue they might have had.

 Technology Read more primary sources at Education Place. www.eduplace.com/kids/hmss/

Visual Summary

1 – 3. ✎➤ Write a description of each item named below.

Illinois and the American Revolution	
Proclamation of 1763	
Taxes	
George Rogers Clark	

Facts and Main Ideas

✔ **TEST PREP** Answer each question below.

4. **History** What happened during Pontiac's Rebellion?

5. **Economics** Why did Britain's government need to raise money?

6. **Government** Who helped write the Declaration of Independence?

7. **History** What did George Rogers Clark do in Illinois during the American Revolution?

Vocabulary

✔ **TEST PREP** Choose the correct word from the list below to complete each sentence.

siege, p. 57
boycott, p. 65
constitution, p. 67

8. State leaders gathered in 1787 to write a _____ for the United States.

9. Pontiac began a _____ to capture Fort Detroit.

10. Colonists showed Britain that they did not want to pay taxes by choosing to _____ certain British goods.

Apply Skills

✔ **TEST PREP Cause and Effect** Read the passage below. Then use what you have learned about cause and effect to answer each question.

> Britain decided to have colonists help pay the money it owed from the French and Indian War. Britain passed a tax on tea. The colonists held a protest and dumped tea into Boston Harbor. They also began a boycott of certain British goods. In the spring of 1775, Britain and the colonies went to war.

11. Which of the following is the effect of the other events in the passage?

A. Britain decided to tax the colonists.
B. Colonists boycotted British goods.
C. The colonists protested a tax on tea by dumping tea into Boston Harbor.
D. Britain and the colonies went to war.

12. Which of the following events caused Britain to tax the colonies?

A. In 1775, Britain and the colonies went to war.
B. Britain needed to pay money it owed from the French and Indian War.
C. The colonists dumped tea into Boston Harbor.
D. The colonists began a boycott of certain British goods.

Critical Thinking

✔ **TEST PREP** Write a short paragraph to answer each question below.

13. Analyze Why do you think many colonists ignored the Proclamation of 1763?

14. Infer Why were George Rogers Clark's victories at Kaskaskia and Vincennes important?

Timeline

Use the Chapter Summary Timeline above to answer this question.

15. How many years after the Boston Tea Party did the United States become a country?

Activities

Art Activity Create an illustrated timeline that shows at least three important events from the American Revolution.

Writing Activity Write an essay that compares life in the colonies under British rule and life after the American Revolution.

Technology
Writing Process Tips
Get help with your essay at
www.eduplace.com/kids/hmss/

Vocabulary and Main Ideas

✓ **TEST PREP** Write a sentence to answer each question.

1. Why did **missionaries** such as Jacques Marquette come to North America?

2. What kind of business would a **voyageur** do with American Indians?

3. Why did Pontiac lead a **siege** of Fort Detroit?

4. What was the purpose of Britain's **taxes** in the colonies?

5. Why did colonists want their **independence** from Britain?

6. Why did state leaders work together to write a **constitution** for the United States?

Critical Thinking

✓ **TEST PREP** Write a short paragraph to answer each question.

7. **Cause and Effect** What effect did Pontiac's Rebellion have on the way Britain ruled its lands in North America?

8. **Fact and Opinion** Is the statement "George Washington was an effective leader" a fact or an opinion? Explain.

Apply Skills

✓ **TEST PREP** Use what you have learned about making a timeline to answer each question.

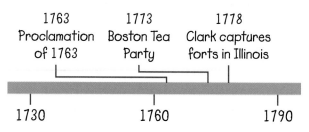

1763
Proclamation of 1763

1773
Boston Tea Party

1778
Clark captures forts in Illinois

1730   1760   1790

9. The American colonies declared their independence in 1776. Where does this event belong on the timeline?

   A. to the left of 1730
   B. between 1730 and 1760
   C. between 1760 and 1790
   D. to the right of 1790

10. Which of the following events would be placed before 1730 on this timeline?

    A. In 1682, La Salle began building Fort St. Louis.
    B. In 1763, the French and Indian War ended.
    C. The American colonies declared their independence in 1776.
    D. In 1765, the British took Fort de Chartres.

Unit Activity

Create a "Why I Came to Illinois" Cartoon

- Choose an explorer, soldier, or colonist. Find out why that person came to Illinois.

- Draw a cartoon with three or four frames that shows the person in Illinois.

- Write statements in speech balloons to explain why the person wanted to come to Illinois.

At the Library

Go to your school or public library to find these books.

Jolliet and Marquette: Explorers of the Mississippi River by Daniel E. Harmon

Learn more about Jolliet and Marquette's travels in Illinois.

George Rogers Clark: Boy of the Northwestern Frontier by Katharine E. Wilkie

A young George Rogers Clark goes on many adventures.

CURRENT EVENTS
WEEKLY (WR) READER

Current Events Project

Learn about famous people from one of the fifty states.

- Choose one state. Find information about famous people who came from that state.

- Draw an outline of the state.

- List some of the state's famous people in your drawing.

- Post your drawing in the classroom.

 Technology

Weekly Reader online offers social studies articles. Go to **www.eduplace.com/kids/hmss/**

Growth and Expansion

The Big Idea

In what ways do people change places?

❝ *I have fixed on this spot in Illinois, and am the better pleased with it the more I see of it.* ❞

Morris Birkbeck,
Illinois settler and author, 1818

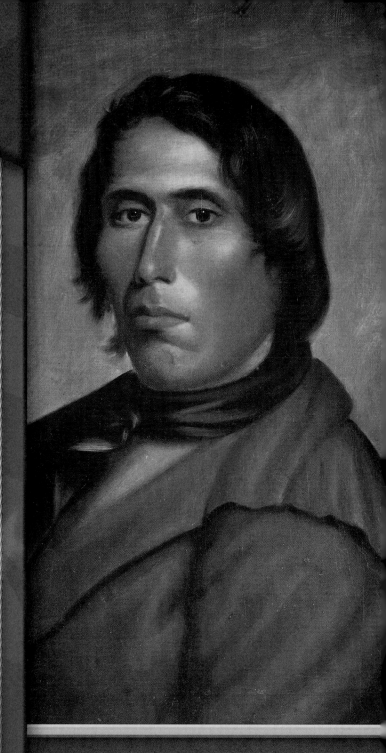

Tecumseh
1768?–1813

Tecumseh was a Shawnee chief whose name meant "Shooting Star." He wanted to bring together American Indians to stop settlers from moving west. **page 88**

History Makers

Nathaniel Pope
1784–1850

Why is Chicago in Illinois today? Pope suggested moving the state's border north to Lake Michigan. Chicago grew along the lake's shoreline. **page 99**

Mary Bickerdyke
1817–1901

Why was this woman famous in Illinois during the Civil War? Bickerdyke was a nurse. She improved conditions at many Union military hospitals. **page 129**

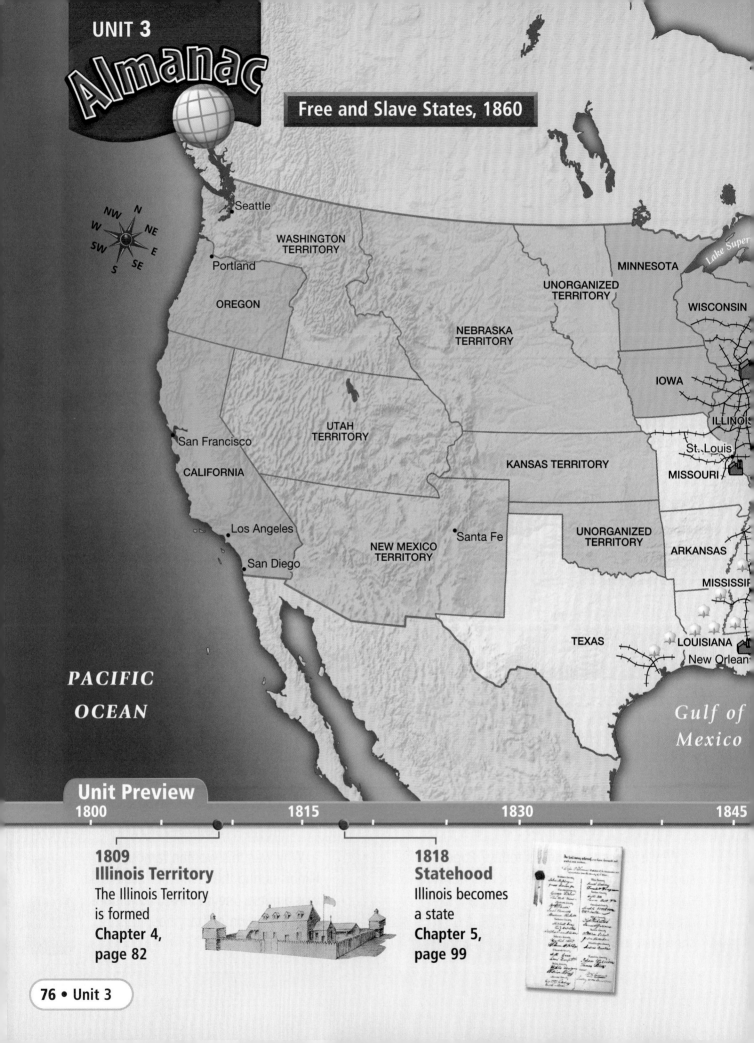

N
NW NE
W   E
SW SE
S

Seattle

WASHINGTON
TERRITORY

Portland

OREGON

MINNESOTA

UNORGANIZED
TERRITORY

WISCONSIN

Lake Super

NEBRASKA
TERRITORY

IOWA

ILLINOIS

UTAH
TERRITORY

San Francisco

CALIFORNIA

St. Louis

MISSOURI

KANSAS TERRITORY

Los Angeles

San Diego

NEW MEXICO
TERRITORY

•Santa Fe

UNORGANIZED
TERRITORY

ARKANSAS

MISSISSIP

PACIFIC

OCEAN

TEXAS

LOUISIANA

New Orlean

Gulf of
Mexico

Unit Preview

1800   1815   1830   1845

1809
Illinois Territory
The Illinois Territory
is formed
**Chapter 4,
page 82**

1818
Statehood
Illinois becomes
a state
**Chapter 5,
page 99**

ATLANTIC OCEAN

MICHIGAN
L. Huron
L. Ontario
Lake Erie
Rochester
Chicago
NEW HAMPSHIRE
VERMONT
MAINE
NEW YORK
Manchester
Lowell
Boston
MASSACHUSETTS
New Bedford
Providence
RHODE ISLAND
CONNECTICUT
New York
NEW JERSEY
Philadelphia
PENNSYLVANIA
INDIANA
OHIO
DELAWARE
MARYLAND
VIRGINIA
Richmond
Louisville
KENTUCKY
NORTH CAROLINA
TENNESSEE
SOUTH CAROLINA
ALABAMA
GEORGIA
FLORIDA

LEGEND
- Slave states
- Free states
- Territories
- +++ Railroad line
- Manufacturing city
- Large manufacturing city
- Cotton-producing area

km 0   200   400
mi 0   200   400

1860

1861
Civil War
The Civil War begins
**Chapter 6,
page 123**

1875

**Chapter 6,
page 123**

Connect to
The Nation

Illinois Population

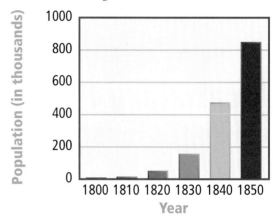

In the early 1800s, settlers from the United States moved to Illinois.

United States Population

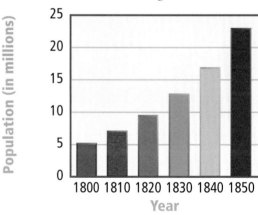

In what ten-year period did the populations of Illinois and the United States increase the most?

CURRENT   EVENTS
WEEKLY (WR) READER

Current events on the web!

Read social studies articles about current events at
www.eduplace.com/kids/hmss/

Chapter 4

The Illinois Territory

Technology

e • **glossary**
e • **word games**
www.eduplace.com/kids/hmss/

Vocabulary Preview

territory

Land that was added to the United States was called a **territory.** Later, these large areas of land were divided into different states. **page 81**

governor

In 1809, Ninian Edwards became the **governor** of Illinois. He led the government in Illinois. **page 82**

Chapter Timeline

1787
Illinois becomes part of Northwest Territory

| 1770 | 1780 | 1790 | 1800 |

Reading Strategy

Question As you read the lessons in this chapter, ask yourself questions about the important ideas.

Quick Tip Stop and ask yourself questions about the text. You can reread to learn the answers.

expedition

Lewis and Clark led an **expedition.** The purpose of this journey was to find a route from the Missouri River to the Pacific Ocean. **page 83**

confederation

Some American Indian nations formed a **confederation.** Some nations still work together today on issues such as pollution and peace. **page 89**

1809
Illinois Territory is formed

1812
War of 1812 begins

1810

1820

New Territory

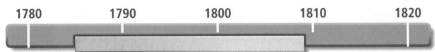

1780   1790   1800   1810   1820

1785–1809

Build on What You Know What if there were no walls inside your school? How would you know where one classroom ended and another began? The early settlers of Illinois had to come up with ways to divide the land.

Looking West

Main Idea After the American Revolution, United States settlement spread westward.

After the American Revolution, the United States controlled more land in North America. This new land extended from the Great Lakes to the Mississippi River. It included what is now present-day Illinois. In the late 1700s, states in the East claimed lands in the West. In 1778, one of those states, Virginia, claimed Illinois as a county. A county is a part of a state. It has its own government. At the time, Illinois was larger than it is today.

As more settlers moved to Illinois, governing the county became more difficult. Virginia did not want to govern such a faraway place. In 1784, it gave the Illinois county to the American government.

VOCABULARY

ordinance
territory
governor
expedition

Vocabulary Strategy

territory

Terra is a word meaning "land." The word **territory** means a large area of land.

READING SKILL
Main Idea and Details
As you read, list details that support the main idea.

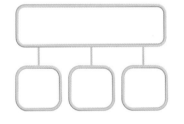

Westward Settlement
In the late 1700s, people traveled to western lands such as Illinois on rafts made of logs.

Growing Nation Western lands became territories of the American government after the American Revolution.

SKILL **Reading Maps** What natural feature formed the western border of the United States in 1787?

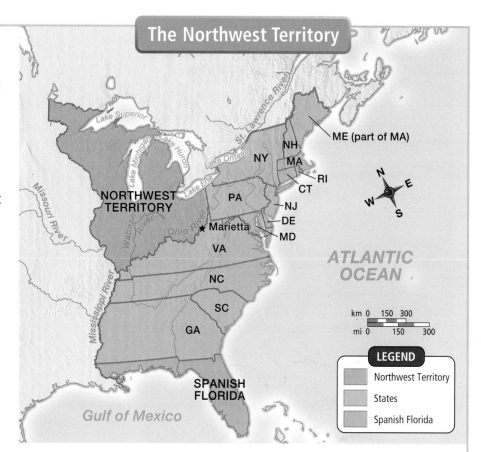

The Northwest Territory

ME (part of MA)
NH
NY
MA
RI
CT
NORTHWEST TERRITORY
PA
NJ
DE
★ Marietta
MD
VA
NC
SC
GA
SPANISH FLORIDA

Lake Superior
Lake Michigan
Lake Huron
Lake Ontario
Lake Erie
St. Lawrence River
Missouri River
Mississippi River
Wabash River
Ohio River

ATLANTIC OCEAN

Gulf of Mexico

km 0   150   300
mi 0   150   300

LEGEND
Northwest Territory
States
Spanish Florida

The Northwest Ordinance

Congress wanted to organize the new land. In 1785, it passed a land ordinance that made rules about how to measure, divide, and sell the land. An **ordinance** is a law made by a government. In 1787, Congress passed the Northwest Ordinance, which set up the Northwest Territory and a plan for settling it. A **territory** is a part of the United States that is not a state. Present-day Illinois was part of the Northwest Territory.

The Northwest Ordinance explained how land in the Northwest Territory could become a new state. When there were 5,000 voters in a territory, they could elect lawmakers. When a territory had 60,000 people, the people could ask to become a state.

Settlers Arrive

Settlers from the United States and other places traveled to the Northwest Territory. In the late 1700s, **Jean Baptiste Point du Sable** came from Haiti. He began a trading post at the site of the present-day city of Chicago.

Conflicts over land arose between American Indians and newcomers. In 1794, U.S. troops defeated American Indians at the Battle of Fallen Timbers in present-day Ohio. After that battle, several American Indian leaders signed the Treaty of Greenville. In this treaty, American Indians gave up most of present-day Ohio and other lands to the United States government.

REVIEW What was the Northwest Ordinance?

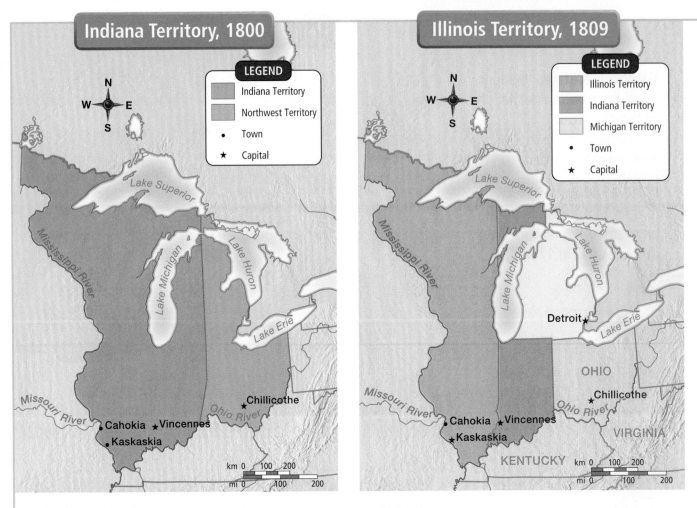

Indiana Territory, 1800

LEGEND
- Indiana Territory
- Northwest Territory
- • Town
- ★ Capital

Lake Superior
Mississippi River
Lake Michigan
Lake Huron
Lake Erie
Missouri River
Ohio River
★ Chillicothe
• Cahokia ★ Vincennes
• Kaskaskia

km 0 100 200
mi 0 100 200

Illinois Territory, 1809

LEGEND
- Illinois Territory
- Indiana Territory
- Michigan Territory
- • Town
- ★ Capital

Lake Superior
Mississippi River
Lake Michigan
Lake Huron
Detroit ★
Lake Erie
OHIO
Missouri River
Ohio River
★ Chillicothe
• Cahokia ★ Vincennes
★ Kaskaskia
VIRGINIA
KENTUCKY

km 0 100 200
mi 0 100 200

Dividing Territory The United States government divided and renamed western territories twice between 1800 and 1809. **SKILL** **Reading Maps** What change was made to the Indiana Territory between 1800 and 1809?

Dividing the Territory

Main Idea As settlement increased, the U.S. government formed new territories.

In 1788, **Arthur St. Clair** became the first governor of the Northwest Territory. A **governor** is an official who leads a state or territorial government. St. Clair worked in the territory's capital, Marietta, in what is present-day Ohio. In 1790, St. Clair visited what is present-day Illinois. He formed the territory's first county. He named it **St. Clair,** after himself.

Illinois Territory

Over time, more and more people came to Illinois. By 1808, about 10,000 settlers lived there. Many of these new settlers wanted the territory's government to be closer to them.

In response, the United States government set up the Illinois Territory in 1809. The Illinois Territory included land in what is present-day Illinois and southern Wisconsin. Kaskaskia was chosen as the capital. **Ninian Edwards** was named the territory's first governor.

The United States Grows

The boundaries of the United States also changed in the early 1800s. President **Thomas Jefferson** agreed to buy a large area of North American land from France. The purchase of this land, called the Louisiana Purchase, doubled the size of the United States. Before the Louisiana Purchase, Illinois was on the western edge of the United States. Now, it was in the center of the country.

Thomas Jefferson He was the third President of the United States.

Meriwether Lewis and **William Clark** led an expedition through the Louisiana Purchase and the land beyond it to look for a route to the Pacific Ocean. An **expedition** is a journey with a special purpose. Lewis and Clark kept a record of what they saw.

REVIEW Who was the first governor of the Illinois Territory?

Lesson Summary

- As the United States grew, Congress made laws to organize western lands.

- In 1809, the Illinois Territory was formed.

Why It Matters ...

Illinois moved closer to statehood when it became a territory in 1809.

Lesson Review

1787 Northwest Territory formed | 1803 Louisiana Purchase | 1809 Illinois Territory formed

1785 — 1790 — 1795 — 1800 — 1805 — 1810

1 **VOCABULARY** Write a paragraph using the words **ordinance, territory,** and **expedition** to describe the American settlement westward.

2 **READING SKILL** What **details** show the steps that Illinois took toward statehood in the early 1800s?

3 **MAIN IDEA: History** What was the name of the law that created the Northwest Territory?

4 **MAIN IDEA: Government** What did the United States government do to organize the West into territories?

5 **TIMELINE SKILL** Which territory was formed first, the Northwest Territory or the Illinois Territory?

6 **CRITICAL THINKING: Cause and Effect** What effect did the Louisiana Purchase have on the position of Illinois in the United States?

HANDS ON **MAP ACTIVITY** On a large sheet of paper, draw a map showing the Northwest Territory as it was in 1787. Make dark lines to show how the territory was divided in 1800 and again in 1809.

Lewis AND Clark

President Thomas Jefferson bought the Louisiana Territory in 1803. At the time, he knew little about the huge piece of land he had bought. He sent Meriwether Lewis and William Clark to explore and map the land west of the Mississippi River.

The journey of Lewis and Clark was a major event in U.S. history. Their explorations led others to journey to the West. Trace their journey on the map, starting in St. Louis.

5 Fort Clatsop
Columbia River

4 Traveler's Rest
Missouri River
Great Falls
Three Forks
Lemhi Pass

Meriwether Lewis

William Clark

"Ocean in view! O! the joy!"

— William Clark, November 7, 1805

1 May 1804:
The Journey Begins!

Lewis, Clark, and their team of more than 40 men headed up the Missouri River into land unexplored by Europeans. It would be a two-year trip.

2 September 1804:
Across the Plains

In the grasslands of what is now South Dakota, the group saw "new" animals such as prairie dogs, pronghorn antelope, coyotes, and jackrabbits. They also saw herds of thousands of buffalo.

3 October 1804–April 1805:
The First Winter

The group built a winter fort near the villages of the Mandan and Hidatsa people. Here, a Shoshone Indian woman named Sacagawea (sak uh guh WEE uh) helped the men find food.

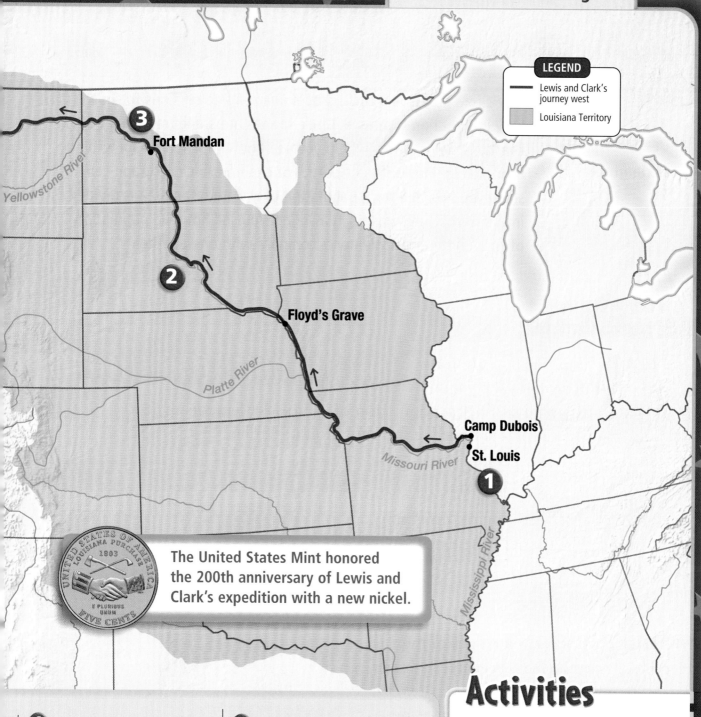

LEGEND
— Lewis and Clark's journey west
▓ Louisiana Territory

3 **Fort Mandan**

2

Yellowstone River

Floyd's Grave

Platte River

Missouri River

Camp Dubois

St. Louis

1

Mississippi River

The United States Mint honored the 200th anniversary of Lewis and Clark's expedition with a new nickel.

4 June 1805:

The Great Falls

Five huge waterfalls blocked the group's travel. It took nearly a month to carry boats and supplies 18 miles to a safe spot up the river.

5 December 1805–March 1806:

The Pacific!

The group spent the winter at Fort Clatsop, waiting for the right time to head home. By the time they completed their journey in September 1806, they had traveled about 8,000 miles.

Activities

1. **CONNECT TO TODAY** Lewis and Clark showed **courage** by going on their journey. Tell about someone you know who has done something courageous.

2. **RESEARCH IT** Read more about Lewis and Clark's journey. Write a series of journal entries about how Sacagawea helped the expedition.

Read a Circle Graph

VOCABULARY
circle graph

A **circle graph** is a circle that is divided into sections to show how information is related. Circle graphs are sometimes called pie charts. Circle graphs can help you see how the whole of something is broken up into different parts. For example, a circle graph can show you how the total population of a state or an area is divided into different settlements. It also lets you see how the populations of these different settlements compare with one another.

Learn the Skill

Step 1: Read the title to find out what information the graph presents. This graph shows the population of Illinois settlements in 1800. The whole circle represents the area's population of settlers.

Population in Illinois Settlements, 1800

Step 2: Read the labels for each section of the circle. Each section of this graph represents the number of settlers living in a particular settlement.

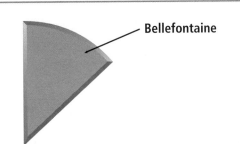

Step 3: Compare the sizes of the different sections. In this graph, a larger section means that more settlers live in that settlement. A smaller section means that fewer settlers live in that settlement.

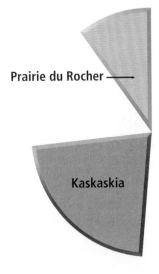

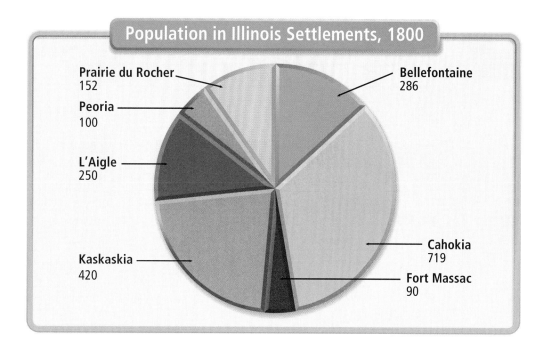

Population in Illinois Settlements, 1800

Prairie du Rocher
152

Peoria
100

L'Aigle
250

Kaskaskia
420

Bellefontaine
286

Cahokia
719

Fort Massac
90

Practice the Skill

Use the circle graph to answer the questions.

1 List the settlements in Illinois in 1800.

2 Which settlement had the largest population in 1800?

3 Which settlement had a larger population in 1800, Kaskaskia or Bellefontaine?

Apply the Skill

Create a circle graph to show how you spend your time during a typical school day. First, draw a circle that stands for the whole school day. Then divide the circle into sections to show all of your activities and the time you spend on each of them.

Tecumseh and the War of 1812

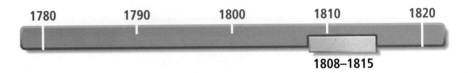

1780   1790   1800   1810   1820

1808–1815

VOCABULARY

unite
confederation

Vocabulary Strategy

confederation

The prefix **con-** means "together." People join together in a **confederation.**

 READING SKILL
Cause and Effect Fill in the chart to show why Tecumseh wanted to stop western settlement.

Build on What You Know Have you ever tried to get people to work together? In this lesson, you will learn how Tecumseh tried to bring together several groups of American Indians.

Tecumseh

Main Idea Tecumseh tried to bring together groups of American Indians to stop western settlement.

In the early 1800s, settlement increased in the Illinois Territory. Not everyone, however, was pleased about the growth of western settlement. Groups of American Indians often battled settlers over land. The settlers usually won. **Tecumseh** hoped to change that.

Tecumseh was born in what is now present-day western Ohio. He understood the effect that western settlement was having on American Indians. Tecumseh and his brother **Tenskwatawa** (tens kwah TAH wah) decided to join with others to stop settlers from moving on to American Indian land.

The Prophet Tenskwatawa, also known as "the Prophet," worked with Tecumseh to stop western settlement.

Shawnee Leader Tecumseh, also known as "Shooting Star," was famous as a public speaker. Today, Tecumseh's likeness appears on a silver dollar (above).

Tecumseh Finds Allies

Tecumseh did not trust settlers. As a child, he learned that settlers had destroyed Shawnee villages. During the American Revolution, Tecumseh fought on the side of the British against the Americans.

Tecumseh visited American Indian leaders west of the Appalachian Mountains. He wanted to unite American Indians. To **unite** means to bring people together for a common purpose. He believed that if they were united, American Indians could stop western settlement.

After the Battle of Fallen Timbers, Tecumseh refused to sign the Treaty of Greenville. He knew that American Indians had lost a lot of land in treaties.

Prophetstown

Tecumseh and his brother formed a confederation of American Indians. A **confederation** is a group united for a purpose. In 1808, the brothers started a village near the Tippecanoe River in the Indiana Territory. People of many Indian nations came to live in Prophetstown, as the village was known.

William Henry Harrison was the governor of the Indiana Territory. He wanted to take more Indian land. In 1811, he led an army to the area near Prophetstown. The two sides fought at the Battle of Tippecanoe. Although neither side won, Prophetstown and the confederation were destroyed. Tecumseh went to Canada.

REVIEW Why did Tecumseh want American Indians to unite?

War of 1812

Main Idea In 1812, the United States went to war against Britain.

In the early 1800s, Britain and the United States were headed toward war again. The British were capturing United States sailors and forcing them to serve in the British navy. Britain also supplied Tecumseh and other American Indian leaders with weapons to use against settlers.

On June 18, 1812, the United States declared war on Britain. American Indians joined the British side in what became known as the War of 1812. American Indians wanted to end U.S. settlement on western lands. They trusted the British. They remembered that the British had tried to stop western settlement with the Proclamation of 1763.

Future President William Henry Harrison battled American Indians and British soldiers during the War of 1812.

Fighting the War

American Indians fought with the British in the former Northwest Territory. In 1812, **Ninian Edwards** was the territorial governor of Illinois. He warned that American Indians might attack Illinois settlers. Edwards was right. In August, American Indians attacked Fort Dearborn.

American Indians fought with the British against U.S. troops several other times during the War of 1812. Tecumseh and British forces captured Fort Detroit, in present-day Michigan. They invaded Ohio. In 1813, they marched to Canada. There, they fought William Henry Harrison and his troops at the Battle of the Thames (tehmz). The United States won that battle, and Tecumseh was killed.

Fort Dearborn It was located where Chicago is today.

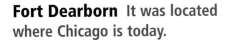

Effects of the War

After two years of fighting, neither Britain nor the United States was winning the war. In 1814, they agreed to end it. The two sides signed a peace treaty. The United States did not gain or lose land in the war. One thing did change, however. The British stopped helping American Indians fight the United States.

Without British support, American Indians lost their power in the Illinois Territory. Although raids by American Indians stopped, settlement in the Illinois Territory did not increase immediately. It would, however, increase in coming years.

REVIEW Why did American Indians join with the British against the United States in the War of 1812?

Lesson Summary

> In the early 1800s, Tecumseh formed a confederation of American Indians to prevent western settlement.

> In 1811, William Henry Harrison and his army destroyed Tecumseh's confederation.

> In 1812, Tecumseh and British forces captured Fort Detroit.

> In 1813, Tecumseh and British forces fought and lost to United States forces at the Battle of the Thames.

Why It Matters...

Loss of British support for American Indians after the War of 1812 allowed settlement in the Illinois Territory to grow.

Lesson Review

| 1808 | 1810 | 1811 Battle of Tippecanoe | 1812 War of 1812 begins | 1812 | 1814 | 1816 |

① **VOCABULARY** Where was Tecumseh's **confederation** located?

② **READING SKILL Cause and Effect** What effect did the lack of British help have on American Indians after the War of 1812?

③ **MAIN IDEA: History** Why did Tecumseh distrust settlers?

④ **MAIN IDEA: History** What conflicts between Britain and the United States led to the War of 1812?

⑤ **TIMELINE SKILL** Which happened first, the War of 1812 or the Battle of Tippecanoe?

⑥ **CRITICAL THINKING: Draw Conclusions** In what way did the War of 1812 affect settlement in the Illinois Territory?

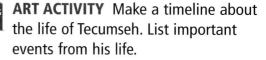

ART ACTIVITY Make a timeline about the life of Tecumseh. List important events from his life.

HANDS ON

Ninian Edwards

1775-1833

From an early age, Ninian Edwards knew what he wanted to do with his life. He wanted to serve his country, just as his father, a member of the United States Congress, had done.

Edwards studied law in Pennsylvania before moving to Kentucky. There, he was elected as a state representative at age 20, or before he was even old enough to vote.

In 1809, Edwards began his service to Illinoisans as the first governor of the Illinois Territory. He was considered by many to be an old-fashioned politician. Edwards wore a powdered wig and dressed in fancy, formal clothes that set him apart from the people he served. Edwards also was wealthy. He used his money to help others, sometimes even buying houses for people.

The U.S. Capitol as it looked during Ninian Edwards's term as senator.

Major Achievements

1796
Elected as state representative in Kentucky

1809
Appointed first governor of Illinois Territory

1818
Elected to the United States Senate

1826
Elected governor of the state of Illinois

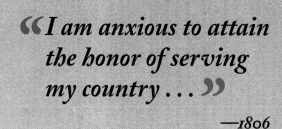

"I am anxious to attain the honor of serving my country . . ."

—1806

Activities

1. **TALK ABOUT IT** Why do you think Ninian Edwards chose a career in public service?

2. **RESEARCH IT** Write three questions about Ninian Edwards's life. Then find the answers to your questions.

 Technology Read more biographies at Education Place. www.eduplace.com/kids/hmss/

Visual Summary

1 – 3. ✏ Write a description of each item named below.

Important Events in Illinois Settlement	
Northwest Ordinance, 1787	
Treaty of Greenville, 1795	
War of 1812	

Facts and Main Ideas

✓ **TEST PREP** Answer each question below.

4. **Geography** What effect did the outcome of the American Revolution have on western settlement?

5. **History** What town was the capital of the Illinois Territory?

6. **History** What did Tecumseh believe American Indians would stop if they united?

7. **History** Why did American Indians fight on the side of Britain in the War of 1812?

Vocabulary

✓ **TEST PREP** Choose the correct word from the list below to complete each sentence.

territory, p. 81
governor, p. 82
expedition, p. 83
unite, p. 89

8. A(n) _____ is an official who leads a state or territorial government.

9. A journey with a special purpose is called a(n) _____.

10. A(n) _____ is a part of the United States that is not a state.

11. To _____ means to bring people together for a common purpose.

CHAPTER SUMMARY TIMELINE

1787
Illinois becomes part of Northwest Territory

1809
Illinois Territory is formed

1812
War of 1812 begins

1770   1780   1790   1800   1810   1820

Apply Skills

 TEST PREP Read a Circle Graph

Study the circle graph below showing the land size of present-day states that made up the Northwest Territory. Then use the graph to answer each question.

Land Size in the Northwest Territory

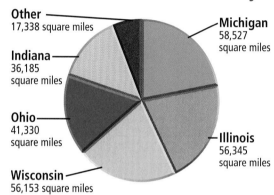

Other
17,338 square miles

Michigan
58,527
square miles

Indiana
36,185
square miles

Ohio
41,330
square miles

Illinois
56,345
square miles

Wisconsin
56,153 square miles

12. What information is presented in this circle graph?

   A. population of present-day states in the Louisiana Purchase

   B. population of counties in the Northwest Territory

   C. land size of present-day states in the Northwest Territory

   D. land size of present-day states in the Louisiana Purchase

13. Which present-day state covered the most land in the Northwest Territory?

   A. Michigan
   B. Ohio
   C. Indiana
   D. Illinois

Critical Thinking

 TEST PREP Write a short paragraph to answer each question below.

14. **Cause and Effect** What effect did the Battle of Tippecanoe have on Tecumseh's confederation?

15. **Analyze** What important change occurred after the end of the War of 1812?

Timeline

 TEST PREP Use the Chapter Summary timeline above to answer the question.

16. What happened first, the formation of the Illinois Territory or the War of 1812?

Activities

 Art Activity Create a poster that might encourage new settlers to move to Illinois.

Research Activity Find out more facts about the War of 1812. Use library or Internet resources to get information. Then write an article.

Technology
Writing Process Tips
Get help with your article at
www.eduplace.com/kids/hmss/

Vocabulary Preview

Technology

e • glossary
e • word games
www.eduplace.com/kids/hmss/

delegate

Elias Kent Kane helped write the state's first constitution. As a **delegate** to the state constitutional convention, Kane worked with others and made laws. **page 99**

capital

In 1820, Illinois leaders moved the state **capital** to Vandalia. This city became the new center of state government in Illinois. **page 99**

Chapter Timeline

1818	1825	1839
Illinois becomes a state	Erie Canal opens	National Road reaches Vandalia

1810 • 1820 • 1830 • 1840

Reading Strategy

Monitor and Clarify As you read, check your understanding of the events in this chapter.

Quick Tip If you are confused about events in a lesson, reread or read aloud.

canal

People in Illinois dug a **canal** to connect the Mississippi River to Lake Michigan. Boats traveled on the canal between the lake and the river. **page 109**

grain elevator

The **grain elevator** allowed farmers to store wheat. The wheat was then shipped to other parts of the country. **page 113**

1856
Illinois Central Railroad completed

1850   1860   1870

Statehood

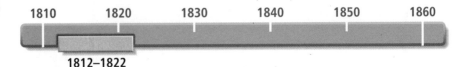

1810   1820   1830   1840   1850   1860

1812–1822

Build on What You Know Today, Illinoisans have the right to vote for leaders in the United States government. People living in the Illinois Territory wanted it to become a state so that they could vote.

Working for Statehood

Main Idea Illinois became the twenty-first state in 1818.

In the years following the War of 1812, the population of Illinois continued to grow. People came to Illinois on foot, by wagon, and on flatboats. By 1815, about 20,000 people lived in the Illinois Territory. Some Illinoisans began thinking about statehood. To gain statehood, Illinois first needed a population of 40,000 people. Illinois leaders also needed to write a plan for statehood and a plan for state government.

In 1817, newspaper editor **Daniel Pope Cook** put in writing what many Illinoisans thought about statehood. They wanted statehood so that they could vote for people to represent them in the United States government. They also wanted money from the federal government to improve roads.

VOCABULARY

delegate
capital
article
amendment

Vocabulary Strategy

amendment

Find the word **mend** in amendment. An **amendment** is a way to mend, or fix, a problem.

READING SKILL

Sequence As you read, note the order of events that led to statehood for Illinois.

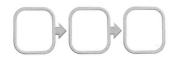

Flatboats Some settlers used them to transport their families, belongings, and even livestock over river to Illinois.

The Plan for Statehood

In December 1817, the Illinois General Assembly met in Kaskaskia. The General Assembly makes laws in Illinois. Cook attended the meeting both as a newspaper reporter and as the new clerk of the Illinois House of Representatives. As clerk, Cook worked in the House of Representatives for Illinois statehood.

Soon, Cook asked Illinois officials to put together a written plan for statehood. Cook's uncle, **Nathaniel Pope,** presented the plan to the United States Congress. Pope was a delegate from Illinois. A **delegate** is a person chosen to act for others. In a change to the plan, Pope suggested that Illinois's northern border be moved north about 40 miles. This would give the new state a shoreline on Lake Michigan. Illinoisans then could transport goods by boat to cities in the East.

The Plan for Government

In August 1818, a group of delegates met in Kaskaskia to write a constitution. A constitution is a plan for state government. Illinois had the 40,000 people it needed for statehood. Now it needed a constitution. **Elias Kent Kane** and other delegates studied the constitutions of other states. They decided what to include in the Illinois Constitution. They also discussed the best place for a state capital. A **capital** is the city where a state or national government is located.

By September, Illinois officials had completed their work on a state constitution. That same month, Illinois voters chose **Shadrach Bond** as governor. **Ninian Edwards** represented Illinois in the United States Senate. On December 3, 1818, Illinois became the twenty-first state.

REVIEW Why did Illinoisans such as Daniel Pope Cook want statehood for Illinois?

Daniel Pope Cook He wrote about the idea of statehood in the *Illinois Intelligencer* newspaper.

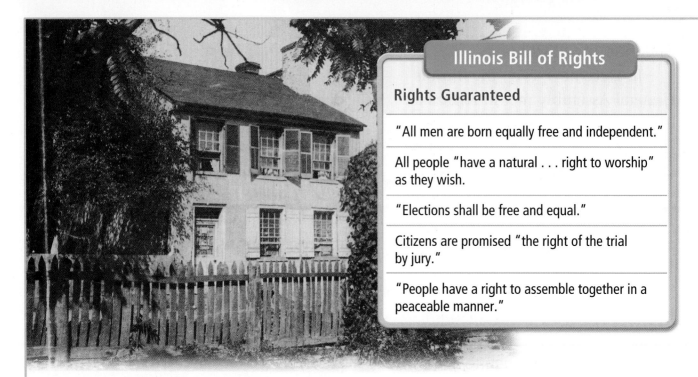

Illinois Bill of Rights

Rights Guaranteed

"All men are born equally free and independent."

All people "have a natural . . . right to worship" as they wish.

"Elections shall be free and equal."

Citizens are promised "the right of the trial by jury."

"People have a right to assemble together in a peaceable manner."

Kaskaskia, the First Capital The first Illinois Constitution was written in this capitol building.

A New State

Main Idea The Illinois Constitution set up the state's government and limited slavery.

The first Illinois Constitution was used from 1818 until 1848. It had an introduction and eight articles. An **article** is a part or section of a document. One article in the Illinois Constitution included a bill of rights. Like the Bill of Rights in the United States Constitution, the Illinois bill of rights protected people's rights to freedom of speech and religion.

The Illinois Constitution explained how the state's government should be set up and run. The constitution said where the state's borders were and named Kaskaskia as the capital. It also stated new rules about slavery in Illinois.

The Debate About Slavery

When the delegates wrote the Illinois Constitution, they agreed on all issues except slavery. Until 1818, slavery was allowed in Illinois. The Illinois Constitution did not immediately change that. People who were enslaved before the Illinois Constitution remained enslaved.

Some Illinoisans, such as Governor Shadrach Bond, supported slavery. Other people believed that slavery in Illinois should end. The Illinois Constitution of 1818 did not end slavery in the state, but it did include an important change. It said that no new slaves could come to Illinois. Illinois was called a free state because its state constitution stopped the future growth of slavery. Other states in which slavery was legal were known as slave states.

A New Capital and Governor

In the first years of statehood, some Illinoisans were unhappy with Kaskaskia as the state capital. Instead, they wanted a capital in the middle of the state, a place where people could visit easily. In 1820, the capital was moved from Kaskaskia in the southwest corner of the state to Vandalia in the center.

In 1822, Illinois voters elected **Edward Coles** as the state's second governor. Over the next two years, some people asked for an amendment to the Illinois Constitution. An **amendment** is a change. These Illinoisans wanted to allow slavery throughout the state. Governor Coles, however, persuaded people to keep Illinois as a free state.

REVIEW Why did the capital move from Kaskaskia to Vandalia?

New Capitol The Vandalia Statehouse is the state's oldest surviving capitol building.

Lesson Summary

- Illinois became a state in 1818.
- The Illinois Constitution determined the state's borders, its capital, and how its government should be run.
- Illinois was a free state.

Why It Matters...

Illinoisans continue to enjoy freedoms that were in the state's first constitution.

Lesson Review

1812   1814   1816   1818   1820   1822

1818 Illinois becomes a state

1820 Vandalia becomes the capital

❶ **VOCABULARY** Explain how an **article** is different from an **amendment.**

❷ **READING SKILL** What **sequence** of events led to changing the northern border of Illinois?

❸ **MAIN IDEA: History** Why did some Illinoisans want to gain statehood?

❹ **MAIN IDEA: Government** What effect did the first Illinois Constitution have on slavery in Illinois?

❺ **TIMELINE SKILL** How long after Illinois became a state did its capital move to Vandalia?

❻ **CRITICAL THINKING: Summarize** Why is having a constitution important to a new state?

WRITING ACTIVITY Write a news article about Illinois becoming a state.

THE Illinois Constitutional Convention

It is August of 1818. The leaders of the Illinois Territory have written a state constitution. What does this mean for the people in the Illinois Territory? In Shawneetown, people are awaiting news from James Elliott, who went to the convention.

Elaine Cooper

※CHARACTERS※

Lovena Jackson: teacher

James Elliott: lawyer

Maybelle Autrey: reporter

Arthur Card: farmer

Isaac Cooper: shopkeeper

Elaine Cooper: shopkeeper

Maybelle Autrey

Elaine Cooper: Mr. Elliot, you've returned. I'm glad you stopped by the store.

Lovena Jackson: We've all been waiting to hear about the convention in Kaskaskia. Tell us what happened.

James Elliott: Certainly. I was just telling Maybelle about it. I'm sure she won't mind if we stop to talk to you folks as well.

Maybelle Autrey: Of course not. I'd like to know what they have to say about your news.

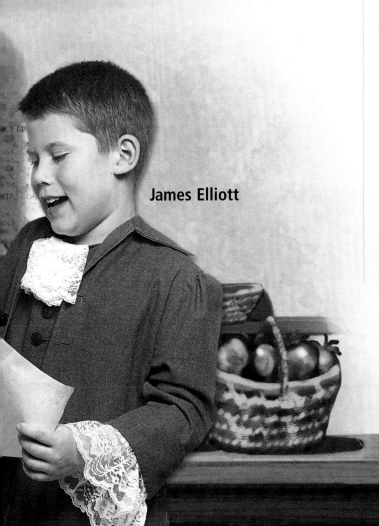

James Elliott

Arthur Card: I wanted to go to the convention in Kaskaskia, but I had to take care of my farm. I support Elias Kane, who wrote the new state constitution.

James Elliott: Then I have good news for you. It passed!

Isaac Cooper: Statehood! I'm glad to hear it. That will bring more people and more business to the town. I'd like to see more people in my store.

Elaine Cooper: I'm also happy to hear that Illinois is becoming a state. We'll have more say in what the country does now.

James Elliott: That's the idea. Illinoisans will elect people to represent them in government. Those representatives will speak and vote for our interests, so we'll have a voice now. The first election will be held this September.

Isaac Cooper: How exciting!

Maybelle Autrey: James, who will be voting in those elections?

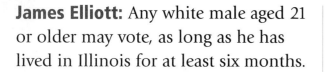

James Elliott: Any white male aged 21 or older may vote, as long as he has lived in Illinois for at least six months.

Maybelle Autrey: The constitution doesn't recognize women's right to vote?

James Elliott: Not yet, Maybelle.

Elaine Cooper: We'll have to work on that.

James Elliott: Well, state leaders can suggest changes to the constitution. If you want to change something, let your representative know.

Maybelle Autrey: Is it true that statehood will change our borders?

Isaac Cooper: Our borders! What are they doing to our borders?

Lovena Jackson: I heard that our northern border is moving 41 miles farther north.

Lovena Jackson

Arthur Card

Arthur Card: That's more land then. Why are they adding 41 miles?

Maybelle Autrey: Because it will give Illinois a shoreline on Lake Michigan. That includes the port of Chicago.

James Elliott: The port will make it easier to travel to and from Illinois. People are talking about building a canal. We'll have a water route from the East Coast to the Mississippi River.

Elaine Cooper: That means more people and trade! Thank you for the good news, Mr. Elliott.

Arthur Card: So, it's all settled then?

James Elliott: Not quite. The delegates signed the new constitution, but we need the approval of the United States government.

Maybelle Autrey: And the signature of the President of the United States.

James Elliott: There's still work to do.

Arthur Card: I'll let you two do it. I have to get back to my fields. When we become a state, maybe I can send some of my crops north to those extra 41 miles.

Lovena Jackson: Statehood will be good for us all, I think.

Maybelle Autrey: I think so, too. It will let us work for more changes for Illinois and the nation. Let's hope the national government approves it.

Activities

1. **TALK ABOUT IT** What part of the constitution do you think some of the characters would want to change? Explain your reasons.

2. **WRITE IT** What else might people from Shawneetown have to say about the new constitution? Write a page of dialogue for one of the characters above as well as for a new character.

Skillbuilder

Make a Map

When Illinois became a state, people made maps to show the new state boundaries. Some early state maps showed the routes between towns. A **route** is a path from one place to another. You can make a map showing the route you take on your way to school.

▶ **VOCABULARY**
route

Learn the Skill

Step 1: List the starting point, stops along the way, and the ending point of the route you take to school.

> 1. My house
> 2. Lara's house
> 3. Peter's house
> 4. School

Step 2: Make an outline map of your community. Label each point from Step 1.

Step 3: Choose a color for the line you will draw to show the route on the map. Label the line. Use that color to draw a line in a legend.

Step 4: Draw the route.

Step 5: Add a map title.

My Route to School

Practice the Skill

Read the paragraph about the route a delegate took to get to Kaskaskia. Use an outline map of Illinois to mark the delegate's route.

> One delegate's journey began at Edwardsville. He traveled south to Cahokia on foot. Then he walked southwest to the town of Bellefontaine. The next day the delegate rode on a horse to Prairie du Rocher. Finally, he traveled southeast to Kaskaskia.

Apply the Skill

Make a map of your own travels in Illinois. You can show a route you have actually taken or one you would like to take.

Western Expansion

VOCABULARY

canal
industry
grain elevator

Vocabulary Strategy

industry

Industry comes from a French word meaning "to work hard." People work in different **industries** to produce goods and services.

READING SKILL
Main Idea and Details
List each main idea and three details that support it.

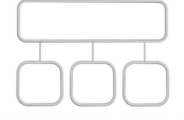

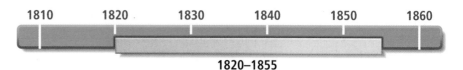

1810   1820   1830   1840   1850   1860

1820–1855

Build on What You Know How do you travel in your state today? In the 1800s, settlers in Illinois found faster and better ways of traveling and working.

A Growing Population

Main Idea In the early 1800s, most people in Illinois settled close to rivers where they could farm and trade.

Statehood brought more settlers to Illinois, but those settlers came slowly in the early 1800s. Settlers came looking for land and new opportunities. It took them a long time to reach Illinois. They traveled overland from Virginia, Tennessee, and Kentucky, or followed the Ohio River from Ohio and Pennsylvania. Most of these people settled in southern Illinois along the Mississippi, Ohio, and Wabash rivers. As more people came, some followed smaller rivers into central Illinois.

Heading to Illinois Many early settlers traveled by wagon. Sometimes, oxen pulled the wagons. The oxen wore wooden yokes like the one below.

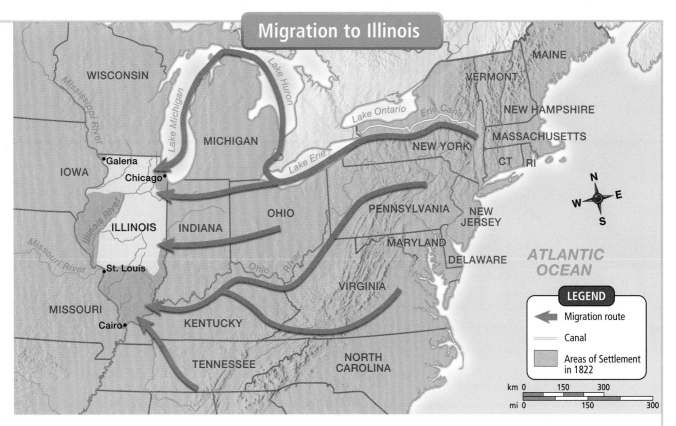

Migration to Illinois

LEGEND

Migration route

Canal

Areas of Settlement in 1822

The New Illinoisans Following statehood, people began to migrate, or move, to Illinois from different parts of the United States.

More Settlers Come

Two developments opened northern Illinois to settlement in the 1820s: the Erie Canal and the Galena lead mines. A **canal** is a human-made waterway. In 1825, the Erie Canal opened a northern route to Illinois. The Erie Canal linked the Great Lakes to northeastern states such as New York and Massachusetts. New settlers followed this water route into northern Illinois.

Some of these settlers moved into central Illinois near the Illinois River. They stayed close to the rivers and woods where they thought their crops would grow well and where they could hunt. The rivers also made it easier to travel and trade.

Other new settlers stayed in northern Illinois, moving to places such as Chicago. Chicago was a small fur trading village in 1820. When the Erie Canal completed the water route between the Midwest and the Northeast, more people settled in Chicago to start businesses and build homes.

The Galena lead mines attracted more people to work in northwestern Illinois. In 1823, builders completed a large factory to melt the lead and make it usable. Lead was shipped down the Mississippi River and then east to be made into tools and other goods.

REVIEW In the first years following statehood, where did most new Illinoisans settle?

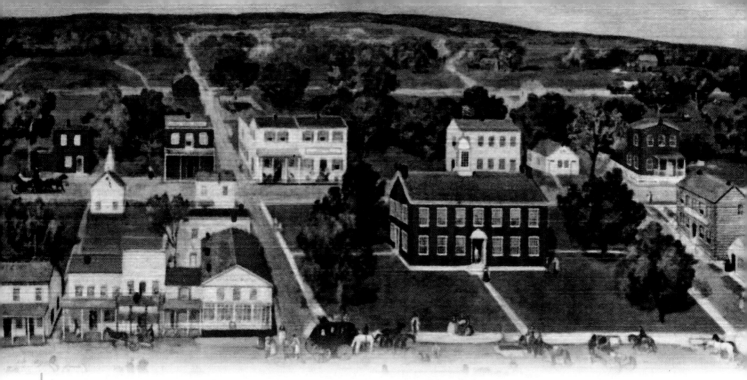

Early Town Vandalia was the capital of Illinois from 1820 to 1839.

Life in Illinois

Main Idea Increasing settlement led to many changes in the new state.

As more people came to Illinois, they settled across the state and learned more about the land. They farmed in new places and built towns. However, life was hard. Families worked every day, building, hunting, farming, and doing other chores.

Those who settled in southern Illinois had to clear the land of trees before they could farm. They used axes to chop down trees. From this wood, settlers made cabins, fences, and simple furniture.

The more the settlers built, the more land they wanted. Over time, this would lead to conflict with American Indian nations in Illinois.

Building Towns

Some Illinoisians built towns near old trading posts and government centers. Often located on the rivers, these towns were centers of trade and travel. Shawneetown was the first town in Illinois. Kaskaskia, the first state capital, followed in 1818. By 1821, Alton, Belleville, Carmi, Edwardsville, and Vandalia had all become towns.

Towns were organized to serve the people who lived in and worked near them. In 1826, Galena began to serve the lead mining communities. Chicago grew into a town to support traders. People opened businesses to serve their neighbors. The government opened land offices to help settlers buy and sell land. State banks allowed settlers to borrow and save money. Some children attended early public schools.

Population of Illinois Settlements, 1840	
Settlement	Population
Chicago	4,853
Lockport	2,977
Springfield	2,579
Joliet	2,558
Quincy	2,349
Alton	2,340
Peoria	2,319
Galena	1,843

Growing Population By 1840, Illinois towns were growing quickly.

Setters and American Indians

The settler population in Illinois increased from 55,000 in 1820 to 150,000 in 1830. As more settlers came, they moved closer to the last American Indian lands in northern Illinois. Here, the Sauk (sahk) and Fox still had villages and farms.

Settlers did not want to share the land with American Indians. In 1831, a Sauk leader named Black Hawk took his people into Iowa to avoid fighting. The Sauk had trouble farming in Iowa, though, and came back to Illinois in 1832. This worried some settlers, who called on the government to prevent American Indians from moving onto the land. The settlers and American Indians battled for 15 weeks in what became known as the Black Hawk War.

The Black Hawk War was the last fight for American Indian lands in the Great Lakes region. It ended with Black Hawk's defeat at the Battle of the Bad Axe.

After the war, the United States government wanted to make sure it could keep Illinois land. In 1833, the government and American Indian nations signed the Treaty of Chicago. In the treaty, American Indians were forced to give up their claim to the lands left in the area. The remaining American Indian groups had to move west of the Mississippi River.

REVIEW In what way did settlement lead to conflict with American Indians?

Black Hawk The Sauk leader fought to keep American Indian lands.

Growth in Illinois

Main Idea New waves of people and new technologies brought growth to Illinois.

Following the Black Hawk War, settlement in Illinois increased. By 1840, more than 450,000 people lived in Illinois. Many soldiers who fought in the war stayed to build farms on the prairie. New opportunities and improvements in travel brought many new people.

In 1839, the National Road connected Illinois to the East Coast. It stretched from Cumberland, Maryland, to Vandalia, Illinois. Another road linked Cumberland to Baltimore, Maryland. Many people reached Illinois by foot or by wagon along these roads. However, travel by foot or wagon was slow.

Travel by water was faster. People could travel along the Erie Canal from the East Coast to the Great Lakes. However, they still had to travel over land when they reached Illinois. Then, in 1848, the Illinois and Michigan Canal opened. It linked the Great Lakes to the Mississippi River.

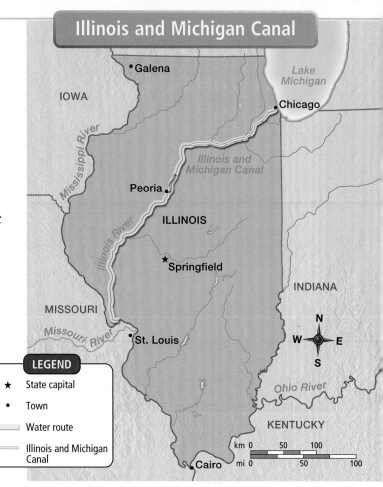

Illinois and Michigan Canal

LEGEND
★ State capital
• Town
Water route
Illinois and Michigan Canal

New Waterways This canal improved trade in Illinois.

This made it faster and less costly to move people and goods. The completed water routes put Illinois at the center of the nation's trade. Railroads such as the Illinois Central Railroad also helped with trade.

Railroads in Illinois They made travel within the state faster.

Industry Inventions

As trade grew, so did some Illinois industries. An **industry** is a group of businesses that provide similar goods or services. New inventions such as the grain elevator helped the farming industry sell and trade more goods. A **grain elevator** is a tall building used to load and store grain. Grain elevators located along canals and railroads made it easier to move grain to sell.

John Deere and **Cyrus McCormick** invented other new farming tools. Deere's steel plow let farmers plow land for planting in less time. McCormick's reaper, which cut grain, made it easier to harvest crops.

REVIEW In what way did canals and railroads improve transportation?

Lesson Summary

- The Black Hawk War and the Treaty of Chicago ended American Indian settlement in Illinois.

- Improvements in transportation and industry helped Illinois grow quickly.

Why It Matters...

Changes in population and transportation in the 1800s helped improve industries that are important to Illinois today.

Grain Elevators
Grain elevators, such as this one in Chicago, helped the farming industry in Illinois grow.

Lesson Review

1825	1832	1848
Erie Canal completed	Black Hawk War	Illinois and Michigan Canal opens

1810   1820   1830   1840   1850   1860

❶ **VOCABULARY** Tell how **canals** and railroads were used by **industry** in Illinois.

❷ **READING SKILL** What **detail** supports the **main idea** that increasing settlement led to many changes in Illinois?

❸ **MAIN IDEA: Geography** Why did many early settlers stay close to the rivers in central and southern Illinois?

❹ **MAIN IDEA: Economics** In what ways did canals help trade in Illinois?

❺ **TIMELINE SKILL** How many years after the Erie Canal was completed did the Illinois and Michigan Canal open?

❻ **CRITICAL THINKING: Infer** Why did people build towns in Illinois?

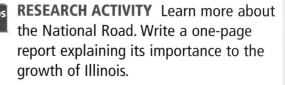

HANDS ON

RESEARCH ACTIVITY Learn more about the National Road. Write a one-page report explaining its importance to the growth of Illinois.

Farming in Illinois

Early farming in Illinois was harder than it is today. Farmers had to clear thick prairie grasses that had deep roots. Harvesting crops took a great deal of time and much tiring work. Two inventions changed farming and made it possible for small Illinois farms to grow into major producers of wheat, corn, and other crops.

John Deere's Steel Plow

Early Illinois farmers used heavy wood and iron plows to break the soil. Sticky prairie soil clung to the plow blade. Farmers had to stop every few yards to clean their plows. In 1837, John Deere invented the steel plow. Its light frame and steel blade made it easier to use. Soil slid right off the blade. Farmers using Deere's plow could clear more land in less time, so they could plant more crops.

Cyrus McCormick's Mechanical Reaper

Farmers had trouble harvesting everything that they planted. In the early 1800s, harvesting had to be done by hand. In 1831, Cyrus McCormick's reaper made that work easier. A reaper is a harvester. McCormick's reaper had blades that moved back and forth to cut grain quickly. A reel pushed the cut grain onto the back of the reaper. With McCormick's reaper, two people could do the work of many. Farmers harvested more crops in less time. The reaper gave them more time for other activities, such as selling extra food at market.

Activities

1. **DESCRIBE IT** Look at the images of the plow and reaper. What can you tell about how they worked? Explain your answer.

2. **COMPARE IT** Learn about another invention that has changed the way people work. Write a paragraph comparing its effect with the effects of the plow and the reaper.

Visual Summary

1 – 3. ✎➤ Write a description of each item named below.

Growth of Illinois		
	Statehood	
	New Settlement	
	Transportation	

Facts and Main Ideas

✔ **TEST PREP** Answer each question below.

4. **Geography** Why did leaders in Illinois want the state border to be moved north?

5. **History** Why was Illinois called a free state?

6. **Geography** What methods did new settlers use to reach Illinois in the early 1800s?

7. **History** What led to the Black Hawk War?

8. **Economics** Name three changes that helped industry in Illinois in the mid-1800s.

Vocabulary

✔ **TEST PREP** Choose the correct word from the list below to complete each sentence.

delegate, p. 99
amendment, p. 101
industry, p. 113

9. A(n) _____ is a group of businesses that make a product or offer a service that can be sold to people.

10. Nathaniel Pope was the _____ who presented Illinois's plan for statehood to the United States Congress.

11. A(n) _____ is needed to change the Illinois Constitution.

1818 Illinois becomes a state	1825 Erie Canal opens	1839 National Road reaches Vandalia	1856 Illinois Central Railroad completed

1810   1820   1830   1840   1850   1860   1870

Apply Skills

✔ **TEST PREP** **Make a Map** Study the map of Illinois below. Then use your map skills to answer each question.

12. To show a settler's route from Chicago to Cairo, which of the following should you add to the map?

  A. a fort at Cairo
  B. a black dot symbol
  C. a color line with the settler's name
  D. a star symbol

13. To add other Illinois towns to the map, which symbol would you use?

  A. ▬
  B. ★
  C. 🏰
  D. ●

Critical Thinking

✔ **TEST PREP** Write a short paragraph to answer each question below.

14. **Infer** In what ways might Illinois be different if Nathaniel Pope had not suggested that the state of Illinois have a shoreline on Lake Michigan?

15. **Summarize** Describe settlement in Illinois in the 1820s, 1830s, and 1840s.

Timeline

✔ **TEST PREP** Use the Chapter Summary Timeline above to answer the question.

16. When did Illinois become a state?

Activities

HANDS ON **Research Activity** Research the debate about slavery in Illinois. What did the Illinois Constitution of 1818 forbid and what did it allow? Write a short summary of what you learn.

Writing Activity Write a paragraph about farm life on the Illinois prairie in the mid-1800s. Include information about the types of work that families did.

Technology
Writing Process Tips
Get help with your paragraph at:
www.eduplace.com/kids/hmss/

Chapter 6

The Civil War

Technology
e • glossary
e • word games
www.eduplace.com/kids/hmss/

Vocabulary Preview

abolitionist

Owen Lovejoy was an **abolitionist** from Princeton, Illinois. He spoke out against slavery.
page 121

election

Abraham Lincoln won the **election** of 1860. Voters chose him to become the 16th President of the United States.
page 122

Chapter Timeline

1845
Slavery outlawed in Illinois

1830   1840   1850

Reading Strategy

Question As you read the lessons in this chapter, ask yourself questions to check your understanding.

Quick Tip Stop and ask yourself questions. Do you need to go back and reread for the answers?

regiment

Groups of soldiers from Illinois trained and served together. One of those **regiments** was made up of African Americans.
page 129

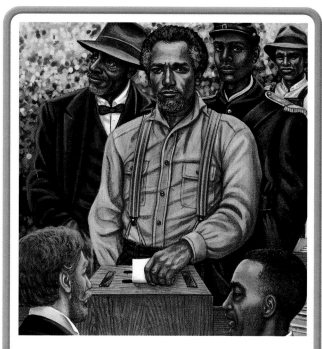

Reconstruction

During **Reconstruction,** Confederate states rejoined the United States. They also recognized the right of African American men to vote. **page 131**

1861
Civil War begins

1863
Emancipation Proclamation

1860

1870

A Nation Divided

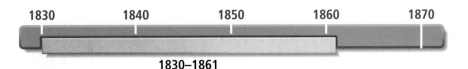

1830   1840   1850   1860   1870

1830–1861

Build on What You Know Have you ever disagreed with someone? In the mid-1800s, people in northern and southern states disagreed so much that they went to war.

VOCABULARY

economy
abolitionist
election
secede

Vocabulary Strategy

election

To **elect** means to choose. In an election, people vote to choose someone for a job.

READING SKILL

Cause and Effect As you read, note the issues that caused the Civil War.

Cause → Effect

Civil War

Work in the South Plantation owners depended on enslaved people to pick cotton, the South's most important crop.

Free States and Slave States

Main Idea Many people in the United States relied on slavery for economic reasons, but others wanted to end slavery.

In the mid-1800s, people in the United States argued about the issue of slavery. Some states, such as Illinois, were free states. Others were slave states. Slave states allowed enslaved Africans to be bought and sold as property. Over time, the issue of slavery would divide the United States.

Many people in the South wanted to keep slavery. Their economy depended on it. An **economy** is the way that people choose to use resources to produce goods and services. In the South, enslaved Africans were forced to work without pay. By using slavery, the South produced cotton and other crops at low cost. Workers in the North were paid for their work.

Opposition to Slavery

Illinoisans disagreed about the issue of slavery. Some came from the South. People accepted slavery there. Others came from free states in the North. Many Illinoisans became abolitionists. An **abolitionist** is someone who wants to end slavery. Abolitionists worked to end slavery in different ways.

In the 1830s, an Illinois journalist named **Elijah Lovejoy** wrote and printed articles that supported the end of slavery. He tried to convince other people that slavery was wrong. These articles angered people who supported slavery. Some people tried to stop Lovejoy from writing against slavery.

Elijah Lovejoy's brother, **Owen Lovejoy**, also became an important abolitionist. He wrote articles and gave powerful speeches to convince people to stop slavery.

Owen Lovejoy This abolitionist helped people escape from slavery and went on to speak for the people of Illinois in Congress.

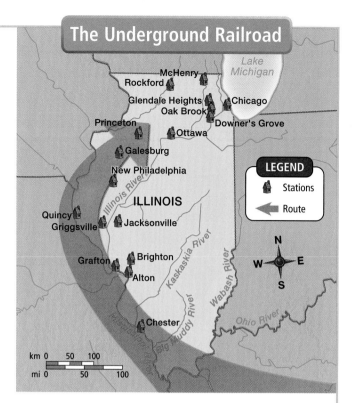

The Underground Railroad

LEGEND
🏠 Stations
← Route

km 0   50   100
mi 0   50   100

Escape Routes The Underground Railroad had many "stations" in Illinois.

Abolitionists led enslaved people to freedom along the Underground Railroad. The Underground Railroad was a system of escape routes to bring enslaved people to freedom in the North. It was not an actual railroad. Illinois had "stations," or stops, that provided food, clothes, and places to hide. Owen Lovejoy's house in Princeton was one station.

Many free African Americans helped the Underground Railroad. **John Jones** and his wife, **Mary Jones,** hid escaped slaves at their home in Chicago. They wrote antislavery articles and supported other abolitionists. In 1845, abolitionists won an important victory. An Illinois court outlawed slavery in the state.

REVIEW What did abolitionists in Illinois do to oppose slavery?

121

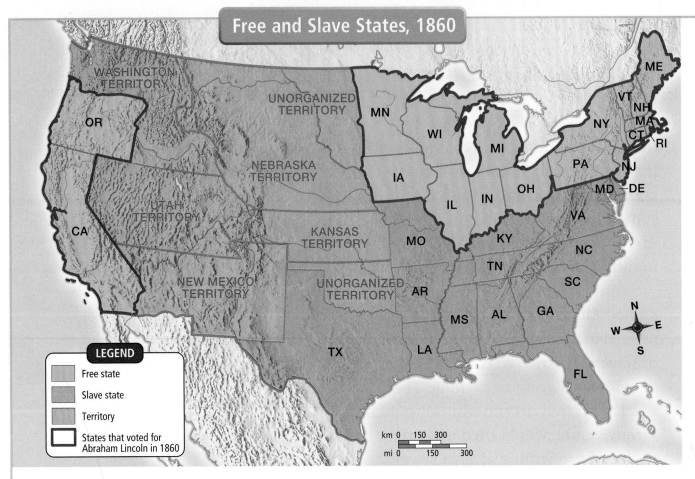

Free and Slave States, 1860

ME
VT
NH
MA
NY CT RI
WASHINGTON TERRITORY
OR
UNORGANIZED TERRITORY
MN
WI
MI
PA
NJ
NEBRASKA TERRITORY
IA
OH
MD DE
UTAH TERRITORY
IL IN
VA
CA
KANSAS TERRITORY
MO
KY
NC
NEW MEXICO TERRITORY
UNORGANIZED TERRITORY
AR
TN
SC
MS AL GA
TX
LA
FL

N
W   E
S

LEGEND
Free state
Slave state
Territory
States that voted for
Abraham Lincoln in 1860

km 0   150   300
mi 0   150   300

Lincoln's Election Abraham Lincoln did not win in any
slave states, but he won the election of 1860.

SKILL **Reading Maps** How many states did Lincoln win?

Election of 1860

Main Idea After Abraham Lincoln was
elected President, 11 states left the Union.

People in the United States
government tried to compromise on
slavery. To compromise is to reach an
agreement. Congress tried to have an
equal number of free and slave states.
By 1860, though, leaders could no
longer compromise. Many people
believed that the United States had to
accept or reject slavery entirely. One of
these people was **Abraham Lincoln.**

Lincoln was a lawyer in Illinois
who had served in the United States
Congress. In 1858, Lincoln spoke
against slavery when he ran against
Stephen Douglas for the United States
Senate from Illinois. Douglas won, but
Lincoln earned a lot of attention.

In 1860, Lincoln ran against
Douglas for President of the United
States. Lincoln won this election.
An **election** is a way of choosing
someone by voting. Lincoln was the
first Illinoisan to be elected President
of the United States.

War Begins

Many southerners worried that Lincoln would end slavery. Seven southern states seceded from the Union, which is another name for the United States. To **secede** means to separate from the country and form a new nation. These states formed the Confederate States of America, also known as the Confederacy.

On April 12, 1861, the Confederacy attacked a Union fort in South Carolina. Lincoln called for soldiers to fight the Confederacy. Four more southern states chose to secede. The Civil War had begun.

REVIEW Why did southern states secede?

Fort Sumter The Civil War began when Confederate soldiers fired on this fort in South Carolina.

Lesson Summary

- People in Illinois and across the nation disagreed about slavery.
- After Abraham Lincoln was elected President, several states seceded.

Why It Matters ...

The Civil War divided the nation. It would affect people for many years to come.

Lesson Review

| 1845 | 1860 |
| Slavery outlawed in Illinois | Abraham Lincoln elected |

1830   1840   1850   1860   1870

❶ **VOCABULARY** Write two sentences using the words **election** and **secede.**

❷ 🕑 **READING SKILL Cause and Effect** What **effect** did the attack on Fort Sumter have?

❸ **MAIN IDEA: History** What was one reason people disagreed about slavery?

❹ **MAIN IDEA: History** What did Congress do to try to compromise on slavery?

❺ **TIMELINE SKILL** When did Illinois outlaw slavery?

❻ **CRITICAL THINKING: Summarize** Summarize the different opinions that people held about slavery in the 1800s.

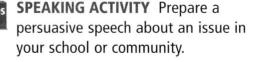

SPEAKING ACTIVITY Prepare a persuasive speech about an issue in your school or community.

📖 **Primary Sources**

Galena Goes to War
A MEMOIR

★ ★ ★ ★ ★ ★ ★

Ulysses S. Grant takes us back more than 100 years. In 1884, Grant wrote a history of his life. Grant told not only his own story but also the history of the Civil War. At the start of the war, Grant was living in Galena, Illinois. President Lincoln called for 75,000 men to serve in the Union army. Grant wrote about how people in Galena responded.

① *"As soon as the news of the call for [people to serve] reached Galena, posters were stuck up calling for a meeting of the citizens at the court-house in the evening. Business ceased entirely; all was excitement; for a time there were no party distinctions; all were Union men. . . . In the evening the courthouse was packed. . . .*

② *"After the speaking was over [people] were called for to form a company. . . . The company was raised and the officers and non-commission officers elected before the meeting adjourned. . . .*

(3) *"The ladies of Galena were quite as patriotic as the men. They could not enlist, but they conceived [came up with] the idea of sending their first company to the field uniformed. They came to me to get a description of the United States uniform for infantry; subscribed and bought the material; procured [hired] the tailors to cut out the garments, and the ladies made them up. In a few days the company was in uniform and ready to report at the State capital for assignment. . . ."*

(4) *"There were so many more [people] than had been called for that the question of who to accept was quite embarrassing to the governor, Richard Yates. . . ."*

(1) When people learned that Lincoln had called for soldiers, they decided to have a meeting. In what way did they find out about the meeting?

(2) People in Galena agreed to send a group of soldiers to join the Union army. In what way did people choose leaders?

(3) Women in Galena wanted to take part in the war effort. They made uniforms for the men who were joining the army. What did they do to find out what the uniforms should look like?

(4) More people wanted to join the army than had been expected. Why was Governor Richard Yates embarassed?

Activities

1. **TALK ABOUT IT** According to the passages above, in what ways did the people of Galena respond to the call to war?

2. **WRITE ABOUT IT** Explain three things that you learned about Galena and the Civil War from the passage above.

Understand Point of View

Citizenship Skills

▶ **VOCABULARY**
point of view

People in the southern United States disagreed about whether to secede from the Union. To understand their ideas, it is important to understand their points of view. A **point of view** is the way a person thinks about an issue, an event, or another person. Understanding a person's point of view can help you understand why people make certain choices or act in different ways.

Learn the Skill

Step 1: Identify the author's point of view. Look for words such as "I" and "our." These words help show what the author thinks about a subject.

_____

Step 2: Describe the author's point of view in your own words.

_____

Step 3: Learn about the person who is writing. Find out what experiences may have influenced the author's point of view.

_____

All of you know that I am opposed to secession.... To secede from the Union and set up another government would cause war. I advise you to remain in the Union. If you go to war with the United States, you will never conquer her, as she has the money and the men.

> **Sam Houston**
> **State Conference of Secession**
> **January 28, 1861**
> **Texas**

It is our sincere desire to separate from the States of the North in peace, and leave them to develop their own civilization to their own sense of duty and of interest. But if, ... they decide otherwise, then be it so.

> **Governor Francis Wilkinson Pickens**
> **Inaugural Message to the House of Representatives**
> **December 18, 1860**
> **South Carolina**

Practice the Skill

Read the comments above about secession. Then answer the questions that follow.

1 What is Sam Houston's point of view?

2 What words tell you Sam Houston's point of view?

3 What is Governor Pickens's point of view?

4 What words tell you Governor Pickens's point of view?

Apply the Skill

Find out more about Sam Houston and Governor Pickens. Note different experiences in their lives. Talk about how their experiences might have contributed to their points of view.

Fighting the War

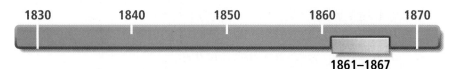

1830   1840   1850   1860   1870

1861–1867

Build on What You Know Has anyone ever asked you to help do something? During the Civil War, Illinoisans helped the Union fight the war, take care of the soldiers, and produce food and supplies.

Illinois and the Civil War

Main Idea Men and women in Illinois helped the Union's efforts during the Civil War.

Illinois became a center of the Union war effort in the West. The Union built a large military camp at the city of Cairo, Illinois. The Ohio and Mississippi rivers meet at Cairo. The Mississippi River was a main water route for both the Union and the Confederacy. Soldiers and their supplies sailed from Cairo to support Union armies fighting in the South.

Illinois helped the war effort in other ways. Farms produced food for the Union army. Mines produced coal for fuel and metals for tools and weapons. Railroads such as the Illinois Central carried supplies. Many Illinoisans served as soldiers, doctors, and nurses.

War in the West
Steamboats on the Mississippi River carried Union soldiers south from Cairo, Illinois.

Fighting for the Union Many Union states, including Illinois, formed African American regiments such as the one shown here.

Illinoisans Support the Union

When the Civil War began in 1861, the Union did not have a large army. Each state was asked to send people willing to serve. More than 250,000 Illinoisans joined the Union army. About 1,800 of those people were African Americans. In 1863, Illinois governor **Richard Yates** formed the 29th U.S. Colored Infantry. It was the first African American regiment in Illinois. A **regiment** is a group of soldiers who train and serve together.

Illinois sent nearly 150 regiments to the Union army during the war. Some were organized by soldiers' backgrounds or skills. For example, some Illinois regiments were made up of Irish or German soldiers. Others consisted of lead miners from Galena or farmers from Rock River.

Women contributed to the war in several important ways. Some women, such as **Frances Hook** and **Jennie Hodgers,** dressed as soldiers and went into battle. Hook called herself "Frank Miller." She served in the Union army for 10 months.

Other women nursed wounded soldiers. One Illinois woman, **Mary Livermore,** collected money and supplies for Union army hospitals. **Mary Ann Bickerdyke** and **Lizzie Aiken** worked hard to care for soldiers in the field.

Illinoisans also contributed to the war effort at home. Women and children did more work on farms and in factories. Many of the men who did those jobs had gone to join the fighting. Some women sewed uniforms and made flags.

REVIEW In what ways did Illinoisans help the Union during the Civil War?

Vicksburg Surrenders The Union victory at Vicksburg gave the Union control of the whole Mississippi River.

The War Ends

Main Idea After four years of fighting, the South surrendered and rejoined the Union.

The South won many battles at first. In 1862, though, Confederate General **Robert E. Lee** invaded Maryland. After a fierce battle, the Union army forced him to retreat. This victory gave President **Lincoln** the confidence to issue the Emancipation Proclamation. **Emancipation** is freedom from slavery. The Proclamation freed all slaves in states at war with the Union.

In July 1863, the Union won two important battles. The first was at Gettysburg, Pennsylvania. Then General **Ulysses S. Grant** of Galena, Illinois, won a battle at Vicksburg, Mississippi. By capturing Vicksburg, the Union cut Texas and Arkansas off from the rest of the Confederacy.

Fighting continued for two more years, but the Confederacy never regained its strength. The Union had more soldiers and supplies. In April 1865, the Confederacy surrendered.

People in the Union celebrated the end of the war. However, six days later President Lincoln was killed by **John Wilkes Booth.** Booth was a southerner who disagreed with Lincoln's policies. **Andrew Johnson** became the next President.

Declaration of Freedom Lincoln's Emancipation Proclamation freed people enslaved in states fighting the Union.

Reconstruction

President Johnson made plans for Reconstruction. **Reconstruction** was the time when the South rejoined the Union. Congress brought the southern states back into the Union under military control. They forced the southern states to end slavery. All states had to recognize the right of African American men to vote.

The war had hurt the South's economy. The South had relied on slavery. After the war, it had to rebuild without slavery. The war had helped northern industries, though. Growth in Illinois and other northern states helped Reconstruction.

REVIEW What laws changed after the Civil War?

Freedom After the Civil War, African American men gained the right to vote.

Lesson Summary

The Civil War was fought to keep the United States together. Illinois supported the Union war effort in many ways and helped the nation rebuild when the war ended. After the end of the war, slavery was outlawed in all states.

Why It Matters . . .

The Civil War led to many changes in the government and the economy of Illinois and the nation.

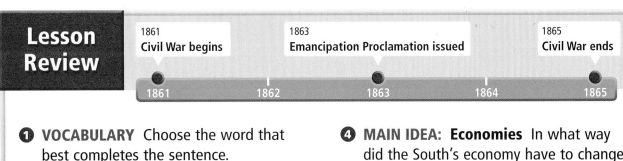

Lesson Review

1861 Civil War begins	1863 Emancipation Proclamation issued	1865 Civil War ends

1861 1862 1863 1864 1865

❶ **VOCABULARY** Choose the word that best completes the sentence.
emancipation   regiment

The _____ of the slaves changed the South's economy and government.

❷ **READING SKILL** What **sequence** of events led to the end of the Civil War?

❸ **MAIN IDEA: Citizenship** In what ways did women from Illinois help the Union war effort?

❹ **MAIN IDEA: Economies** In what way did the South's economy have to change after the war?

❺ **TIMELINE SKILL** When did the Civil War end?

❻ **CRITICAL THINKING: Analyze** In what ways did Reconstruction affect the South?

WRITING ACTIVITY Write a news article reporting on President Lincoln's Emancipation Proclamation.

Illinois Women
in the Civil War

The Civil War is not only the story of great men, great speeches, and great battles, but also the story of great women who took part in the war. Many Illinois women chose to use their skills to serve the Union cause. They saved lives and helped change beliefs about what women could do.

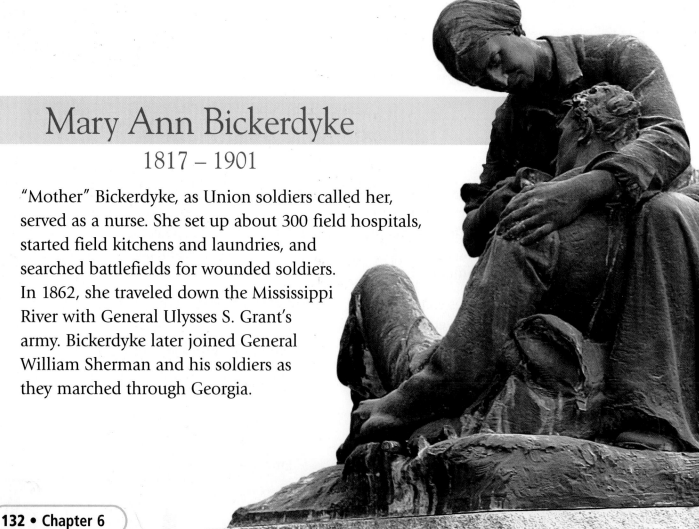

Mary Ann Bickerdyke
1817 – 1901

"Mother" Bickerdyke, as Union soldiers called her, served as a nurse. She set up about 300 field hospitals, started field kitchens and laundries, and searched battlefields for wounded soldiers. In 1862, she traveled down the Mississippi River with General Ulysses S. Grant's army. Bickerdyke later joined General William Sherman and his soldiers as they marched through Georgia.

Jennie Hodgers
1843? – 1915

In 1862, Jennie Hodgers dressed as a man and joined the Union army saying her name was Albert D.J. Cashier. Hodgers served in the 95th Illinois Infantry for more than three years. She fought in more than 40 battles, including one at Vicksburg. Hodgers was captured by the Confederate army once, but escaped.

Mary Livermore
1820 – 1905

Mary Livermore was a Chicago journalist who worked to improve medical care and hospital conditions during the war. As a member of the United States Sanitary Commission, Livermore traveled to Union army hospitals and camps. She made sure that they were clean and well supplied. She also organized events to raise money for the Sanitary Commission's work.

Activities

1. **TALK ABOUT IT** Describe ways in which Bickerdyke, Hodgers, and Livermore showed **patriotism**.

2. **RESEARCH IT** Learn more about one of the women discussed here. Write a paragraph about what she did before the war and a paragraph about what she did after the war.

Visual Summary

1 – 3. ✏️ Write a description of each item named below.

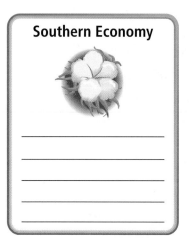

Southern Economy

_____
_____
_____
_____

Election of 1860

_____
_____
_____
_____

Emancipation

_____
_____
_____
_____

Facts and Main Ideas

✔️ **TEST PREP** Answer each question below.

4. **Economics** In what ways were the economies of the North and South different?

5. **History** What was the Underground Railroad?

6. **Geography** In what way did the Union army use Cairo, Illinois, in the Civil War?

7. **Government** What did the Emancipation Proclamation do?

Vocabulary

✔️ **TEST PREP** Choose the correct word from the list below to complete each sentence.

economy, p. 120
abolitionist, p. 121
election, p. 122
Reconstruction, p. 131

8. Elijah Lovejoy was a(n) _____ who printed articles that said slavery was wrong.

9. Abraham Lincoln won the _____ of 1860.

10. The South rejoined the Union during the time called _____.

11. The _____ of the South depended on slavery.

1845
Slavery outlawed in Illinois

1863
Emancipation Proclamation

1830   1840   1850   1860   1870

Apply Skills

✔ TEST PREP **Understand Point of View** Study the letter below. Then use what you have learned about understanding point of view to answer each question.

April 7, 1865

Dearest Mother,

It seems that this war has dragged on forever, but there is hope. We've heard that General Grant asked the Confederates to surrender before any more blood is shed. Although our Union troops have won many battles, there's no happiness in this ugly war. We all want the war to end. Perhaps we can return home to our families soon!

Your loving son,
John

---

12. Which of the following statements summarizes John's point of view?

   A. The Confederate army will win.
   B. The Union army wants more fighting.
   C. The war brings happiness to both sides.
   D. The war should end.

13. Which of the following statements helps you understand John's point of view?

   A. The Union can win more battles.
   B. The war has gone on for too long.
   C. General Lee is about to attack again.
   D. General Grant wants to surrender.

Critical Thinking

✔ TEST PREP Write a short paragraph to answer each question below.

14. **Analyze** Why was winning the Battle of Vicksburg important to the Union?

15. **Infer** What might have happened if the Union had lost the Civil War?

Timeline

✔ TEST PREP Use the Chapter Summary Timeline above to answer the question.

16. How many years after slavery was outlawed in Illinois did President Lincoln issue the Emancipation Proclamation?

Activities

HANDS ON **Interview Activity** Prepare at least five questions a reporter might have wanted to ask Abraham Lincoln about his decisions during the Civil War.

Research Activity Learn more about Reconstruction. Make a list of things that had to be done to help the nation rebuild after the Civil War.

Technology
Writing Process Tips
Get help with your research at
www.eduplace.com/kids/hmss/

Early Years

Abraham Lincoln was born in a one-room log cabin in Kentucky. Like most pioneer children, young Lincoln helped clear land, plant crops, carry water, and chop wood.

Lincoln went to school when he could. He loved to read and learn. At fifteen, Lincoln started working for money on neighbors' farms and in town. He often carried a book with him and read it when he had time.

In 1831, Lincoln moved to New Salem, Illinois. There he worked in the general store. Customers enjoyed the funny stories Lincoln told. They also trusted him. People called him "Honest Abe."

> **"**Upon the subject of education, . . . I can only say that I view it as the most important subject which we as a people can be engaged in.**"**
>
> —*March 9, 1832, from first political announcement*

The Rail Splitter To earn money, Lincoln split wood for fences and firewood. Over time, his skill with an axe earned him the nickname "the Rail Splitter."

Major Events

1809
Lincoln is born on February 12

1815–1820
Lincoln attends school when possible and learns reading and math

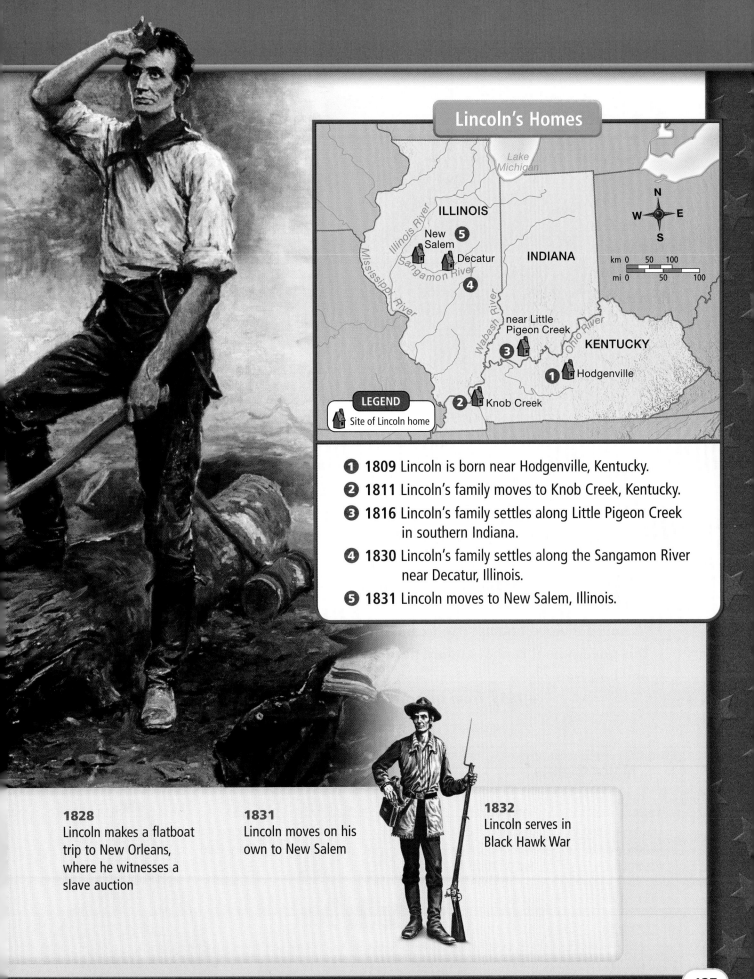

Lincoln's Homes

ILLINOIS

INDIANA

KENTUCKY

Lake Michigan

Illinois River

Mississippi River

Sangamon River

Wabash River

Ohio River

New Salem **5**

Decatur **4**

near Little Pigeon Creek **3**

Hodgenville **1**

Knob Creek **2**

LEGEND
Site of Lincoln home

1 **1809** Lincoln is born near Hodgenville, Kentucky.

2 **1811** Lincoln's family moves to Knob Creek, Kentucky.

3 **1816** Lincoln's family settles along Little Pigeon Creek in southern Indiana.

4 **1830** Lincoln's family settles along the Sangamon River near Decatur, Illinois.

5 **1831** Lincoln moves to New Salem, Illinois.

1828
Lincoln makes a flatboat trip to New Orleans, where he witnesses a slave auction

1831
Lincoln moves on his own to New Salem

1832
Lincoln serves in Black Hawk War

Politician

In 1832, Lincoln first ran for the Illinois General Assembly and lost. In 1834, he ran again and won. In 1841, Lincoln was elected to the U.S. House of Representatives. Then the United States went to war against Mexico. Lincoln made speeches against the war. Many voters in Illinois did not like these speeches, so he did not run for re-election.

Lincoln's concern about slavery brought him back into politics. He wanted to keep slavery from expanding. In 1855, he ran for a seat in the U.S. Senate and lost. In 1858, he ran again. This time, he debated his opponent, Stephen Douglas. Their debates earned Lincoln national attention. He lost the election, but he won the respect of many people. In 1860, Lincoln ran for President and won.

Before the Beard
Lincoln posed for this photo in 1858.

66 **A house divided against itself cannot stand. I believe this government cannot endure permanently half slave and half free.** 99

—1858, from speech accepting nomination for the U.S. Senate

Major Events

1834
Lincoln elected to Illinois General Assembly

1837
Lincoln moves to Springfield, Illinois, and practices law

1842
Lincoln marries Mary Todd

The Debates This painting by Robert Marshall Root shows Lincoln and Douglas at their fourth debate, in Charleston, Illinois on September 18.

1846
Lincoln elected to U.S. House of Representatives

1858
Lincoln loses to Stephen Douglas in U.S. Senate race

1860
Lincoln elected President of the United States on an antislavery message

139

President

Shortly after Lincoln was elected, seven southern states seceded. Lincoln did not want the nation to be broken into two parts. He raised an army to force the southern states to stay in the Union.

In July 1863, Union and Confederate armies fought one of the largest battles of the war at Gettysburg, Pennsylvania. Four months later, Lincoln went to the battlefield to honor those who had died. His speech there, the Gettysburg Address, became one of the most famous speeches in American history.

In November 1864, Lincoln was re-elected. The Union won the war less than six months later. Lincoln began making plans to bring the southern states back into the United States. He did not get the chance to carry out his plans. On April 14, Lincoln was shot by John Wilkes Booth. The President died the next morning.

> **66 . . . Government of the people, by the people, for the people shall not perish from the earth. 99**
>
> —*1863, from the Gettysburg Address*

Final Portrait This photograph was taken on April 10, 1865, four days before Lincoln died.

Major Events

March 4, 1861
Lincoln becomes 16th President of the United States

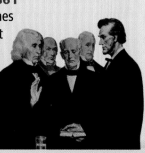

April 12, 1861
Civil War begins and Lincoln visits Union camps throughout the nation

January 1, 1863
Lincoln issues Emancipation Proclamation

Emancipation Proclamation Lincoln presents the proclamation to his advisors for approval on September 22, 1862. Francis Bicknell Carpenter painted this scene in 1864.

> **". . . [O]n the first day of January, in the year of our Lord one thousand eight hundred and sixty-three, all persons held as slaves within any State or designated part of a State, the people whereof shall then be in rebellion against the United States, shall be then, thenceforward, and forever free. . . ."**
>
> —*January 1, 1863, from the Emancipation Proclamation*

November 19, 1863
Lincoln delivers
Gettysburg Address

April 9, 1865
Civil War ends

April 15, 1865
Lincoln dies and is
later buried in a
tomb in Springfield

Legacy

Today, few presidents are as honored as Abraham Lincoln. Even while he was alive, people had strong opinions both for and against Lincoln's actions and ideas. Some historians think he made mistakes, but many wonder if the nation could have survived without him. Lincoln's words still inspire people to work for freedom and equality. The United States honors Lincoln in many ways.

Library and Museum Lincoln's life, challenges, and accomplishments are featured at the new Abraham Lincoln Presidential Library and Museum in Springfield, Illinois.

> **66** Fellow citizens, we cannot escape history. We of this Congress and this administration will be remembered in spite of ourselves. . . . **99**
>
> —*1862, from a message to Congress*

Mount Rushmore The memorial at Mount Rushmore in South Dakota honors four Presidents: George Washington, Thomas Jefferson, Theodore Roosevelt, and Abraham Lincoln.

Money Lincoln was the first President to appear on a U.S. coin. In 1909, the penny with Lincoln's image was made to celebrate Lincoln's 100th birthday. In 1914, Lincoln's portrait first appeared on the five dollar bill.

Lincoln Memorial This giant statue is the Lincoln Memorial. In the statue, Lincoln's left hand is clenched, showing his strength and determination. His right hand is open, showing his kindness.

Review

Art Activity Make a poster entitled "The Life of Lincoln." Divide the poster into four sections. Write and illustrate four events from Lincoln's life that show his childhood, his early years in Illinois, his efforts as a lawyer and politician, and his time as President.

Writing Activity Learn more about one of the places where Lincoln lived in Illinois. Write an article about the town or city, explaining why people would want to live there today.

Speaking Activity Read the Gettysburg Address. Choose an idea in that speech and prepare your own speech about the importance of that idea to the United States today. Discuss what the idea means to you, why you think it is important, and what effect the idea has on the lives of people in the nation.

Research Activity Research the Lincoln–Douglas debates. Think of questions to ask the two politicians. Write your questions on note cards, and take turns with classmates answering one another's questions.

Review and Test Prep

Vocabulary and Main Ideas

✔ **TEST PREP** Write a sentence to answer each question.

1. What did a **territory** need to become a state?

2. What did Tecumseh do to **unite** American Indians?

3. What important work did **delegates** do in Kaskaskia in 1818?

4. In what ways did **canals** change life for people in Illinois?

5. What role did slavery play in the South's **economy**?

6. Which group of people gained **emancipation** in 1863?

Critical Thinking

✔ **TEST PREP** Write a short paragraph to answer each question.

7. **Infer** Why do you think so many settlers came to Illinois?

8. **Summarize** What were some of the events that led to the Civil War?

Apply Skills

✔ **TEST PREP** Use what you have learned about circle graphs to answer each question.

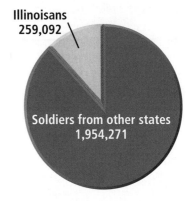

Union soldiers

Illinoisans
259,092

Soldiers from other states
1,954,271

9. What does the circle graph show?

   A. Union nurses in the Civil War
   B. Union soldiers in the Civil War
   C. Union soldiers who died during the Civil War
   D. States in the Union

10. What can you conclude from the information shown on the circle graph?

    A. Illinoisans contributed more than half of the Union soldiers.
    B. Illinoisans contributed less than half of the Union soldiers.
    C. Illinoisans contributed more Union soldiers than any other state.
    D. Illinoisans contributed fewer Union soldiers than any other state.

Unit Activity

Design a Magazine Cover

- Look back at Unit 3. Choose an event that changed Illinois.

- Research to find facts that explain how the event changed Illinois.

- Design a magazine cover to feature the event. Give the magazine a name. Find ways to combine words and pictures on the cover.

At the Library

Learn more by finding books like these at your school or public library.

Tecumseh by Don McLeese

This short illustrated biography tells the story of the great Shawnee chief.

Eyewitness: Civil War by John Stanchak

Photographs, illustrations, and text show many different facts about the Civil War.

CURRENT EVENTS
WEEKLY (WR) READER

Current Events Project

Plan a trip to a place that you would like to see.

- Find an article about a place that you find interesting.

- Locate the place on a map. Think about how to get there. Would you travel by car, train, boat, or plane?

- Write a description of your trip. Draw a picture of one part of the trip.

Technology
Weekly Reader online offers social studies articles. Go to **www.eduplace.com/kids/hmss/**

UNIT 4

Illinois Grows

The Big Idea

Why do people and places change over time?

" . . . Let us now have libraries, galleries of art, scientific museums, . . . and public parks. . . . "

Isaac Arnold, cofounder of Chicago Historical Society

Marshall Field
1834–1906

In 1881, Marshall Field took control of Illinois's first department store. Today, Marshall Field and Company has stores throughout the Midwest. **page 155**

History Makers

Frances Willard
1839–1898

Frances Willard wanted to vote with her brother. She worked to gain women's suffrage and to form the National Council of Women in 1888. **page 161**

THE NATIONAL COUNCIL
NCW
of WOMEN

Harold Washington
1922–1987

Chicago Mayor Harold Washington worked hard against discrimination. In 1983, he became the first African American mayor of Chicago. **page 202**

Washington!
For Chicago

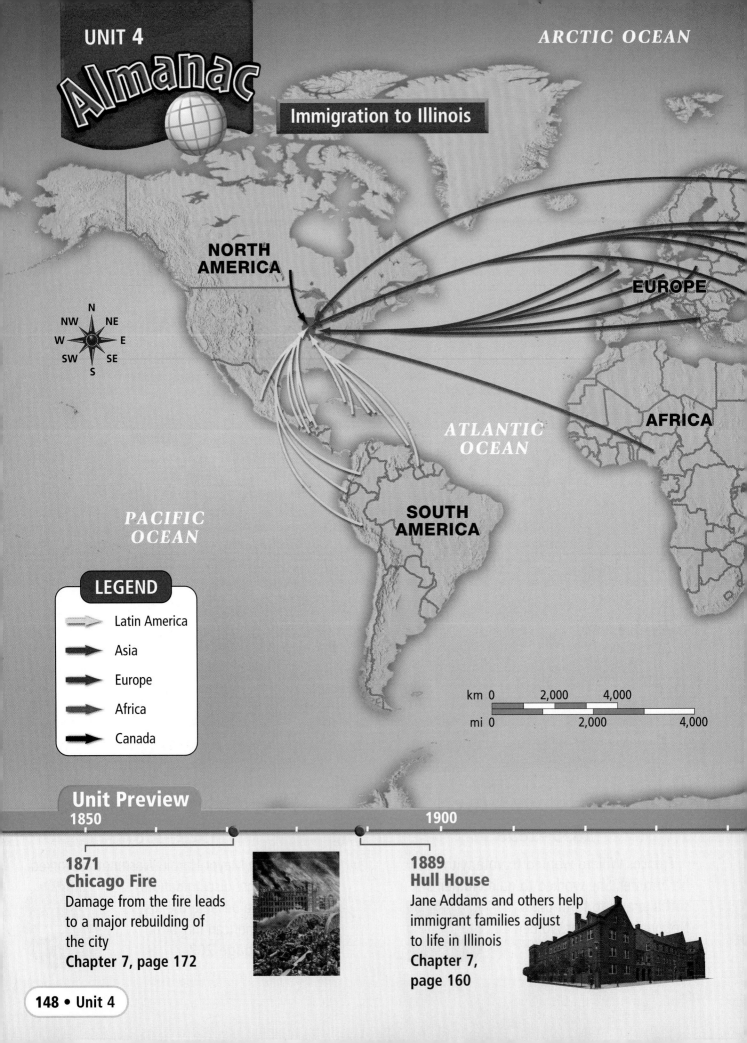

Almanac

Immigration to Illinois

ARCTIC OCEAN

NORTH AMERICA

EUROPE

AFRICA

ATLANTIC OCEAN

PACIFIC OCEAN

SOUTH AMERICA

N
NW   NE
W   E
SW   SE
S

LEGEND

→ Latin America
→ Asia
→ Europe
→ Africa
→ Canada

km 0   2,000   4,000
mi 0   2,000   4,000

Unit Preview

1850   1900

1871
Chicago Fire
Damage from the fire leads
to a major rebuilding of
the city
Chapter 7, page 172

1889
Hull House
Jane Addams and others help
immigrant families adjust
to life in Illinois
**Chapter 7,
page 160**

ASIA

AUSTRALIA

INDIAN OCEAN

ANTARCTICA

1950

2000

1970
Illinois Constitution
Lawmakers rewrite the
state constitution of 1870
Chapter 7,
page 192

Illinois Population, 1900–2000

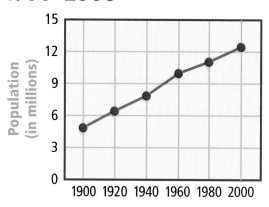

Population (in millions) vs. Years (1900, 1920, 1940, 1960, 1980, 2000), y-axis 0 to 15

Top Five State Populations, 2004

State	Population
California	35,893,799
Texas	22,490,022
New York	19,227,088
Florida	17,397,161
Illinois	12,713,634

How many states have larger
populations than Illinois?

CURRENT EVENTS
WEEKLY WR READER

Current events on the web!

Find out about current events that
connect to this unit. See activities at:
www.eduplace.com/kids/hmss/

Vocabulary Preview

manufacturing

In the late 1800s, many Illinoisans worked in **manufacturing.** They built farm equipment, furniture, steel goods, and other products. **page 152**

immigrant

Immigrants often settled in ethnic communities. They lived near others who shared their language and culture. **page 158**

Chapter Timeline

| 1871 Chicago fire | 1878 Refrigerated train car | 1913 Suffrage for Illinois women | 1929 Stock market crash |

1865   1895   1925

Reading Strategy

Summarize Use this strategy as you read the lessons in this chapter.

Quick Tip Look for important details that support the main ideas in each lesson.

depression

During the Great **Depression,** many people lost their jobs. They had little money for things such as food, clothes, and housing. **page 165**

innovation

Many people came to Chicago for the 1893 World's Columbian Exposition. They wanted to see **innovations** such as the Ferris wheel and electricity. **page 172**

1945
World War II ends

1966
Dr. Martin Luther King Jr. in Chicago

1955

1985

Illinois Industry

| 1850 | 1900 | 1950 | 2000 |

1850–1900

Build on What You Know Have you ever wondered who makes the clothes, furniture, or food sold in so many stores? In the late 1800s, many Illinoisans began processing these things in factories.

Farming and More

Main Idea In the late 1800s, Illinois's agricultural industry grew to include more than just farming.

After the Civil War, new tools and equipment, such as the steel plow and the mechanical reaper, changed farming. Farmers produced more crops faster and at less cost. Manufacturing made these tools easier and less costly to make. **Manufacturing** means making goods by hand or with machines in a factory. The production of farm equipment formed a new industry.

New crops and products also expanded Illinois's agricultural industry. Factories manufactured food products, such as flour. Farmers planted new crops, such as soybeans. By 1900, the agricultural industry included manufacturing and farming.

Manufacturing
Workers produced new kinds of farm equipment, such as reapers, at this McCormick factory.

Refrigerated Train Car

Roof hatch

Food product

Door

SWI
REFRIGE
LIN

... as it passed over ice bunkers on the side of each train car.
...eat and other food products within the car cool.

Industry

In the late 1800s, railroads made Illinois industries grow. Illinois's location near main waterways helped it become a transportation center. **Transportation** is the way that people and goods move from one place to another.

The Illinois Central and other railroads connected Illinois towns and cities, including Cairo, Galena, and East St. Louis. Trains carried crops and livestock from farms to cities. Chicago became the center for buying and selling cattle.

In 1878, Chicago livestock dealer **Gustavus Swift** asked engineer **Andrew Chase** to build a refrigerated train car. Chase designed cars that stayed cool by passing air through bins of ice.

Refrigerated cars kept meat fresh as it was shipped to markets in other states. A **market** is a setting in which goods and services are bought and sold. Swift, **Nelson Morris, Philip Armour,** and other meatpackers built meatpacking factories in Chicago, St. Louis, and other cities.

Steamships carried other goods to and from Chicago across the Great Lakes. From Chicago, goods traveled by trains or by boats along canals and rivers throughout Illinois and the Midwest. All these goods had to be loaded and unloaded. Ships and trains had to be taken care of. Many people found jobs in the transportation industry.

REVIEW In what way did the refrigerated train car help Chicago's industries?

Factories, Mines, and Stores

Main Idea Transportation and manufacturing helped many other Illinois industries grow.

As the transportation and manufacturing industries grew, fewer people in Illinois worked on farms. Cities grew along railroad lines, and more people worked in factories.

The John Deere factory in Moline produced farm equipment. In 1874, **Joseph Glidden** and **Isaac Ellwood** began manufacturing barbed wire fencing in DeKalb to protect crops and control cattle. **Frederick Weyerhauser** started a lumber company on Rock Island. Factories in towns such as Rockford, Peoria, and Quincy produced clothes, furniture, and household appliances.

The Illinois mining industry also grew at this time. Mining means taking resources from underground. Coal mines in Belleville, Kingston, and other areas provided fuel for transportation and manufacturing.

Underground Miners dug deep into the earth to reach coal and other resources.

Illinois clay was used to make bricks in Murphysboro and pottery around the state.

In the mid-1800s, Illinois factories began using iron ore to make steel, a strong metal. Ships carried iron from Minnesota across the Great Lakes to Chicago. Mills in Chicago, Joliet, and Alton melted the iron and added other minerals to turn it into steel. Other factories turned the steel into finished products.

Steel Mill Illinois factories turned iron ore into steel.

Retail Industry

As factories grew, they hired more workers. People with jobs had money to spend in stores. Stores are part of the retail industry. **Retail** is the sale of goods to a customer.

In 1852, **Potter Palmer** built the state's first department store. His store sold clothes, furniture, and other goods made in factories back east. Later, Potter went into business with **Marshall Field** and **Levi Leiter.** The store was renamed Marshall Field and Company.

Montgomery Ward and Sears and Roebuck sold goods through mail-order catalogs. Customers ordered tools, clothing, and equipment such as plows and stoves from these Chicago companies. Railroads and boats carried these goods to distant farms.

REVIEW What new industries developed in Illinois in the late 1800s?

Lesson Summary

New tools and equipment changed Illinois farming in the late 1800s. Illinois's location made it a transportation center. Factories, mining, and the retail industry became important in the late 1800s.

Why It Matters ...

The industries of the 1800s changed the economy of Illinois.

Marshall Field and Company The department store began in Chicago and expanded throughout the Midwest.

Lesson Review

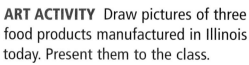

1852
Palmer opens first department store

1878
Swift uses refrigerated train car

1850   1875   1900

1. **VOCABULARY** Describe ways that **transportation** and **manufacturing** helped Illinois industries grow.

2. **READING SKILL** State the **main idea** of the second page of the lesson in your own words.

3. **MAIN IDEA: Economics** In what way did manufacturing help farming?

4. **MAIN IDEA: History** Why did the retail industry in Illinois grow in the late 1800s?

5. **TIMELINE SKILL** In what year did Chicago's first department store open?

6. **CRITICAL THINKING: Draw Conclusions** Why did mail-order companies such as Sears and Roebuck do well in rural areas?

ART ACTIVITY Draw pictures of three food products manufactured in Illinois today. Present them to the class.

A Railroad Economy

Chicago was at the center of the national economy. In the late 1800s, railways, shipping lines, and roads connected most of the nation. Chicago was located almost midway between the East and the West. This meant that many natural resources and finished products passed through the city's rail stations and shipyards. Chicago quickly became the nation's transportation hub, or center.

Natural resources from the West traveled thousands of miles to factories in the Midwest and the East. Products from those factories traveled all across the nation, even all the way back west. Most of the trains and ships carrying these resources and goods passed through Chicago.

① Natural resources such as wood came from the forests of the Northwest.

② Wood traveled to Chicago by train, along with many other goods and resources.

LEGEND
— Railroad line
• City

km 0   250   500
mi 0   250   500

Gulf of Mexico

3 Wood was used in the East for building or made into products such as furniture.

4 Products from factories in the East were shipped around the country. Many passed through Chicago on the way to new markets.

Activities

1. **TALK ABOUT IT** In a group, choose a natural resource found in Illinois and discuss the ways in which it can be used. What products can be made from the natural resource?

2. **RESEARCH IT** Choose an item such as a piece of clothing that you own. Find out what company made the item and where it was made and sold. In what way do you think the item traveled from where it was made to where it was sold?

157

Changing Times

1850   1900   1950   2000

1885–1940

Build on What You Know What do new students need to learn about your school? In the late 1800s, many people moved to Illinois. They had to learn many things.

Moving to Illinois

Main Idea Newcomers faced challenges in Illinois.

After the Civil War, many immigrants came to Illinois from Italy, as well as from Poland and other countries in Eastern Europe. An **immigrant** is someone who moves to another country. Most immigrants settled in mining towns, such as Galena, and in cities near factories and railroads, such as Chicago and Joliet. Often, immigrants from one country settled in the same neighborhood.

In the late 1800s, many African Americans also moved to Illinois in search of new opportunities. They did not have money to buy land, but they hoped to find jobs in factories. They did not find the great opportunities that they expected.

Vocabulary Strategy

immigrant

The prefix **im-** means "into." An immigrant is a person who moves into a new country.

READING SKILL
Cause and Effect As you read "Social and Labor Reforms" on page 160, list reforms and the effects that they had on people.

Reformer	Effect

A Neighborhood Store Many immigrants settled in communities where people shared their traditions and language.

Challenges and Changes

In the late 1800s and early 1900s, newcomers did much of the work that helped Illinois grow. Unfortunately, Illinois did not have enough jobs for all of the people who came. Those who found work often earned low pay. Others could not find work at all.

Newcomers faced discrimination. **Discrimination** is unjust treatment of a group of people. Illinois outlawed separation of students in schools according to their race and discrimination in public places such as restaurants. Still, many people did not follow the laws. Many businesses would not hire African Americans. Often, the only neighborhoods open to immigrants and African Americans were poorly kept and overcrowded.

Open Doors Provident Hospital and Training School for Nurses opened in 1891. In 1893, Daniel Hale Williams performed the first open heart surgery there.

Ida Wells Barnett
This Chicago journalist worked to stop violence against African Americans.

Some people worked to end discrimination. **Ida Wells Barnett,** a Chicago journalist, wrote newspaper stories to stop violence against African Americans. **Daniel Hale Williams** founded Provident Hospital to hire and train nurses and doctors of all races. In 1915, **Oscar Stanton de Priest** became the first African American elected to Chicago's city council. Later, he was elected to the U.S. Congress. He worked for laws against discrimination.

REVIEW What challenges did new Illinoisans face?

Social and Labor Reforms

Main Idea Illinoisans have worked to change Illinois for the better.

In the late 1800s, Illinoisans worked for many reforms. A **reform** is a change that makes something better.

In 1889, **Jane Addams** and **Ellen Gates Starr** opened Hull House. There, they helped immigrants learn English, find jobs, and take care of their families. Addams and others also worked for better government and to improve public health.

Many reformers worried about children in Illinois who worked on farms, in factories, and in mines. In 1912, the U.S. government formed the United States Children's Bureau. This action led to laws that increased the minimum working age and required children to attend school.

Upton Sinclair His book about workers in Chicago industries was called *The Jungle*.

Other efforts also brought change. **Upton Sinclair** wrote a novel about the hard lives of immigrants in Chicago. His descriptions of poor conditions in the meatpacking industry led to new laws.

In the 1870s, farmers formed groups called granges. By acting as a group, they won lower railroad and shipping costs and their efforts led to laws that allowed government to regulate, or oversee, business.

Other groups of workers came together to form labor unions to improve working conditions. **Eugene V. Debs** led the American Railroad Union. **Mary Harris "Mother" Jones** and the United Mine Workers pushed for reforms in the mining industry.

Unions held strikes to gain shorter work hours, safer conditions, and more pay. A strike is a protest in which workers refuse to work.

In 1892, workers and farmers helped elect Governor **John P. Altgeld.** He worked to stop child labor and make workplaces safer. In the 1900s, reformers gained minimum pay for workers and an eight-hour workday.

In the Factories Many men, women, and children worked long hours for little money.

Suffrage

Women worked for political reform and demanded suffrage. **Suffrage** means the right to vote. **Susan B. Anthony** led the national fight for women's suffrage. Many Illinois women such as **Frances Willard, Ellen Martin,** and **Grace Wilbur Trout** also worked for suffrage. Willard helped start the National Council of Women to work for suffrage, healthcare, and other concerns of women.

In 1913, Illinois women won suffrage in presidential elections. Three years later, 5,000 women marched in Chicago to demand national suffrage. In 1919, the U.S. Congress guaranteed suffrage for women across the nation.

REVIEW Explain two ways that people in Illinois came together to work for change.

Lesson Summary

In the late 1800s, many African Americans and immigrants came to Illinois for jobs. They faced low pay and poor conditions. Reformers worked for better conditions for many different people. Women in Illinois and the nation won suffrage.

Why It Matters...

Reformers helped people in Illinois and around the nation gain rights that we enjoy today.

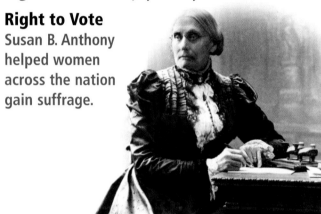

Right to Vote
Susan B. Anthony helped women across the nation gain suffrage.

Lesson Review

| 1889 | | 1913 | |
| Hull House opens | | Illinois women win suffrage | |

1880 — 1900 — 1920 — 1940

❶ **VOCABULARY** Use these vocabulary words in a sentence.
discrimination   reform

❷ **READING SKILL** List two **effects** of reformers in Illinois.

❸ **MAIN IDEA: Economics** Why did immigrants and African Americans move to Illinois after the Civil War?

❹ **MAIN IDEA: Government** Explain some changes that the U.S. government made to help workers, women, and children.

❺ **TIMELINE SKILL** When did women gain the right to vote in Illinois?

❻ **CRITICAL THINKING: Draw Conclusions** Were the reformers successful in bringing about needed changes? Explain your answer.

HANDS ON

CITIZENSHIP ACTIVITY Find out about some of the challenges that modern immigrants face. Work with a partner or small group and write a proposal about ways that you can help.

Hull House Reformers

When Jane Addams co-founded Hull House in the late 1800s, she had an idea. She wanted to make Hull House a place where people could come to get what they needed. Her idea worked. Some people came to get health care from nurses. Others came because they needed a safe place to leave children while they worked.

Still others came from around the world to learn from Addams. Many of them set up programs like Hull House in other cities. Others worked for reforms in government, health care, and factories. They also worked for women's suffrage, in Illinois and the nation.

Jane Addams, 1860–1935
Addams worked to improve conditions for women and children.

Julia Lathrop, 1858–1932
Lathrop started the first children's court in the world. She also made sure that laws protecting children were obeyed.

Florence Kelley, 1859–1932
Kelley inspected factories to improve health and safety. Her reports led to laws against child labor.

Alice Hamilton, 1869–1970
Hamilton ran a medical clinic at Hull House. She tried to make workplaces safer and to get help for people who were injured at work.

Activities

1. **THINK ABOUT IT** In what way do you think the work of Hull House reformers affects you today? Discuss your ideas in groups.

2. **PRESENT IT** Learn more about one reformer on this page. Make a timeline of events from her life. Present your findings.

Core Lesson 3

War and Growth

1850 1900 1950 2000

1910–2000

Build on What You Know What kinds of work have you done with other people? In the early 1900s, Illinoisans worked together to help two war efforts.

From War to Depression

Main Idea The early 1900s brought war and economic problems.

In 1917, the United States entered World War I, a war that began in Europe. Illinois sent more than 314,000 soldiers to serve. Farmers grew food to send to the troops, and factories made equipment. Volunteers made clothes and hospital supplies and gave money.

Factories needed workers. Women and immigrants filled many jobs, and thousands of African Americans came from the South to work. When the war ended, businesses kept growing. Factories that had built tanks and battleships manufactured things for people to buy, such as cars.

VOCABULARY

depression
scarcity
suburb
segregation
civil rights

Vocabulary Strategy

civil rights

Civil describes something connected with ordinary citizens. **Civil rights** are the rights of all citizens.

READING SKILL

Problem and Solution
What problems did people face in the 1930s? What solutions did President Roosevelt offer?

Problem	Solution

Illinois Soldiers These men were among more than 350,000 African Americans who served during World War I.

Soup Kitchen People without jobs waited in lines for free food and coffee during the Depression.

The Great Depression

In 1929, businesses in Illinois and across the nation began to fail. This was the beginning of the Great Depression. A **depression** is a period of time when many businesses fail, prices drop, and jobs are hard to find.

During the Depression, most people had less money to buy things. Many factories closed. Mines shut down because fewer factories bought coal for fuel. One-third of workers in Illinois lost their jobs. Farmers could not sell crops because people did not have money to buy as much food.

The problem of scarcity was made much worse. **Scarcity** means that people's wants are greater than their resources can provide. Many families did not have enough money to buy food and clothes. They had to make tough decisions about how to use their money. Many people sold their cars and lost their homes.

The New Deal

President **Franklin Delano Roosevelt** started a program called the New Deal to help people during the Depression. He promised to put people across the nation back to work.

The Civilian Conservation Corps (CCC) was a New Deal program that provided jobs and training. More than 100,000 Illinoisans worked on roads, parks, telephone lines, forestland, and farmland for the CCC.

Another New Deal program, the Works Progress Administration (WPA), hired Illinoisans to build roads, sidewalks, schools, airports, and playgrounds. It also created jobs for artists, actors, and writers. In the late 1930s, these programs and others helped people in Illinois and the rest of the nation recover from the Depression.

REVIEW In what way did the New Deal change life for Illinoisans and other Americans?

CCC Poster Many Illinoisans found jobs in the Civilian Conservation Corps.

Illinois and World War II

During the war, posters such as the one shown here asked people to grow their own food so crops could be sent to those in the military. These men were among one million sailors who trained at Great Lakes Naval Training Base between 1941 and 1945. Here, they learn to use radios for communication. This woman worked in a factory in East Moline making parts for harvesting machines.

YOUR VICTORY GARDEN
counts more than ever!

World War II

Main Idea World War II changed the way people in Illinois worked and lived.

In 1941, the United States entered another war that started in Europe. Farmers met a new call for crops, and factories made more food products.

Other factories made machinery and supplies. Dodge made airplane engines. The Pullman Company made tank and airplane parts. The town of Seneca made ships and became known as the "Prairie Shipyard."

Other Illinois factories made goods such as clothing and electronic parts. Mines produced coal for fuel. Many factory workers left Illinois to fight. More workers were needed. Many women went to work in factories for the first time and gained new skills.

More than one million Illinoisans served in the war as soldiers, pilots, sailors, nurses, and other workers. Military bases in Illinois trained many of those who served. Camp Grant near Rockford trained medical workers. Scott Field near Belleville was a training field for pilots. More than one million sailors went through the Great Lakes Naval Training Base outside Chicago.

Illinois was one of the few places where African Americans could receive military training. Harlem Airport in Oaklawn trained African American pilots. African Americans at Camp Robert Smalls learned industrial skills.

Illinoisans recycled scrap metal and stopped buying unnecessary goods. People planted "victory gardens" in their yards, on rooftops, and in any other space that they could find so that farm crops could go to the soldiers.

Post-War Growth

The war ended in 1945. Some Illinoisans returned from the war and went back to work. Others went to school. The U.S. government gave money to men and women who had been in the military to go to college.

During the war, many resources had been used to make ships, tanks, and other supplies. After the war, factories started making clothes, shoes, washers and dryers, and cars. Illinois factories produced televisions, radios, and other electronic items.

Many people bought new homes. The suburbs grew quickly. A **suburb** is a community near a city where people live who work in the city. Most suburban houses were larger than city homes, and many people felt safer away from city traffic and crime.

As people moved to the suburbs, businesses followed them. More people had cars. Gas stations, grocery stores, and shopping malls, such as Old Orchard Shopping Center in Skokie, were built. New highways made it easier for people to get to these businesses. Governor **Adlai Stevenson** encouraged much of this growth.

After the war, agricultural production increased but many small farmers could not keep up. Often, farmers who could not buy machinery and more land lost their farms. Illinois's farms grew bigger and bigger.

REVIEW Why were new highways built in Illinois after World War II?

The Television
Illinois became a leading producer of televisions such as this one made in Chicago in 1955.

Ending Discrimination Civil rights activists worked to end housing segregation.

Civil Rights Movement

Main Idea Many Illinoisans worked to make sure that all people had equal rights.

Not everyone could move to the suburbs. Despite laws against discrimination, many people and businesses in Illinois refused to hire, rent to, and sell to African Americans. Even the military treated African Americans unfairly until it ended segregation in 1948. **Segregation** means the separation of people of different races.

Some people wanted the government to guarantee equal rights for all citizens. This fight for equal rights at home became known as the civil rights movement. **Civil rights** are basic rights that are protected by the government.

Civil Rights Dr. Martin Luther King Jr. led protests in Chicago to end discrimination.

Civil Rights Leaders in Illinois

Civil rights leaders organized nonviolent actions such as marches and boycotts. **Dr. Martin Luther King Jr.** and **Jesse Jackson** worked for equal rights in Illinois. In 1966, Dr. King worked to end housing segregation in Chicago. Jackson and others organized boycotts in Chicago, Cairo, and East St. Louis to end job discrimination.

U.S. Senator **Everett Dirksen** from Illinois helped pass the 1964 Civil Rights Act. This law made segregation and discrimination illegal. A year later, the Voting Rights Act removed state laws that made people take a test to vote. In 1967, Illinois Governor **Otto Kerner** ordered an end to housing segregation in Illinois.

Diversity in Illinois

African Americans have held important positions throughout Illinois. **Gwendolyn Brooks** and **Richard Wright** were famous authors and poets working in Illinois. **Vernon Jarrett** has spent his life working for Chicago newspapers, radio, and television. In 1975, he cofounded the National Association of Black Journalists.

People from many countries have come to Illinois. Most recently, immigrants from Mexico, China, Iran, and Japan have brought their traditions to Illinois and increased the state's diversity. **Diversity** means variety. Diversity has led to many changes.

REVIEW What did the civil rights movement want the government to guarantee?

Lesson Summary

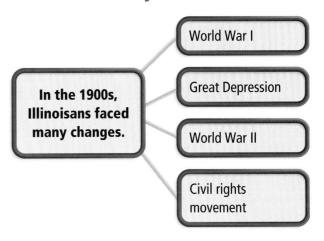

In the 1900s, Illinoisans faced many changes.
- World War I
- Great Depression
- World War II
- Civil rights movement

Why It Matters ...

Illinoisans have worked through hard times to help make Illinois a good place to live.

Lesson Review

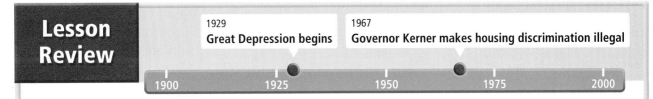

1929 Great Depression begins

1967 Governor Kerner makes housing discrimination illegal

1900   1925   1950   1975   2000

1 **VOCABULARY** Write two to three sentences using the words **depression** and **scarcity**.

2 **READING SKILL** What were two **solutions** that President Franklin Roosevelt found to put people back to work during the Great Depression?

3 **MAIN IDEA: Economics** In what way did the Great Depression affect the choices that people made?

4 **MAIN IDEA: History** What was the civil rights movement?

5 **TIMELINE SKILL** When did the Great Depression begin?

6 **CRITICAL THINKING: Analyze** In what way did the two world wars affect women?

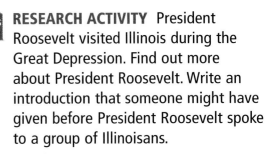

HANDS ON

RESEARCH ACTIVITY President Roosevelt visited Illinois during the Great Depression. Find out more about President Roosevelt. Write an introduction that someone might have given before President Roosevelt spoke to a group of Illinoisans.

Your Illinois

What do you like best about Illinois? Dr. Kevin Stein pulls together many ideas in his poem "Your Illinois." Dr. Stein is the Illinois Poet Laureate. A poet laureate works to help people understand and connect with poetry. As you read, think of how Dr. Stein's words connect with your life and your Illinois.

When you come to school and sit in your chair,
you flip pages in this book of your place
and history. When you daydream and stare
out the schoolroom's sun-washed window, you face
land that glaciers shaped and wide rivers cut,
leaving rich soil and round hills but no ice.
When you get up and cross the room to shut
the door, you may step where the Illinois grew
squash and beans in the earth's fertile loam
and built longhouses and wigwams too,
making the villages that were their home.
When you play ball with friends, you're having fun
where Jolliet and Marquette paddled canoes
to trade and bring their faith where rivers run.

When you walk along a city street, your shoes
may tread where the Peoria and Cahokia tribes once
roamed the prairie, or where men worked long days
digging a canal to link the work and lives
of the Mississippi with the seaways
of Lake Michigan. When you see Chicago sky,
you feel the same blue freedom Lincoln said
was yours, no matter the color of skin or eye.
When you eat your dinner, perhaps you're fed
by corn grown in this Land of Lincoln, this state
whose mills and factories make things people need,
this place your home no matter what great
distance you traveled to get here. When you plead
to stay up late although it's time for you
to sleep, the stars that float above your bed
wink their promises for you. All this is true.

—Dr. Kevin Stein,
Illinois Poet Laureate

Activities

1. **DRAW IT** Reread this poem. What things do you
see in your mind as you read? Create a poster to
illustrate the poem based on your ideas.

2. **WRITE ABOUT IT** What does this poem tell you
about Illinois? Write an essay about the ways in
which this poem relates to what you know about
Illinois history, geography, and culture.

Chicago

1850   1900   1950   2000

1870–2000

Build on What You Know What would you like to see in Chicago? Chicago has a little bit of everything, from towering skyscrapers to vast parks to unique neighborhoods that reflect the city's many cultures.

Chicago Changes

Main Idea After the Great Fire of 1871, Chicagoans rebuilt their city to be big, strong, and exciting.

No one knows exactly how the Great Fire started. Legend says that a cow kicked over a lantern and started the blaze. The fire began in Patrick and Catherine O'Leary's barn on the night of October 8, 1871. Strong winds pushed the fire across the river and through Chicago. The fire burned through the wooden buildings until October 10 and damaged much of the city.

Chicagoans began to rebuild immediately. Before the fire, Chicago was a small city at the heart of the country. After the fire, Chicago became a center of growth and industry. The new Chicago attracted new immigrants, new businesses, and new innovations. An **innovation** is a new idea or a new way of doing something.

VOCABULARY

innovation
architecture
skyscraper
conservatory
entrepreneur

Vocabulary Strategy

entrepreneur

Entrepreneur comes from a French word meaning "to undertake" or "take on." An entrepreneur takes on starting a business.

READING SKILL

Predict Outcome
Predict what life will be like in Chicago after the Great Fire of 1871. Then check your predictions.

Prediction	Was it correct?

The City Burns The Great Fire of 1871 burnt down 18,000 buildings over 2,000 acres. Chicagoans worked hard to rebuild.

Grand Display In 1893, Chicago stunned the world with its World's Columbian Exposition.

Boom Town

Chicago grew rapidly. Limited space meant that builders had to build up. Around 1885, **William LeBaron Jenney** designed the first skyscraper for the Home Insurance Company. A **skyscraper** is a very tall building. The skyscraper had a steel skeleton and many windows. Chicago led the way in this new style of architecture. **Architecture** means the method and style of building.

Wealthy Chicagoans gave money to build the first Art Institute of Chicago. They donated paintings and other artwork. Many people helped rebuild the Chicago Public Library. People from around the world, including Queen Victoria of England, donated books to replace those lost.

In 1893, Chicago hosted the World's Columbian Exposition to celebrate the 400th anniversary of Columbus's voyage. An exposition is a public show.

Large buildings made to look like palaces displayed technology, art, and culture from 46 countries. Thousands of electrical lights lit the area at night. People called it the Great White City.

Canals and trains carried the millions who came to see the fair. Many rode on the world's first Ferris wheel, designed by Illinoisan **George Washington Gale Ferris.**

REVIEW In what ways did Chicagoans change Chicago after the Great Fire?

Chicago Today

Main Idea Chicago has many special communities and places.

Today, Chicago's Museum of Science and Industry is the largest museum in the United States. It is in the only building that remains from the 1893 fair. Other museums include the DuSable Museum of African American History and the Field Museum of Natural History.

Chicago has 552 parks, 33 beaches, 10 bird and wildlife gardens, and 2 nature conservatories. A **conservatory** is a place for growing and protecting plants. Grant Park contains the Buckingham Fountain, one of Chicago's most famous features. In 2004, the newest park, Millennium Park, opened. Many of the city's parks host musical events, farmers' markets, and other activities.

Chicago has seventy-seven different communities that reflect the city's ethnic groups. The central Douglas and Grand Boulevard neighborhoods have strong African American traditions. Different groups of Hispanic Americans, Asian Americans, and European Americans all have distinct neighborhoods.

The 110-story Sears Tower stands over Chicago's downtown, called the Loop. Skyscrapers house many businesses and government offices. The Magnificent Mile and other shopping strips draw thousands of visitors.

Many jazz and blues musicians, such as **Louis Armstrong,** have called Chicago home. The Chicago Symphony Orchestra, the Lyric Opera, and the city's many theater companies are world famous. Sports teams such as the Cubs, the White Sox, and the Bulls draw millions of fans each year.

Today Chicagoans continue to find ways to improve their city in the 21st century.

Navy Pier Once a military base, this amusement park and meeting center is now Chicago's most visited site.

Chicagoans helped build the nation's mass media industry. Mass media means the businesses that provide entertainment and information to large numbers of people. **Robert R. McCormick,** an entrepreneur, made the *Chicago Tribune* one of the most widely read newspapers in the nation. An **entrepreneur** is someone who takes risks to start a business.

Chicago is still a busy transportation center. National railroads still meet in the city. O'Hare International Airport serves more than 190,000 people every day. People from all over the world come to Chicago to explore, do business, and make new homes.

REVIEW What are three places you can visit in Chicago?

Lesson Summary

- The Great Fire of 1871 and the World's Columbian Exposition led to growth and innovation.

- Chicago has many unique features and distinct communities.

Why It Matters...

Growth, industry, and culture have made Chicago one of the most important cities in the United States.

Lesson Review

1893
World's Columbian Exposition

1974
Sears Tower completed

1850 — 1900 — 1950 — 2000

❶ **VOCABULARY** Choose the word that completes the sentence.

entrepreneur   architecture

Chicago buildings show many unique styles of _____.

❷ 🔄 **READING SKILL** Review your **prediction.** Was it correct? What happened in Chicago after the fire?

❸ **MAIN IDEA: Technology** In what ways did architecture change in Chicago after the Great Fire?

❹ **MAIN IDEA: Culture** Name three ethnic groups that have formed large communities within Chicago.

❺ **TIMELINE SKILL** When was the World's Columbian Exposition?

❻ **CRITICAL THINKING: Analyze** Why do you think people might want to visit Chicago today?

HANDS ON **ART ACTIVITY** Collect images of people and places in Chicago. Make a collage that shows the city's diversity.

175

Chicagoans
MAKING NEWS

Chicagoans take pride in their tough city and its lively citizens. Chicago has produced writers, musicians, artists, politicians, social reformers, entrepreneurs, philanthropists, scientists, and others who have changed the city and the nation.

Oprah Winfrey

Oprah Winfrey gained national attention through her television talk show, but she stays busy with other work as well. Winfrey is a successful Chicago businesswoman. She started her own production company, helped found a company to produce programs for women, and began her own magazine. She uses her success to support the education and health of children, women, and families through several charities.

Dr. Mae Jemison

Dr. Mae Jemison discovered her interest in science while growing up in Chicago. After medical school, she worked as a doctor in Asia and Africa. She joined NASA in 1986. In 1992, Jemison flew into space aboard the shuttle *Endeavor*, becoming the first African American female astronaut. Jemison now has her own technology company. She works on many educational projects, such as an international space camp.

Marca Bristo

Marca Bristo has made news because of her courage and dedication. In 1979, she helped found Access Living, a program in Chicago to improve conditions for people with disabilities. Bristo later became the first person with a disability to head the National Council on Disability. In that job, she has worked for civil liberties in the United States and around the world. Bristo also helped develop the Americans with Disabilities Act, a law which protects the rights of people with disabilities.

Activities

1. **WRITE ABOUT IT** What skills do you have that you could use to improve your community? Write a paragraph to explain your answer.

2. **RESEARCH IT** Research someone in your town who has helped the community. In what way have that person's actions improved the community?

Identify Primary and Secondary Sources

▶ **VOCABULARY**

primary source
secondary source

A primary source comes from a person who witnessed an event. A secondary source is written by someone who did not witness the event. Primary and secondary sources can offer different points of view on the same topic. The sources below are about the Great Fire of 1871.

No one knows exactly how the Great Fire started. Legend says that a cow kicked over a lantern and started the blaze. The fire began in Patrick and Catherine O'Leary's barn on the night of October 8, 1871. Strong winds pushed the fire across the river and through the city. The fire burned through the wooden buildings until October 10 and damaged much of the city.

—*Illinois Studies*
  Boston: Houghton Mifflin Company, 2005

Everybody was talking about the fire. Everybody had [a] different story as to how the fire started. I am sure Mrs. O'Leary's cow started the fire. I was talking to a man who lived next door to Mrs. O'Leary and he told me. . . . The house where I lived was burned down.

—*Mr. Hyman Bernstein*
  as told to Hilda Polacheck, 1937–1938

Learn the Skill

Step 1: Identify the subject of both sources.

Step 2: Read both passages. Look for clue words such as **I, my, we,** and **our.** These are often used in primary sources. Also look for personal details. Secondary sources do not include personal information about the event. Often, secondary sources summarize or analyze an event.

Step 3: Identify each passage as being a primary or secondary source. To help you determine this, ask yourself questions such as these: *Who wrote this passage? Was the writer at the event?*

Practice the Skill

Use the passages on page 178 to answer the questions.

1 Which is the primary source, and which is the secondary source? How do you know?

2 Which facts are the same in both sources?

3 What details do you learn from the secondary source that the primary source does not include?

Apply the Skill

Using a newspaper, find one example of a primary source and one example of a secondary source. Write a paragraph explaining how the two sources are similar and how they are different.

Visual Summary

1 – 3. Write a description of each concept or event named below.

Growth in Illinois	
Industry	
Great Chicago Fire	
Reform	

Facts and Main Ideas

TEST PREP Answer each question below.

4. **Geography** In what way did Illinois's location help it become a center of transportation and industry?

5. **Technology** In what way did transportation changes help industry?

6. **Culture** What difficulties did workers in Illinois face during the 1800s and early 1900s?

7. **History** What did President Roosevelt do to help people during the Great Depression?

8. **Government** What did leaders in the civil rights movement want the United States government to do?

Vocabulary

TEST PREP Choose the correct word from the list below to complete each sentence.

retail, p. 155
reform, p. 160
suburb, p. 167
entrepreneur, p. 175

9. A(n) _____ is a community near a city.

10. When you buy goods from stores, you are helping the _____ industry.

11. A(n) _____ takes risks to start a business.

12. Granges and labor unions worked for _____ in the late 1800s.

1893 World's Columbian Exposition	1938 Congress passes labor laws	1966 Dr. Martin Luther King Jr. in Chicago

1865   1895   1925   1955   1985

Apply Skills

✓ **TEST PREP Identify Primary and Secondary Sources** Use the passage below and what you have learned about primary and secondary sources to answer each question.

> On our first New Year's Day at Hull House we invited the older people in the vicinity [area], sending a carriage for the most feeble [weak] and announcing to all of them that we were going to organize an old Settlers' Party.
>
> — Excerpt from *Twenty Years at Hull House* by Jane Addams

13. This passage is an example of

    A. a secondary source.
    B. a primary source.
    C. a speech.
    D. an encyclopedia entry.

14. A primary source

    A. does not include personal details.
    B. does not use words such as *I* and *my*.
    C. comes from a person who has witnessed an event.
    D. is written by someone who did not witness the event.

Critical Thinking

✓ **TEST PREP** Write a short paragraph to answer each question below.

15. **Draw Conclusions** Do you think the labor reform movement was successful? Explain your answer.

16. **Analyze** Why were so many different industries able to do well in Illinois?

Timeline

Use the Chapter Summary Timeline above to answer the question.

17. How many years after the World's Columbian Exposition did Dr. King come to Chicago?

Activities

 Research Activity Choose one of the innovations or reforms described in this chapter. Find out more information about how it changed people's lives. Present what you learn to the class.

 Writing Activity Write a personal essay about where you live. Do you live in a rural area, a city, or a suburb? Describe the area where you live and what you like about it.

 Technology **Writing Process Tips** Get help with your report at: www.eduplace.com/kids/hmss/

Chapter 8

Government of the People

Technology
e • glossary
e • word games
www.eduplace.com/kids/hmss/

Vocabulary Preview

democracy

Democracy is government by the people. The United States has a form of democracy in which citizens elect representatives to speak and vote for them. **page 184**

citizen

A **citizen** has special rights and responsibilities. Immigrants to the United States can apply to become citizens. **page 184**

Reading Strategy

Question Use this strategy as you read the lessons in this chapter.

Quick Tip List any questions you have. When you finish reading, go back to find the answers.

bill

Every law begins as a **bill.** Lawmakers discuss and vote on these ideas for new laws. **page 194**

volunteer

Schools, hospitals, and other organizations depend on volunteers who work without pay. You can help your community by becoming a **volunteer. page 201**

Core Lesson 1

United States Government

VOCABULARY

democracy
citizen
common good
liberty

Vocabulary Strategy

common good

Common means "relating to the community." The **common good** means the good of the community.

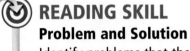

READING SKILL

Problem and Solution
Identify problems that the United States government faces. Tell how the government solves them.

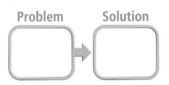

Problem → Solution

Build on What You Know A United States flag probably hangs in your classroom. Schools in all fifty states have this flag. People in all states, including those in Illinois, are part of a larger nation.

Government by the People

Main Idea Our government is made by the people, of the people, and for the people of the United States.

The United States has fifty states. All of them are part of the same nation—the United States.

The United States is a democracy. A **democracy** is a system in which the people hold the power of government. The people decide who will lead them. This means that the United States government is "by the people." The United States government is also "of the people" because each American citizen has a right to participate in the government. A **citizen** is someone who is born in a country or who promises to be loyal to a country. The United States government is "for the people" because it is supposed to protect the people's rights and serve the common good. The **common good** means the good of the whole population, not of just a few people.

Citizens These immigrants are becoming United States citizens. They are raising their hands as they promise to be loyal.

United States Congress United States voters elect officials to represent them in government. Members of Congress represent the people in their states.

How the People Rule

Democracy can take several forms. In many small towns, every citizen may vote on every rule and decision. This does not work well, however, for a huge nation. Suppose that millions of citizens had to vote on every law. It would take far too long to make a decision.

Instead, the government of the United States is a representative democracy. Citizens choose officials to represent them. These officials represent the people in their states and make day-to-day decisions for the government. This system is what makes the United States a democracy.

Citizens decide who will represent them by voting in elections. On election day, voters cast their votes for the people they want to represent them. Whoever gets the most votes usually wins the election. Citizens in a democratic system have a responsibility to vote for their leaders. Voting is one way that citizens participate in their government. Citizens can also participate by writing and calling their representatives about issues.

REVIEW What is the job of representatives in our democratic system?

The Constitution

Main Idea The United States Constitution limits the power of the government.

Leaders wrote the United States Constitution in 1787. The Constitution created a government based on the rule of law. This means that laws should apply to everyone in the same way.

The people who wrote the Constitution knew that ideas about government would change. The writers included a way to change or add to the Constitution. In 1791, lawmakers added 10 amendments, or changes, to protect citizens' rights and liberties. **Liberty** means freedom from control by others.

These amendments became known as the Bill of Rights. They limited the power of the government. For example, the First Amendment guarantees people the right to speak freely and to question government. The Fourth Amendment protects people's privacy in their homes.

Over time, additional amendments were added to recognize the equality of all people. The Thirteenth Amendment makes slavery illegal. The Fifteenth and Nineteenth Amendments guarantee the right to vote for all citizens. These amendments and others protect citizens and keep the government from becoming too powerful.

Some Liberties Protected by the Bill of Rights

Freedom to Practice Your Religious Beliefs

Freedom of Speech

Freedom of the Press

Freedom of Assembly

Sharing Power

The Constitution also lays out a plan for how the government should work. In this plan, the national government has three branches, or parts.

Congress is the legislative branch. It makes the nation's laws. Congress has two parts, the Senate and the House of Representatives. Voters in each state elect people to Congress. Lawmakers can be elected more than once.

The executive branch executes, or carries out, the nation's laws. The President leads the executive branch. Voters elect a President every four years.

Many courts make up the judicial branch. The Supreme Court is the highest court. The President appoints justices, or judges, to the Supreme Court.

The Constitution allows each branch to check, or hold back, the power of the other two branches. This system is called "checks and balances."

For example, the President appoints justices to the Supreme Court, but Congress can reject them. When Congress passes laws, the President can veto, or say no, to the laws. The Supreme Court can decide whether a law is allowed under the Constitution.

REVIEW In what ways does the Constitution limit the powers of government?

Lesson Summary

The U.S. Constitution lays out the plan for the United States government

Protected rights and liberties	Three branches of government	Checks and balances

Why It Matters ...

The government set up by the U.S. Constitution has lasted for more than two hundred years.

Lesson Review

❶ **VOCABULARY** Write a paragraph about the United States government that uses **citizen, common good,** and **democracy.**

❷ 🖑 **READING SKILL** In what way does the Constitution protect rights and liberties?

❸ **MAIN IDEA: Citizenship** What is a representative democracy?

❹ **MAIN IDEA: Government** What are the three branches of government?

❺ **CRITICAL THINKING: Infer** Why do you think people wanted amendments to protect liberty in the Constitution?

✏️ **WRITING ACTIVITY** Write a newspaper editorial that explains why you think people in the United States should participate in government.

★ ★ ★ ★ ★ ★ ★ ★ ★ ★ ★

National Symbols

★ ★ ★ ★ ★ ★ ★ ★ ★ ★ ★

Americans feel proud when they see the stars and stripes of the United States flag waving high overhead. The flag and other national symbols represent important ideas that helped build our nation. These ideas include freedom, democracy, and civil rights.

★ The Statue of Liberty ★

The people of the United States received the Statue of Liberty as a gift from the people of France in 1885. For millions of immigrants arriving in New York, "Lady Liberty" is the first thing they see. It suggests that they can find freedom and opportunity in America. The words below are engraved at the base of the statue.

"Give me your tired, your poor, Your huddled masses yearning to breathe free. . . ."

—from "The New Colossus" by Emma Lazarus

★ The Washington Monument ★

In 1884, Americans finished building a monument to honor George Washington. Inside are 193 memorial stones engraved with messages. Every state sent at least one stone. Many cities, companies, and foreign nations also sent memorial stones.

★ The Liberty Bell ★

The Liberty Bell arrived in Philadelphia in 1752. It was rung when the Declaration of Independence was first read in public. Later, people fighting against slavery named it "The Liberty Bell." It has become a symbol of our nation's struggle for freedom.

Look Closely The Liberty Bell has cracked twice. The first time, it was melted down and made again.

Activities

1. **THINK ABOUT IT** Notice the torch in Lady Liberty's hand. Talk about what this shining light might mean.

2. **DRAW IT** Draw your own memorial stone for the Washington Monument. Use words and pictures to say something important about the United States.

 Technology Explore more primary sources for this unit at Education Place. www.eduplace.com/kids/hmss/

Skillbuilder

Summarize

To **summarize** means to tell the most important points of a piece of writing in your own words. Knowing how to write a summary can help you organize information and understand what you read.

► **VOCABULARY**

summarize

Learn the Skill

Step 1: Find the main idea of the passage. The main idea is what the passage is mostly about.

Step 2: Find important details that tell more about the main idea.

Step 3: Use your own words to tell about the main idea and the important details that you identified.

Main idea

Citizens decide who will represent them by voting in elections. On election day, voters cast their votes for the people they want to represent them. Whoever gets the most votes usually wins the election. Citizens in a democratic system have a responsibility to vote for their leaders. Voting is one way that citizens participate in their government.

Important details

Citizens participate in government by voting. Citizens vote for the officials they want to represent them in government.

The people who wrote the Constitution knew that ideas about government would change. The writers included a way to change or add to the Constitution. In 1791, lawmakers added 10 amendments, or changes, to protect citizens' rights and liberties. **Liberty** means freedom from control by others. These amendments became known as the Bill of Rights. They limited the power of the government.

Practice the Skill

Read the passage above. Then answer the questions that follow.

1 What is the main idea of the passage?

2 Identify two details that support the main idea.

3 Summarize the passage in your own words.

Apply the Skill

Use the steps you learned to help you summarize how the three different branches of government work as described on page 187 of your textbook.

State and Local Government

VOCABULARY

income tax
sales tax
budget
bill

Vocabulary Strategy

budget

A **budget** is a way to keep track of money. The governor makes a budget to show how the government plans to spend money.

READING SKILL
Compare and Contrast
List ways that the governments of the United States and Illinois are alike and different.

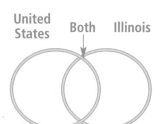

United States Both Illinois

Build on What You Know As a citizen in your classroom, you follow rules. Citizens in Illinois also have to follow certain rules. These rules are called laws.

The Illinois Constitution

Main Idea The Illinois Constitution explains the plan, role, and responsibilities of state government.

The U.S. Constitution allows states to share power with the federal, or national, government. Each state, including Illinois, has a constitution that lays out a plan for its government and laws.

Early leaders in Illinois wrote the state's first constitution in 1818. Over time, Illinois grew and changed. Illinois leaders revised the constitution in 1848 and again in 1870 to adapt to these changes. The Constitution of 1870 governed Illinois for 100 years. Many things changed during that time, so state leaders decided to revise the constitution again in 1970. This new constitution guides the government of Illinois today.

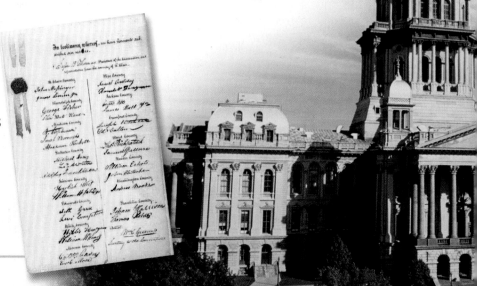

The Illinois Constitution
The government of Illinois was based on the Constitution of 1870 for one hundred years. The constitution used today was written in 1970.

Rights and the Common Good

The governments of Illinois and the United States protect people's rights. Both the United States Constitution and the Illinois Constitution have a Bill of Rights that guarantees freedom of religion, freedom of speech, and other important liberties. People should know their rights under both constitutions.

Both governments are supposed to work for the common good. They collect income taxes to help pay for goods and services. **Income tax** is a tax on money that people earn. It is based on how much money a person earns in a year. The federal government spends this tax money on services such as public education, national parks, national defense, and the interstate highway system.

A state income tax and a state sales tax provide money to the government of Illinois. A **sales tax** is money that goes to the government when people buy certain things. The state uses this money to support public schools and libraries, maintain state roads, and provide public transportation.

The state's constitution requires the governor to make a budget for the state. A **budget** is a plan for spending the state's money. The state constitution also gives guidelines for making state laws and tells how long elected officials can serve. It explains how the state government must divide power among its branches.

REVIEW What are some freedoms guaranteed by the constitutions of the United States and Illinois?

State Capitol The Illinois government meets in the capitol building (left). The inside of the capitol dome is shown at right.

Executive	Legislative	Judicial

Executive

- Oversees the state government
- Reports on how the state is doing

Leader: Governor

Legislative

- Makes laws for the state
- Represents the people of Illinois

Leaders: President of the Senate, Speaker of the House of Representatives

Judicial

- Determines the meaning of the Illinois Constitution and Illinois laws
- Determines whether laws have been broken
- Decides what the punishment for breaking laws should be

Leader: Chief Justice of the Illinois Supreme Court

Three Branches Illinois state government divides power among three branches.

State Government

Main Idea State and local governments share power in Illinois.

Like the federal government, the state government has three branches. The executive branch carries out the state laws. The governor is the leader of the state's executive branch. Every four years, voters elect the governor. Recent Illinois governors include **James Edgar, George Ryan,** and **Rod Blagojevich** (blah GO yeh vihch).

Voters also elect members of the legislative branch. The state legislature is called the General Assembly. It has two parts. The Senate has 59 members. The House of Representatives has 118 members.

Members of the General Assembly meet in Springfield, the state capital. They make the laws of the state. To make a law, they first write a bill. A **bill** is a written idea for a law. For a bill to become a law, more than half of the members of both the Senate and the House of Representatives must vote for it. Then the governor must sign the bill if it is to become a law. The bill does not become a law if the governor vetoes it or if not enough people in the legislature vote for it.

The state's judicial branch includes state courts and judges. The highest state court is the Illinois Supreme Court. Illinois voters elect seven judges to this court. These judges decide whether a law agrees with the state's constitution.

Local Government

The Illinois state government shares power with local governments. Each of the state's 102 counties has its own local government. County governments carry out state laws and provide services. Voters in each county elect a group of commissioners who run the county government.

Cities and towns also have local government. Most cities have a mayor and a city council. Together, the mayor and the city council decide how to run the city. The mayor also represents the city at public events. Citizens can attend city council meetings to give their opinions.

Government Services
Local taxes help pay for schools and libraries.

Local governments receive money from local taxes. The state government and United States government also give money to local governments. Each local government has a budget that plans how to pay for schools, libraries, roads, fire departments, and police. Local governments provide these and other services to the people of Illinois.

REVIEW What public services do local governments in Illinois provide?

Lesson Summary

The government of Illinois is guided by its constitution. The state government shares power with local governments. City, town, and county governments provide public services.

Why It Matters...

The state and local governments of Illinois are designed to protect the common good and individual rights.

Lesson Review

1 **VOCABULARY** Match each vocabulary word with its meaning.
budget bill
(a) a written idea for a law (b) a plan for spending money

2 **READING SKILL Compare** the governments of Illinois and the United States. Describe one way in which they are alike.

3 **MAIN IDEA: Citizenship** Why has the Illinois Constitution changed over time?

4 **MAIN IDEA: Government** What are the three branches of the state government?

5 **CRITICAL THINKING: Evaluate** Why do you think local governments provide fire and police services instead of state government?

ART ACTIVITY Learn more about your local government. Make a poster that shows two parts of your local government and explains what they do.

A Visit to the CAPITOL

When the governor goes to work each day, where does he or she go? In most states, the governor works at the state capitol. Hundreds of other government officials and employees work there, too. In this story, a group of students gets a chance to visit the capitol in Springfield.

CHARACTERS

Narrator

Ms. Frankel: tour guide

Mr. Oates: fourth-grade teacher

Senator Lynch: state senator

James Miller ⎤
Justin Yee ⎥
Erin Watson ⎬ students
Felipe Montez ⎥
Rebecca Kline ⎦

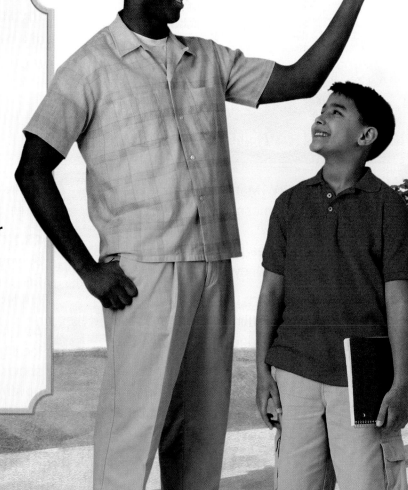

Narrator: The capitol building of Illinois is in the capital city of Springfield. It is the home of the Illinois state government. Mr. Oates has brought his fourth-grade class on a field trip to see it.

James Miller, student: Wow! Check out all of these hallways. How do people keep from getting lost?

Ms. Frankel, tour guide: They learn their way around pretty quickly. Different people have different government jobs.

Mr. Oates, teacher: That's right. We've been learning about what those jobs are. Do you remember what many people here work on?

Felipe Montez, student: Laws! Some people make laws, some people enforce laws, and some people make sure that the laws are fair.

Ms. Frankel: Excellent. That brings us to our first stop. It's where members of our government make the laws.

Justin Yee, student: It's the General Assembly.

Ms. Frankel: Right. This is where members of the Illinois Senate and the House of Representatives work.

Narrator: The students take a tour of the General Assembly. Later, they have lunch in the cafeteria with Sheryl Lynch, one of their state senators.

Rebecca Kline, student: Do these senators and representatives come from all over Illinois?

Senator Lynch: Yes, they do.

Erin Watson, student: But I don't understand why we need people from all over Illinois to make the laws.

Senator Lynch: Think of it this way, Erin. If your class wanted to go on a trip, would you want just one person to decide where you go?

Erin Watson: No way! We should all get to vote. I guess I see your point. The lawmakers represent many different people.

Senator Lynch: Exactly! So, let's say that senators and representatives pass a new law. Who makes sure that law is enforced?

Justin Yee: I know! The governor and the rest of the executive branch.

Ms. Frankel: You've got it. And that's where we're headed next.

Narrator: The class continues talking as they visit the governor's office.

Mr. Oates: So, can anyone tell me what the governor's job is?

Rebecca Kline: The governor makes sure that all of the state laws are carried out.

Felipe Montez: Not only that—the governor plans the **budget** for how much money the government can spend.

Erin Watson: The governor gets help from the lieutenant governor and the cabinet.

James Miller: What do they keep in the cabinet?

Rebecca Kline: Not that kind of cabinet! The cabinet is a group of the governor's advisors.

James Miller: I knew that.

Narrator: The last place the class visits is the Illinois Supreme Court, the highest court in Illinois.

Felipe Montez: This is where the judges decide whether the laws follow the Illinois Constitution.

Ms. Frankel: Maybe you kids should be running this tour! Well, we're just about done. There's only one thing we haven't talked about—the role you all play!

Justin Yee: What do you mean?

Ms. Frankel: Your state government comes from the people. All of you can express your opinions about the government. And when you're older, you'll be able to participate in other ways, too.

James Miller: Right! James Miller for governor in 2040!

Ms. Frankel: Yes, James, and you'll be able to vote long before 2040. Well, that's the end of our tour today. Thank you all for coming.

Mr. Oates: I think we've learned a great deal. Thank you, Ms. Frankel.

Students: Thanks for the tour, Ms. Frankel!

Activities

1. **ACT IT OUT** Organize the class into three groups that represent the Congress, the President, and the Supreme Court. Have your teacher propose a bill. The Congress should debate and pass the bill. The President should sign the bill. The Supreme Court should determine whether the bill is allowed by the Constitution.

2. **WRITE IT** Learn the names of your state senators. Write a letter to one of them, explaining what you think the state government should do to help your school or community.

Your Role in Government

VOCABULARY

jury
volunteer

Vocabulary Strategy

jury

The words **juror** and **jury** have similar meanings. Both have to do with the law.

READING SKILL

Categorize As you read, list the rights and responsibilities of citizens.

Rights	Responsibilities

Build on What You Know Have you ever worked on a project with a group? A project group works in much the same way that the government does. Members must listen to one another to work well together.

Rights and Responsibilities

Main Idea Citizens of Illinois have many rights and responsibilities.

People in the United States enjoy important rights. These rights are guaranteed by the Bill of Rights in the Constitution. The rights include free speech. People have the right to express their opinions, even if they disagree with something that the government has done. They also have the freedom to practice their religion. They are free to assemble, or gather, in groups. Newspapers and magazines are free to print opinions. Citizens in the United States also have the right to vote.

Casting Ballots
To vote in Illinois, a person must be a United States citizen and at least 18 years old.

Participating Young people who work with Habitat for Humanity help others in their community by building homes. Here, (left) people begin to dig a hole where a home will be built. All young people have a responsibility to follow laws, such as obeying traffic signs.

Responsibilities

Along with rights come responsibilities. For government to work well, citizens must participate in it. One way citizens can participate is to vote. Choosing government representatives is an important responsibility. Before an election, voters have a responsibility to learn about candidates and the issues.

People also have a responsibility to pay taxes. Federal, state, and local governments use tax money to provide public goods and services.

Everyone in Illinois has a responsibility to respect the rights of others. They must follow laws written to protect everyone. They also have a responsibility to make sure that their own rights and the rights of others are respected.

Some citizens may be asked to serve on a jury. A **jury** is a group of citizens who decide a case in court. People who serve on juries protect the right to a trial by jury.

Citizens can also work together to improve their communities. They can do this as volunteers. A **volunteer** is a person who agrees to provide a service without pay. Volunteers work for the common good of the community. You can be a responsible citizen by volunteering to help your community.

REVIEW Why do citizens in a democracy have responsibilities?

Government Leaders

Main Idea Illinoisans in federal and state government work for the people.

Citizens elect representatives to work for them in government. This means that elected officials have a responsibility to work for the people they represent. This is true for federal, state, and local government officials. Elected officials have a responsibility to make laws, uphold laws, and provide public goods and services. They must consider the opinions of the people whom they represent as well as the common good when making government decisions.

Many Illinoisans have held important jobs in federal government. **Abraham Lincoln** was the 16th President of the United States. He was the first President elected from Illinois. **Ronald Reagan** was born in Tampico, Illinois. In 1981, he became the 40th President of the United States.

The 40th President Ronald Reagan served as President from 1981 to 1989.

Other leaders from Illinois have represented our state in the federal government. In 1992, Illinoisan **Carol Moseley Braun** became the first African American woman in the United States Senate. She served there until 1999. Moseley Braun ran for President in 2004.

In 1999, Illinoisan **J. Dennis Hastert** became Speaker of the House in the United States House of Representatives. Illinoisan **Donald Rumsfeld** began serving as Secretary of Defense under President **George W. Bush** in 2001.

U.S. Senator Carol Moseley Braun served in the Senate from 1993 to 1999.

Illinois has also had many important state and local leaders. **Richard J. Daley** was a powerful mayor in Chicago from 1955 to 1976. The citizens of Chicago elected him six times. **Jane Byrne** became the city's first female mayor in 1979.

Harold Washington served in the General Assembly of Illinois from 1965 to 1980. He was elected to the United States Congress in 1980. In 1983, he became the first African American mayor of Chicago.

James Thompson was the first Illinois governor to be elected to four straight terms. He served from 1977 to 1990. State Senator **Barack Obama** earned national attention for his speaking ability in 2004. Illinoisans elected him to the United States Senate that year.

REVIEW What are some responsibilities of government leaders?

Lesson Summary

Rights	Responsibilities
voting	voting
freedom of speech	paying taxes
freedom of religion	obeying laws
freedom of assembly	serving on a jury
freedom of the press	staying informed

Why It Matters ...

A representative democracy depends on people's participation.

U.S. Senator In 2004, Barack Obama was elected to the United States Senate.

Lesson Review

❶ **VOCABULARY** Write two sentences. Use the words **jury** and **volunteer.**

❷ **READING SKILL** Look at the activities that you **categorized** as responsibilities. Name the two responsibilities that you think are most important and explain your reasoning.

❸ **MAIN IDEA: Citizenship** Why do citizens have a responsibility to vote?

❹ **MAIN IDEA: Government** What is the main responsibility of Illinoisans who work in federal, state, and local government?

❺ **CRITICAL THINKING: Analyze** What can citizens do if they believe that an elected official is not representing them well?

WRITING ACTIVITY Write four or five questions that you would like to ask of an elected official. You may want to include questions about that official's views on certain issues.

Let's *Vote!*

Eric's sister Gina has just turned 18. Now she can vote for the first time. Gina tells Eric that voting is one of the most important ways that people can participate in a democracy. It's both a right and a responsibility.

How to Vote:

Before the election, Gina registers to vote. She fills out forms and shows proof that she is at least 18 years old and a United States citizen.

Next, Gina gathers information about the candidates, or people who are running for office. She reads news articles and listens to programs to learn their opinions.

3 On election day, Eric and Gina go to their local voting place. Outside, people hold signs showing support for their candidates. Gina already knows for whom she will vote.

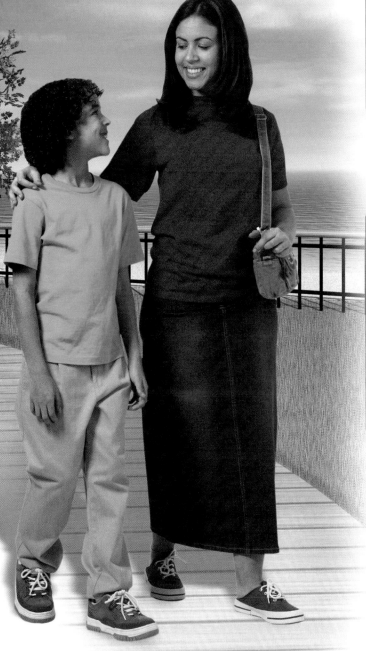

4

Gina stands at a voting booth to vote. Eric cannot go with her because voting is secret.

5

The next morning, the newspaper reports the election. Gina is excited because some of the people for whom she voted have won.

Activities

1. **TALK ABOUT IT** What things should citizens do before they vote? Why?

2. **LIST IT** Learn the names of your local representatives. Make a poster that lists these people and explains their jobs.

Skillbuilder

Make a Decision

The leaders of Illinois must make many decisions about how to govern the state. The decisions they make have consequences. A **consequence** is something that happens because of a decision or an action. Use these steps and a diagram like the one below to help you think about consequences and make good decisions.

▶ **VOCABULARY**
consequence

Learn the Skill

Step 1: Identify the decision you must make.

Step 2: List all of the possible actions you could take.

Step 3: Think about each option. Consider the consequences of each choice, both good and bad.

Step 4: Make your decision. Choose the option with the best possible outcome.

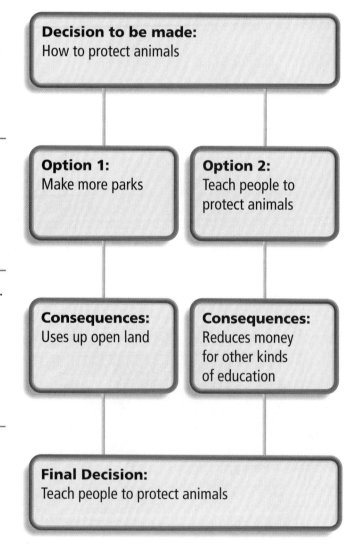

Decision to be made:
How to protect animals

Option 1:
Make more parks

Option 2:
Teach people to protect animals

Consequences:
Uses up open land

Consequences:
Reduces money for other kinds of education

Final Decision:
Teach people to protect animals

Practice the Skill

Suppose that there is a polluted river in your town. Make a decision about what you could do to help solve the problem. You could organize a river cleanup or tell people about the problem by writing a letter to a local newspaper. Think about the consequences of each of these actions. Use a chart like the one on page 206 to decide on the best action.

Apply the Skill

Choose an issue in your state about which people must make a decision. Use the steps you have learned to think about your choices. Fill out a chart to help you make your decision. Then write a paragraph explaining your decision and your reasons for making it.

Chapter 8 Review and Test Prep

Visual Summary

1 – 3. ✏️ Write a description of each item named below.

Levels of Government

National	
State	
Local	

Facts and Main Ideas

✔ **TEST PREP** Answer each question below.

4. **Government** What part does the executive branch play in the United States government?

5. **Government** What are checks and balances?

6. **Economics** Name three ways that state and local governments spend tax money.

7. **History** Who was the first African American mayor of Chicago, and when was that person elected?

Vocabulary

✔ **TEST PREP** Choose the correct word from the list below to complete each sentence.

common good, p. 184
budget, p. 193
jury, p. 201

8. Citizens are sometimes asked to serve on a _____ to decide a case in court.

9. It is the job of the governor of Illinois to create a _____ for the state.

10. The government provides public goods and services to benefit the _____.

Apply Skills

✔ **TEST PREP** **Make a Decision** Use the organizer below and what you have learned about making a decision to answer each question.

Decision to be made:
What can I do to study for my class?

Option 1: Read lessons as assigned and summarize.	**Option 2:** Read lessons right before the test.
Consequences: I will spend some time each night studying. I will have notes to study for the test.	**Consequences:** I can do other things at night. I will have to learn everything in a short amount of time.

Final Decision:

11. What is the first step in making a decision?

   A. Think about all of the possible actions that can be taken.
   B. Identify the decision to be made.
   C. Identify the consequence of each action.
   D. Decide on the best action to take.

12. What should you do after considering all of the options?

   A. Create a chart.
   B. Predict more consequences.
   C. Identify a decision that has to be made.
   D. Make a final decision.

Critical Thinking

✔ **TEST PREP** Write a short paragraph to answer each question below.

13. **Synthesize** Why is it important that the writers of the constitution included a way to amend it?

14. **Analyze** Explain why you think that federal, state, and local governments should or should not provide public goods and services.

Activities

Citizenship Activity Work in groups to suggest ways that students can help in your community. Vote to decide which volunteer activity would best help your community.

Writing Activity Write a research report about your local town or city government and how it works. Describe the jobs of elected officials in your local government.

Technology
Writing Process Tips
Get help with your research report at:
www.eduplace.com/kids/hmss/

209

Review and Test Prep

Vocabulary and Main Ideas

✔ **TEST PREP** Write a sentence to answer each question.

1. Why did **immigrants** come to Illinois in the late 1800s?

2. What was life like during the Great **Depression?**

3. In what ways did **manufacturing** change industry in Illinois?

4. Who chooses **representatives** to serve in Illinois government?

5. What branch of the Illinois state government can write a **bill?**

6. Why do people become **volunteers?**

Critical Thinking

✔ **TEST PREP** Write a short paragraph to answer each question.

7. **Synthesize** Describe the ways in which Chicago changed in the late 1800s.

8. **Summarize** Explain what each of the three branches of federal government does.

Apply Skills

✔ **TEST PREP** Use the chart below and your decision-making skills to answer each question.

Decision to Be Made:
Regina has to choose an aftershool activity.

Option 1:
School band

Option 2:
School soccer team

Consequences:
Regina will learn a musical instrument. She will not be able to play a school sport.

Consequences:
Regina will play an outdoor sport. She will not have time to play in band.

Final Decision: school band

9. What decision did Regina have to make?

   A. if she wanted to participate in an afterschool activity
   B. whether she wanted to participate in band or play soccer
   C. whether she wanted to play an outdoor or indoor sport
   D. if she wanted to play on more than one sports team

10. What will be a consequence of Regina's decision?

   A. She will not learn an instrument.
   B. She will not get to play outside.
   C. She will not participate in an activity.
   D. She will not play on the school soccer team.

Unit Activity

The Big Idea

Make a State Government Poster

- Make a chart of the three branches of state government. List the name of the governor and other top officials.

- Find out when and where the state legislature meets and what law or laws are coming up for a vote. Add the information to your poster.

- Write a sentence stating how you think the legislature should vote on the possible law or laws.

- Present your poster to the class.

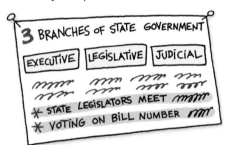

At the Library

Go to your school or public library to find these books.

The Great Fire by Jim Murphy
Learn more about the Great Chicago Fire, how it may have started, and how it could have been stopped.

Harold Washington: Mayor With a Vision by Naurice Roberts
Learn more about Harold Washington's career in Illinois government.

CURRENT EVENTS
WEEKLY (WR) READER

Current Events Project

Create a bulletin board about the freedoms that Americans have.

- Find articles about the Constitution and the Bill of Rights.

- Choose one of the amendments that make up the Bill of Rights. Think about how it keeps Americans free today.

- Write a paragraph about the amendment you chose. Include drawings of people using their freedom.

- Post your paragraph and drawings on a bulletin board.

Technology
Weekly Reader online offers social studies articles. Go to
www.eduplace.com/kids/hmss/

UNIT **5**

Illinois and the World

The
Big
Idea

What will you do to earn a living?

"*Money is necessary —
both to support a family
and to advance causes
one believes in.*"

Coretta Scott King,
civil rights leader

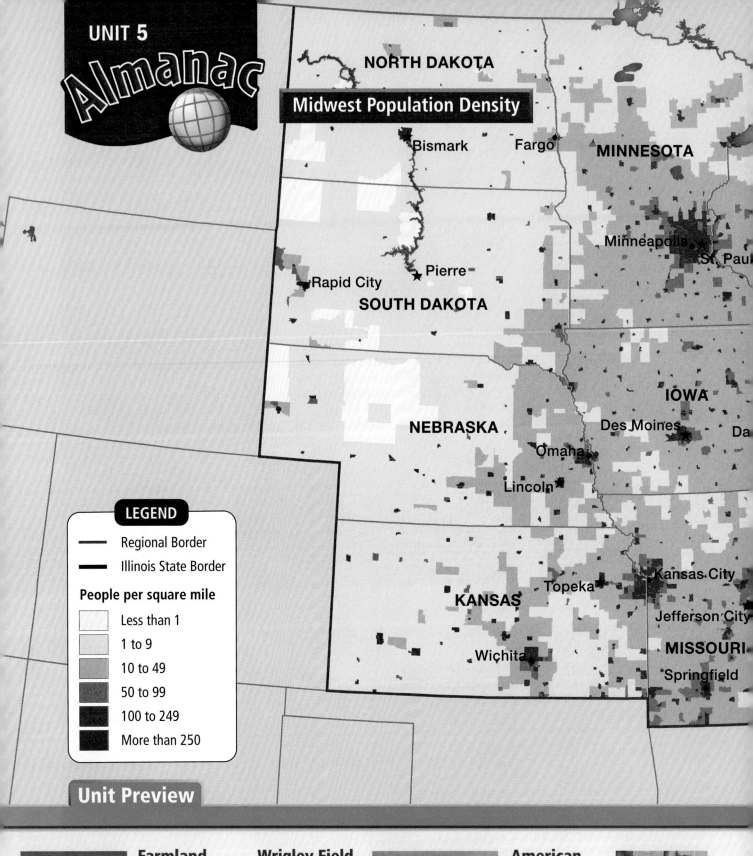

Midwest Population Density

NORTH DAKOTA

Bismark   Fargo   MINNESOTA

Minneapolis   St. Paul

Pierre

Rapid City

SOUTH DAKOTA

IOWA

Des Moines   Da

NEBRASKA

Omaha

Lincoln

LEGEND

— Regional Border

— Illinois State Border

People per square mile

Less than 1
1 to 9
10 to 49
50 to 99
100 to 249
More than 250

Kansas City

Topeka

KANSAS

Jefferson City

MISSOURI

Wichita

Springfield

Unit Preview

Farmland
Much of the
country's farmland
is in the Midwest
**Chapter 9,
page 218**

Wrigley Field
One of the country's
oldest ballparks is
in Chicago
**Chapter 9,
page 232**

**American
Heritage**
Americans share
many traditions
**Chapter 10,
page 246**

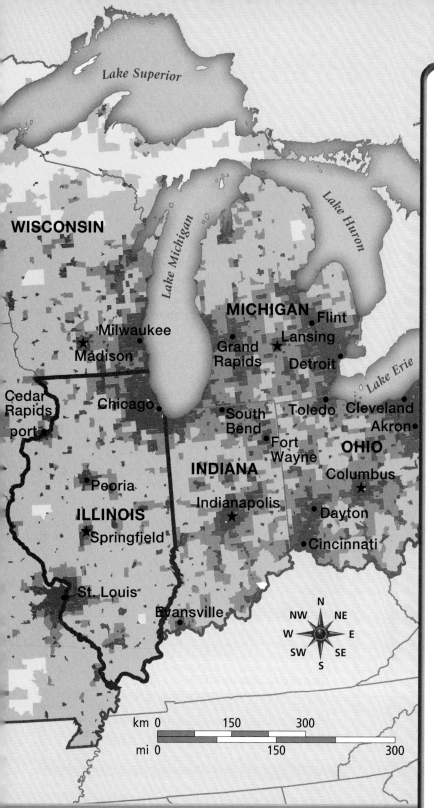

Lake Superior

WISCONSIN

Milwaukee
Madison

MICHIGAN
Flint
Lansing
Grand
Rapids
Detroit

Lake Michigan

Lake Huron

Lake Erie

Cedar
Rapids
port

Chicago

South
Bend
Fort
Wayne

Toledo
Cleveland
Akron

OHIO
Columbus

INDIANA
Indianapolis

Dayton

Peoria

ILLINOIS
Springfield

Cincinnati

St. Louis

Evansville

N
NW   NE
W   E
SW   SE
S

km 0   150   300
mi 0   150   300

United Nations
The United Nations
works for world peace
**Chapter 10,
page 252**

Connect to
The Nation

Illinois Population Growth

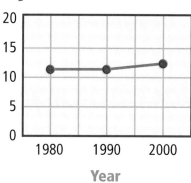

Population (in millions)

20
15
10
5
0

1980   1990   2000
Year

By about how much did Illinois's
population grow from 1980 to 2000?

U.S. Population Growth

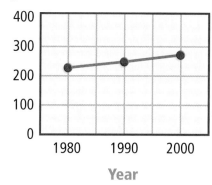

Population (in millions)

400
300
200
100
0

1980   1990   2000
Year

How is Illinois's population growth
different from growth in the United
States?

CURRENT   EVENTS
WEEKLY (WR) READER

Current events on the web!

Read social studies articles about
current events at
www.eduplace.com/kids/hmss/

Chapter 9

Exploring the Midwest

Technology

e • glossary
e • word games
www.eduplace.com/kids/hmss/

Vocabulary Preview

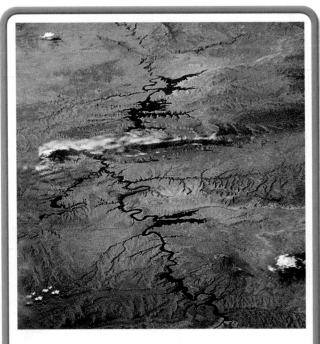

tributary

A **tributary** is a smaller river or stream that flows into a larger river or stream. Each major river has many tributaries that flow into it. **page 219**

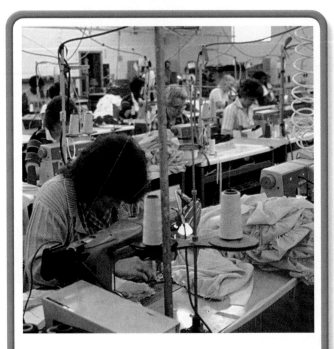

supply

Supply is how much of a product producers will provide at different prices. When prices increase, suppliers produce more. When prices decrease, suppliers produce less. **page 227**

Reading Strategy

Predict and Infer Use this strategy as you read the lessons in this chapter.

Quick Tip Before you read, look at the lesson title and the pictures. What do you think you will read about?

demand

Demand is how much of a product consumers will buy at different prices. At lower prices, consumers buy more. At higher prices, consumers buy less. **page 227**

elevated train

Chicago's first **elevated train** began operating in 1892. You can see it traveling through Chicago and the surrounding areas today. **page 231**

Land and Climate

Build on What You Know Does wind seem harsher out in the open than in a forest? The Midwest has lots of flat, open plains. What might the wind feel like there?

Land and Water of the Midwest

Main Idea The Midwest is a central region of wide open plains, thick woods, and huge waterways.

The Midwest lies in the middle of the country. Canada lies to the north. The Rocky Mountains and the Appalachian Mountains lie on either side of it.

The eastern part of this region features the Great Lakes. The land is mostly flat, with some hilly areas. The rainfall here supports deep forests. Pine forests in the north can withstand the harsh climate. The south has a mix of trees.

West of the Great Lakes are the Great Plains. The climate is drier here. Prairie grasses cover much of the land. People in the Midwest learned to farm the rich soil beneath the prairies. Today, Midwestern farms produce much of the country's wheat and corn.

Iowa Farmland Midwestern farmers have turned grasslands into farmland.

The Midwest

LEGEND
Great Lakes States
Plains States
★ State capital

CANADA

GREAT PLAINS

NORTH DAKOTA
★ Bismarck

SOUTH DAKOTA
★ Pierre

Black Hills

Mesabi Range

MINNESOTA

St. Paul
Minneapolis

Lake Superior

MICHIGAN

Lake Michigan

Lake Huron

Lake Ontario

WISCONSIN

Madison
★ Milwaukee

Lansing
★

Detroit

Lake Erie

Missouri River

Mississippi River

IOWA
Des Moines ★

Chicago

Cleveland

OHIO
Columbus ★

NEBRASKA
Omaha
Lincoln ★

Platte River

Illinois River

Wabash River

ILLINOIS
Springfield ★

Indianapolis ★

INDIANA

Kansas City

N
W E
S

Topeka ★
KANSAS

St. Louis

Jefferson City ★

MISSOURI

Arkansas River

Ohio River

km 0 100 200
mi 0 100 200

Midwest Regions The Midwest includes the Plains States and the Great Lakes States.

Water Resources

The Midwest has two main waterways. The Great Lakes make up one of them. Glaciers created these five lakes. Together, the lakes form the world's largest body of fresh water. Rivers and canals connect the lakes to the Atlantic Ocean and the Gulf of Mexico. Ships reach the lakes through these waterways.

The Mississippi River is the second main waterway. With its major tributaries, the Missouri and Ohio Rivers, it forms the nation's largest river system. A **tributary** is a river or stream that flows into another river. Dams and levees help limit floods on these rivers. A **levee** is a high river bank that stops the river from overflowing.

Before the invention of railroads, travel on waterways was faster and less expensive than land travel. Towns along water routes became trading centers. Some, such as Chicago and Milwaukee, became large cities.

Waterfalls can make river travel difficult. Locks help ships get past waterfalls. A lock is the part of a waterway that is closed off by gates. Ships enter a lock, and people let water into or out of it. As the water level goes up or down, so does the ship. The lock at St. Anthony Falls in Minneapolis raises and lowers ships by 50 feet.

REVIEW What are the major regions and waterways of the Midwest?

Climate, Plants, Animals

Main Idea The Midwest can have severe weather.

The location of the Midwest affects its climate. There is no ocean nearby to warm the land in winter and cool it in summer. As a result, the climate varies more than in coastal regions. In parts of the Midwest, the temperature can change as much as 100°F between winter and summer.

The Great Lakes are not as big as an ocean, but they affect the climate by adding moisture to the air. Areas near the lakes stay cooler in summer and warmer in winter like coastal regions do. In winter, however, moisture from the lakes causes lake effect snow. Fierce snowstorms called blizzards often strike the region. People have had to adapt. They wear layers of clothing. They use covered walkways to get from one building to another.

People have also found ways to enjoy winter. They go skiing, skating, and icefishing. They hold winter festivals.

Tornadoes often hit the plains of the Midwest when cold and warm air masses meet. Tornadoes are strong, spinning storms with high winds.

SKILL **Reading Charts** Which two states have had the highest temperatures?

Extreme Temperatures in the Midwest

State	Highest	Lowest
Illinois	117°F	−36°F
Indiana	116°F	−36°F
Iowa	118°F	−47°F
Kansas	121°F	−40°F
Michigan	112°F	−51°F
Minnesota	114°F	−60°F
Missouri	118°F	−40°F
Nebraska	118°F	−47°F
North Dakota	121°F	−60°F
Ohio	113°F	−39°F
South Dakota	120°F	−58°F
Wisconsin	114°F	−55°F

Lake Effect Snow

❶ Warm, moist air rises from the lake and meets cold, dry air.

❷ The cold air freezes the moisture and drops it as snow over the land.

Midwestern Plants and Animals

Plants and animals have adapted to the region's climate extremes. For example, some prairie grasses have deep roots. They help the plants find moisture. Pine trees keep their needles for years. This saves energy and helps the trees survive harsh weather.

Animals have also adapted. Some birds migrate to warmer places. Prairie dogs dig underground dens that protect them from severe weather. A prairie dog is a rodent, or a small mammal with special teeth for gnawing, that belongs to the squirrel family.

Millions of bison, or buffalo, once roamed the Great Plains. Thick coats of fur kept them warm. Hunters wanted this fur. By 1885, they had killed all but a few hundred bison. Then people started protecting bison. Today, about 150,000 bison live in the United States.

REVIEW How have people and wildlife adapted to the climate of the Midwest?

Lesson Summary

- Landforms of the Midwest include prairies, hills, and forests.
- The two main waterways are the Great Lakes and the Mississippi River system.
- The Midwest is very hot in summer and very cold in winter.

Why It Matters ...

People, plants, and animals have adapted to the Midwest's climate and made it their home.

Prairie Dog The prairie dog, found in the Midwest, is not really a dog. It is a rodent.

Lesson Review

1 VOCABULARY Write a paragraph showing that you know what **levee** and **tributary** mean.

2 READING SKILL Explain one **cause** of the growth of Chicago.

3 MAIN IDEA: Geography Name some land features in the Midwest.

4 MAIN IDEA: Geography How does location affect climate in the Midwest?

5 CRITICAL THINKING: Evaluate In what ways might the Midwest be different without its large rivers and tributaries?

WRITING ACTIVITY Suppose a student from Florida was moving to the Midwest. What clothes should the student bring? Write a letter explaining what the student should pack.

The Mighty Mississippi

The Mississippi River flows through ten of the fifty states. It starts in Minnesota and ends in Louisiana at the Gulf of Mexico. People use the river for many purposes. Its water is used for drinking, for making electricity, and for transporting people and goods. Barges on the Mississippi carry grain, coal, gravel, petroleum products, chemicals, paper, wood, coffee, iron, and steel. This powerful river provides many benefits, but people can never completely tame it.

Water
The Mississippi is a source of fresh water for millions of people who live in nearby towns and cities.

Agriculture
Farmers use water from the Mississippi to grow cotton, corn, soybeans, and rice. Others use the water to raise catfish.

Transportation
For hundreds of years, the river has been like a highway. Today, there is more traffic than ever. Each year, people ship about 500 million tons of cargo on the river.

Recreation

Every year, more than 12 million people visit the upper Mississippi to boat, fish, and enjoy the scenery. These visitors create jobs for people who live near the river.

Floods and Levees

The U.S. government has built **levees** and other structures to try to control the river's yearly floods. However, levees prevent natural wetlands from soaking up extra water. This may make flooding worse downstream.

Towns

Many towns are along the river. When people built levees, they thought it was safe to build near the river's edge. However, flooding still occurs sometimes. Some people think that homes should be built on higher ground.

Activities

1. **DRAW YOUR OWN** Draw a picture of life on the Mississippi. Show people using the river in at least three ways.

2. **RESEARCH IT** Find out about dams and locks. How do they work? Why are they used? How many are there on the Mississippi? Write about your findings.

Resources and Economy

VOCABULARY

consumer
supply
demand

Vocabulary Strategy

demand

When you **demand** something, you say that you want it. In economics, **demand** means that consumers want a certain product or service.

READING SKILL

Categorize Use a chart to categorize the goods and services produced by midwestern businesses.

Manu-facturing products	Farm products	Services

Build on What You Know How often do you go to the market? Do they have many kinds of cereal, cheese, and bread? Many of these foods come from the Midwest.

Using Midwestern Resources

Main Idea Resources provide products and jobs.

The Midwest has many natural resources. Water, rich soil, and minerals helped the region become a major farming and manufacturing center.

People use the Midwest's water resources in many ways. Farmers water their crops. More than 26 million people drink water from the Great Lakes. Rivers and lakes provide transportation. Barges and ships carry resources, such as coal. Large manufacturing centers have grown along waterways.

In parts of the Midwest, the soil and climate support dense forests. Forests provide lumber and wood products, such as plywood and paper.

Wakeboarding Midwesterners enjoy many activities on the region's lakes and rivers.

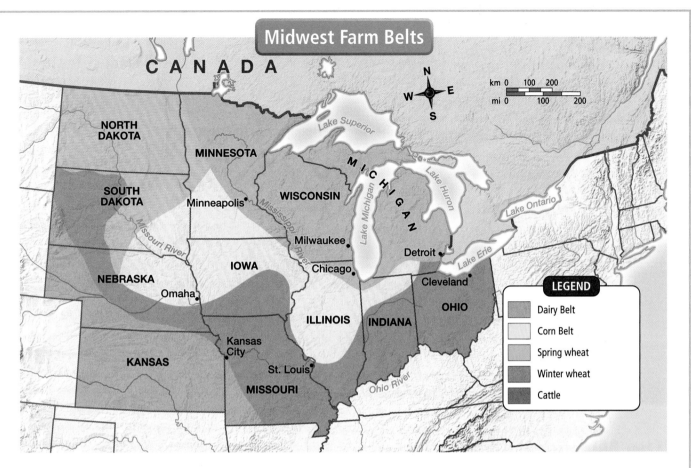

Midwest Farm Belts

Midwest Farm Belts The Midwest has rich soil, hot summers, and plenty of rain. **SKILL** **Reading Maps** Where is spring wheat the most important crop?

A Farming Region

In the early 1800s, the Midwest's rich soil attracted many farmers. Today, fields of wheat, corn, and soybeans stretch for miles. Iowa, Illinois, and Nebraska produce more corn than any other states.

Midwestern farmers also grow hay, fruits, and vegetables. They raise hogs and dairy cows. Wisconsin is called America's Dairyland. Minnesota is called the Bread and Butter State. Many people work in farm-related industries. Some workers make food products such as jam or cereal. Some build tractors. Others ship food around the world.

Mining and Other Industries

Valuable minerals lie below the Midwest's soil. These include rock and minerals used to make cement. Lead is another valuable mineral. People use it to make batteries and computers. Lead, coal, oil, and other minerals can be found in Illinois.

Much of the nation's iron ore comes from Minnesota, Michigan, and South Dakota. Workers use iron ore to make steel. Steel is used to make products that range from tools to planes, boats, bridges, and cars. Detroit, Michigan, is famous for its automobile industry. Its nickname is "Motor City."

REVIEW Name two midwestern industries.

Some Goods and Services from the Midwest

Region	Goods and Services
Plains States	banking, health care, chemical products, insurance, houses, telephone services, auto sales, real estate, tires, hotels
Great Lakes States	health care, banking, airlines, electronic equipment, medicines, engineering, business services, cars and trucks

SKILL **Reading Charts** Which goods and services might a traveler use?

The Midwest's Economy

Main Idea The Midwest's economy was built around its natural resources and the laws of supply and demand.

If you were a manufacturer, you might want to build your factory in the Midwest. The region has many natural resources and many skilled workers. It also has waterways for moving goods. Many manufacturers built factories in the Midwest to make products such as cars and paper.

Service industries have also grown in the Midwest. A service is an activity a person or company does for someone else. For example, the transportation industry provides a service. Factories decide to bring raw materials in and ship finished goods out to consumers.

A **consumer** is someone who buys goods and services. Many midwestern cities have good railroads, streets, and waterways to serve consumers. Indianapolis, Chicago, Kansas City, and other cities in the region serve as transportation hubs.

People and businesses also want banking, health, and communication services. If someone wants to buy or sell a home, the person can talk to a real estate agent. These services and others have become major industries in the Midwest.

Supply and Demand

The laws of supply and demand can help you understand the Midwest's economy—and the economy of all regions. **Supply** is how much of a product businesses will make at different prices. **Demand** is how much of a product consumers will buy at different prices.

Supply and demand affect each other. Suppose a company makes a delicious new cereal. Many people want to buy it. When demand for the cereal rises, the price also rises. That is because people are willing to pay a higher price for what they want. At the higher price, the cereal maker will make more of its new cereal. Over time, the higher price will attract more suppliers. As more suppliers enter the market, the supply increases. Prices begin to go down.

Midwestern farmers supply many products, including milk, corn, and meat. When there is an increase in demand, prices rise. Farmers earn more income, but consumers pay higher prices. When there is an increase in supply, prices fall. Farmers earn less income, but consumers pay lower prices.

REVIEW In what way does the increase in the supply of corn affect farmers?

Lesson Summary

The Midwest has many natural and human resources. As a result, farming and manufacturing industries have grown there. Like industries everywhere, they are affected by supply and demand.

Why It Matters ...

Midwestern businesses grow when there is demand for their products.

Lesson Review

1 VOCABULARY Explain what happens to the **supply** of a product when **demand** for it increases.

2 READING SKILL Which industries did you **categorize** as services?

3 MAIN IDEA: Geography In what ways do people use water resources in the Midwest?

4 MAIN IDEA: Economics How does high demand affect producers?

5 CRITICAL THINKING: Draw Conclusions What makes iron ore such an important mineral?

HANDS ON

DRAMA ACTIVITY Write a skit about a person selling two trading cards. Few people want to buy one of the cards. Many people want the other card. Show how demand affects the price of the cards. Perform the skit with your classmates.

Extend Lesson 2

Economics

Supply and Demand

Most of the world's popcorn is grown in the Midwest. Selling popcorn is a good way for movie theaters to earn money. Theater owners must decide how much popcorn to make each day and what to charge for each box.

Supply

The **supply** of popcorn is how much theater owners are willing and able to sell at different prices. Look at the chart and think about how the price affects the supply.

Supply of Popcorn

Price of one box of popcorn	Amount owners will produce at each price
50 cents	10 boxes
$1	50 boxes
$4	300 boxes
$7	600 boxes
$10	800 boxes

Demand

The **demand** for popcorn is how much people are willing and able to buy at different prices. If the popcorn's price is low, many people will buy it. However, when the price goes up, people will buy less. The chart shows how price affects demand.

Demand of Popcorn

Price of one box of popcorn	Amount people will buy at each price
50 cents	800 boxes
$1	600 boxes
$4	300 boxes
$7	50 boxes
$10	10 boxes

Supply Greater Than Demand	Demand Greater Than Supply	Supply Equals Demand

ECONOMICS

Too Much Popcorn

The seller has set a high price. He planned to sell several boxes of popcorn. But, at this high price, people demanded only a few boxes.

Not Enough Popcorn

The seller has set a low price. He planned to sell only a few boxes of popcorn. But, at this low price, people demanded a lot of boxes.

Just Enough Popcorn

The seller has the right amount of popcorn and customers. According to the charts on page 200, the seller is making 300 boxes of popcorn and charging $4 per box.

Activities

1. **TALK ABOUT IT** Why will the theater owners sell less popcorn if the price rises above $4 per box?

2. **CHART IT** Make your own supply and demand charts for a product.

The Great Lakes States

VOCABULARY

elevated train
wages

Vocabulary Strategy

| **elevated** train

The word **elevate** means to raise. An **elevated train** runs on a track that is raised above the ground.

READING SKILL

Compare and Contrast
Use a Venn diagram to compare and contrast the rural and urban areas of the Great Lakes States.

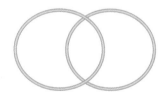

Chicago, Illinois This city of nearly three million people lies on the shore of Lake Michigan.

Build on What You Know Do you enjoy camping and fishing, or would you rather watch a baseball game? Would you like to explore a submarine or tour a cheese factory? You can do all of these things in the Great Lakes States.

Where People Live

Main Idea People in the Great Lakes States live near large lakes, in vast rural areas, and in busy cities and suburbs.

The Great Lakes States include Ohio, Indiana, Illinois, Michigan, Wisconsin, and Minnesota. Each state borders one of the Great Lakes. The northern states, Michigan, Wisconsin, and Minnesota, have thick forests. The southern states have fertile land.

The map on the next page shows some major cities in the Great Lakes States. Most people in the region live in cities or their surrounding suburbs. Beyond the suburbs lies mostly rural land, where people who live on farms produce much of the nation's food.

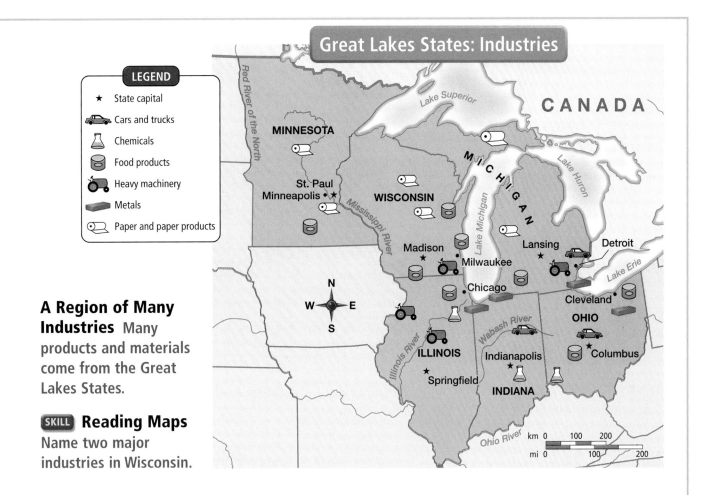

Great Lakes States: Industries

LEGEND
★ State capital
🚗 Cars and trucks
🧪 Chemicals
🥫 Food products
🚜 Heavy machinery
▬ Metals
📄 Paper and paper products

A Region of Many Industries Many products and materials come from the Great Lakes States.

SKILL Reading Maps Name two major industries in Wisconsin.

Living in Chicago

Chicago, Illinois, has more people than any other city in the Great Lakes States. Chicago's location near important waterways, especially Lake Michigan, helped it become a trading center. Today, Chicago is a transportation hub and a leading manufacturing and business center.

People have been moving to Chicago in search of good jobs since the mid-1800s. As the city grew, public transportation became necessary to take workers to and from downtown Chicago. The "L," or elevated train, was built to carry many people without getting in the way of busy city traffic. An **elevated train** is a railway that runs above the ground on raised tracks.

Rural Life

Although most people live in urban areas, the Great Lakes States are mostly rural. The region has more than 400,000 farms. In recent years, these farms have become more productive. However, fewer people work on farms. Today, many people work in manufacturing, as well as in health care, tourism, and other service industries.

In general, people in rural areas earn lower wages than urban workers. **Wages** are payments for work. At the same time, the cost of living is often lower in rural areas. A rural home can cost less than half as much as a similar home in an urban area.

REVIEW What is an advantage of Chicago's elevated train?

Baseball at Wrigley Field Chicago's Wrigley Field—the home of the Chicago Cubs—is the country's second oldest Major League Baseball park.

Things to Do

There are many things to do in the Great Lakes States. People who love the outdoors can go camping, fishing, boating, or swimming. Visitors can tour a lighthouse on the Great Lakes or a cheese factory in Wisconsin. Ice fishing, snowmobiling, and cross-country skiing are popular activities in the winter months.

Cities in the Great Lakes region offer a wide variety of activities. Sports fans can watch events at stadiums or speedways. People can enjoy art museums, theaters, and concerts. Many cities have special museums, such as Detroit's Museum of African American History. Visitors to Chicago can tour a submarine and a coal mine at the Museum of Science and Industry.

Leaving Cities

Main Idea In recent years, many people have left cities to live in suburbs.

For many years, people viewed cities as places where they could earn higher wages and live a better life. People moved to Great Lakes cities from rural areas, other parts of the United States, and different countries. As a result, the cities grew rapidly.

Today, many people live outside of cities. Improvements in transportation allow people to live in suburbs. They travel to cities to work and shop. Improvements in technology allow some people to work at home. As more people have moved out of cities, many businesses also have moved. As a result, some suburbs have become business and industrial centers.

Facing Challenges

Some Great Lakes cities, such as Detroit, have had many people move away. Cities develop problems when people leave. Businesses and schools close because not enough people use them. Buildings and homes may be abandoned, and crime may increase.

Growth in the suburbs can cause environmental problems. Too much building may leave few natural areas for people to enjoy. Suburban life can increase air pollution because so many people drive cars instead of walking.

Many people are finding ways to face these challenges. Cities are rebuilding downtown areas to attract residents. Communities are working to improve public transportation and reduce car use.

REVIEW How can the growth of suburbs affect the environment?

Millennium Park Located in downtown Chicago, this outdoor market space was built atop parking lots and railroad tracks.

Lesson Summary

The Great Lakes States have busy urban areas and large rural areas. Many suburbs are growing as city populations decline. People are working together to face new challenges.

Why It Matters ...

People in the Great Lakes States and across the country are working to adjust to changes in population.

Lesson Review

1 VOCABULARY Use **elevated train** in a paragraph that tells what you might see while riding this kind of train.

2 READING SKILL Compare and contrast activities that take place in urban and in suburban areas.

3 MAIN IDEA: Geography What feature do many major cities of the Great Lakes States share?

4 MAIN IDEA: Culture In what ways can a declining population affect a city?

5 CRITICAL THINKING: Infer Based on the goods and services provided in the Midwest, what can you infer about the types of jobs many people there have?

HANDS ON CITIZENSHIP ACTIVITY Learn more about a city or town near you. In a group, make a list of ways that you as students can help make your city or town a nice place to live. Share that list with the class.

Extend Lesson 3

Literature

Trouble at Fort La Pointe

by Kathleen Ernst

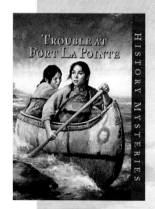

For the Ojibwe people in 1732, La Pointe Island is a place to gather with friends and family during the warm summer months. Suzette Choudoir is the daughter of an Ojibwe woman and a French *voyageur,* or fur trader. She is eager to paddle over to the island. As the story begins, she gazes at it across the sparkling water of Lake Superior.

She took a deep breath, enjoying the damp smell of earth, the lapping of the waves, and the sun warming her shoulders like a trader's wool blanket. Still smiling, Suzette glanced back at the camp. Smoke from morning fires twisted toward the sky, and the first shouts of children at play mixed with the mournful yipping of hungry dogs. It was good to be among more *wiigwams* again!

Ojibwe people moved with the seasons. During the cold winter months, when food was scarce, they scattered into the deep forest in small family camps. At the end of the long winter, it felt wonderful to move on to the sugaring camp, where perhaps a dozen families gathered to tap maple trees for sap to boil into syrup and sugar. And then Ojibwe people all over the mainland began making their way to the great summer village on La Pointe Island, just like Suzette's family. Each day now, more families arrived at the campground along the lakeshore and pitched *wiigwams* among the trees, waiting for good weather so they could cross to the island. Every passing day brought happy reunions with friends and relatives Suzette hadn't seen since last summer. . . .

La Pointe Island in 1732

Mainland

Lake Superior

Big Bay

La Pointe Island

Ojibwe camp

Fort La Pointe

And this year, because of the trappers' competition, her family would have even more to celebrate. This year—

"Suzette!"

Suzette grinned and waved when she saw Gabrielle Broussard emerge from the trees, carrying a copper kettle. Gabrielle was her best friend. They had both been born in the moon of blooming flowers, twelve years earlier. And they both had French fathers.

"*Aaniin*," Gabrielle greeted her. "What are you doing?"

"I'm going to find Papa. He walked out to the point, to get the best view of the lake. Want to come with me?"

Gabrielle splashed into the water to fill the kettle.

"Mama's waiting for me. What's your papa doing there?"

"Can't you guess? He's watching for the *voyageurs!*" Suzette's feet scuffed the earth in a little dance. Any day now, the songs of the French *voyageurs* would ring across the water from the east. They were paddling huge canoes filled with trade goods from a far-off place called Montréal. The trip took many weeks, down mighty rivers and across two great lakes. Their arrival on La Pointe Island would spark the wildly joyous gathering called *rendez-vous* by the French and *maawanji'iwin* by the Ojibwe. By the end of the short summer visit, the *voyageurs'* canoes would be loaded with the furs the Ojibwe trappers had been collecting all year. Then the *voyageurs* would say their good-byes and paddle back to Montréal before snowstorms and iced-over rivers made travel impossible.

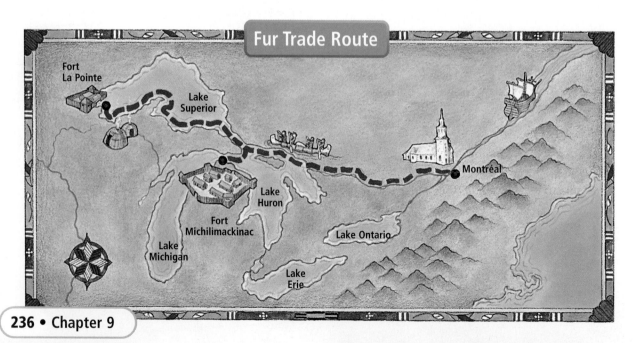

Fur Trade Route

Fort La Pointe

Lake Superior

Lake Huron

Fort Michilimackinac

Lake Michigan

Lake Ontario

Lake Erie

Montréal

"Papa can't wait to see his old friends again," Suzette added. Her own papa had been a *voyageur* for many years.

Gabrielle glanced to the east, her face wistful. "I'm waiting too."

Suzette stopped dancing. For a moment she had forgotten that Gabrielle's father would be among the paddlers. Gabrielle hadn't seen her father since the moon of shining leaves, when the woods blazed with red and yellow and the air held a promise of coming snow. Suzette chewed her lip. "I'm sure your papa will arrive soon, Gabrielle. I'm sure his journeys have been safe."

Voyageurs paddle a canoe along the fur trade route.

Activities

1. **TALK ABOUT IT** Discuss the part of the story that shows that Suzette is a **caring** person.

2. **WRITE ABOUT IT** Write a paragraph explaining how Suzette feels about La Pointe Island.

Skillbuilder

Use a Special Purpose Map

Some maps have a special purpose. They use different symbols to tell about the special features of a place. The map below tells you about resources in the Midwest.

Mineral Resources of the Midwest

LEGEND

Coal		Limestone	
Copper		Natural Gas	
Gold		Oil	
Iron Ore		Silver	
Lead		Zinc	

CANADA

NORTH DAKOTA
Bismarck
Fargo

SOUTH DAKOTA
Pierre
Sioux Falls

NEBRASKA
Omaha
Lincoln

KANSAS
Topeka
Wichita

MINNESOTA
St. Paul
Minneapolis

IOWA
Des Moines
Davenport

Jefferson City
St. Louis
MISSOURI

Lake Superior

MICHIGAN

WISCONSIN
Madison
Milwaukee

Chicago
Gary

ILLINOIS
Springfield
Indianapolis

INDIANA

Lake Michigan
Lansing
Detroit
Lake Huron

OHIO
Columbus
Cincinnati
Lake Erie

Mississippi River
Missouri River
Platte River
Arkansas River
Illinois River
Wabash River
Ohio River

km 0   100   200
mi 0   100   200

Learn the Skill

Step 1: Read the map title to find out what kind of information is shown on the map.

Mineral Resources of the Midwest

Step 2: Study the map's legend. Notice that each symbol represents one of the different mineral resources found in the Midwest.

LEGEND

Coal
Copper
Gold
Iron ore
Lead

Limestone
Natural gas
Oil
Silver
Zinc

Step 3: Note where the symbols from the legend appear on the map. For example, the coal symbol appears in Illinois. This shows that coal is mined in that state.

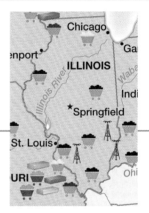

Practice the Skill

Use the map on page 238 to answer the questions.

1 Look at the legend. Name seven mineral resources that are found in the Midwest region.

2 According to the map, which mineral resources are found in the state of Illinois?

3 Based on this map, which mineral resource is found most widely in the Midwest?

Apply the Skill

Study the special purpose map on page 231. Then write a paragraph that summarizes the information shown on the map.

Visual Summary

1 – 3. Write a description of each item below.

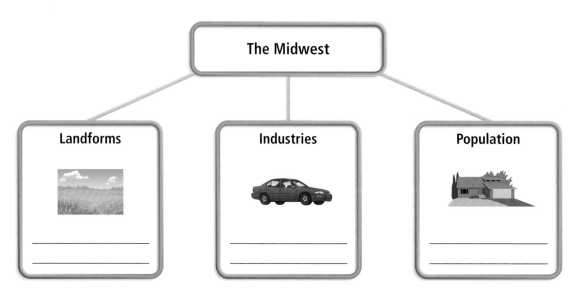

The Midwest

Landforms

Industries

Population

Facts and Main Ideas

☑ **TEST PREP** Answer each question below.

4. **Geography** Why are the Great Lakes and the Mississippi River important?

5. **Geography** Why do so many food products come from the Midwest?

6. **Economics** What happens to prices when there is an increase in demand?

7. **Culture** Name two ways that people in the Midwest have fun in the winter.

8. **Culture** What can happen to cities when a lot of people move away?

Vocabulary

☑ **TEST PREP** Choose the correct word from the list below to complete each sentence.

tributary, p. 219
consumer, p. 226
wages, p. 231

9. The Missouri River is a _____ of the Mississippi River.

10. Workers receive _____ for the work that they do.

11. A _____ makes choices that affect supply and demand.

Apply Skills

✔️ **TEST PREP** **Use a Special Purpose Map** Study the Crystal Lake Beach map below. Then use your map skills to answer each question.

Crystal Lake Beach Visitors Guide

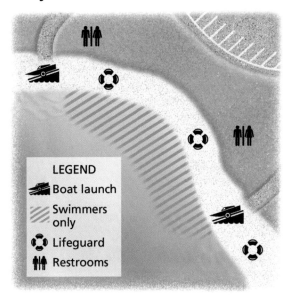

LEGEND
🚤 Boat launch
▨ Swimmers only
🛟 Lifeguard
🚻 Restrooms

12. What is the purpose of the map?

   A. to sell boats
   B. to provide a guide for visitors
   C. to keep people out of the lake
   D. to identify wildlife

13. How many places for people to put their boats into the water does the map show?

   A. two
   B. three
   C. four
   D. none

Critical Thinking

✔️ **TEST PREP** Write a short paragraph to answer each question below.

14. **Problem and Solution** Describe how animals and people have adapted to winters in the Midwest.

15. **Cause and Effect** List some problems caused by people leaving cities and building suburbs.

Activities

HANDS ON **Math Activity** Consumers have to decide how to spend their wages. For example, a woman earns $1,300 in a month. She spends $700 on rent and $500 on other things that she needs. How much does she have left?

 Writing Activity Write an essay about a place where you might want to live. Explain what you would give up if you moved there and what you would gain.

 Technology
Writing Process Tips
Get help with your essay at
www.eduplace.com/kids/hmss/

Chapter 10

Neighbors in the World

Technology

e • **glossary**
e • **word games**
www.eduplace.com/kids/hmss/

Vocabulary Preview

interdependence

Producers in one part of the nation sell goods such as food to consumers in other parts of the nation. This is called **interdependence.** page 245

heritage

People celebrate different cultures and our common **heritage** in festivals across the United States.
page 246

Reading Strategy

Monitor and Clarify Use this strategy as you read the lessons.

Quick Tip If you are confused about information in a lesson, reread or read ahead.

international law

The United Nations works to develop **international law.** Member nations agree to the laws to maintain peace. **page 253**

nongovernmental organization

Nongovernmental organizations such as the American Red Cross work outside of governments. **page 254**

Many Regions, One Nation

VOCABULARY

interdependence
specialize
prosperity
heritage

Vocabulary Strategy

interdependence

The prefix **inter–** means "between." **Interdependence** can mean dependence between people, or people needing each other.

READING SKILL

Draw Conclusions As you read, list facts that support this conclusion.

The government helps create links between Americans.

Build on What You Know Do you have friends or relatives who live in other parts of the country? Although you live far apart, do you feel connected? People all across our nation are connected, too.

Linking Regions

Main Idea Networks of communication, transportation, and trade link people of the United States.

Americans are linked in many ways. We live in the United States. We have a national government. We share a market economy. We share the values of liberty, equality, and justice.

Americans have always searched for new ways to link states and regions. For example, early leaders created a postal system even before there was a United States. Our nation has built roads, canals, and railroads. We have telephone systems, airports, and the Internet. These links change over time, but they have always had the same goal of connecting the states and regions of the country.

Making Connections The United States Postal Service is one system that links Americans.

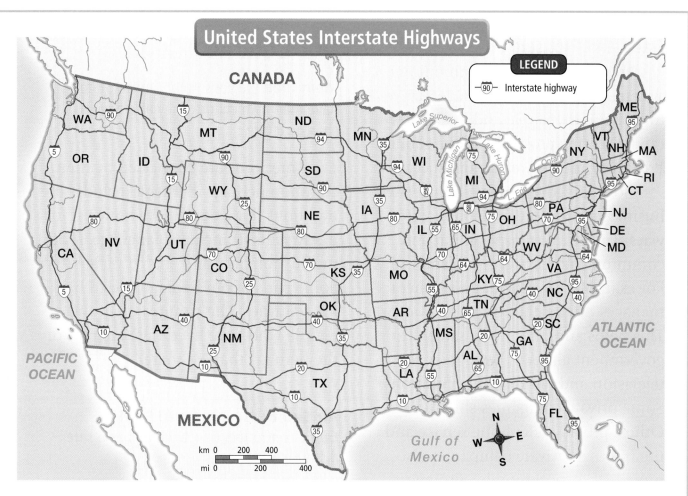

United States Interstate Highways

LEGEND
—90— Interstate highway

CANADA

PACIFIC OCEAN

ATLANTIC OCEAN

MEXICO

Gulf of Mexico

km 0   200   400
mi 0   200   400

Interstate Highways The interstate highway system has made transportation much easier.

Interdependence of Regions

Each link that connects states and regions leads to more interdependence. **Interdependence** is a relationship in which people depend on each other. For example, roads connect the states, so Maryland farmers can sell crops to New Jersey families who eat the farmers' crops. Maryland farmers may specialize in growing one type of crop. To **specialize** means that a person or business makes a few goods or provides one service. Both the farmers and families depend on each other. These kinds of links help people in our country conduct trade, communicate, and live better lives.

The United States government has worked to create some of these links. Today, the United States Postal Service connects people and businesses across the country. It helps people communicate and transport goods. The mail handles billions of dollars in business every day.

The United States government has also helped build a network of roads called the Interstate Highway System. Many of these roads were built in the 1950s and 1960s. Interstate highways help people and goods move easily across the country.

REVIEW In what way does the United States Postal Service link different parts of the country?

Trade and Prosperity

Transportation and communication systems help the nation's trade. Active trade between people and businesses can help bring prosperity to the country. **Prosperity** means wealth and success.

Both the government and private businesses promote trade in many ways. They help transportation and communication systems run smoothly. For example, the federal government manages our air-traffic control system. This helps airplanes travel safely. The government also sets basic rules for television and radio communications. Some private companies ship items. Others provide telephone service and the Internet. Private companies also provide transportation by airplane, bus, and train. The United States has a large private trucking industry that moves goods around the country.

Our government also helps trade by providing a system of money. This makes trade easier, because everyone agrees on how to pay for goods and services. People know what the money is worth.

Our Common Culture

Main Idea Regions in the United States have their own culture. They also have a shared culture.

Americans are connected by their common heritage. **Heritage** includes the traditions that people have honored for many years. It includes language, food, music, holidays, and shared beliefs. Some parts of our heritage stretch back for centuries. The cultures of all the people who have lived here are part of the heritage that we share.

Air Safety One responsibility of air traffic controllers is to keep planes a safe distance apart.

Sharing Traditions

Holidays show our shared heritage. People in every state celebrate Independence Day. On Memorial Day, parades and events across the country honor those who have died in the nation's wars.

People also share a tradition of helping others. After the attacks of September 11, 2001, volunteers from around the country came to New York City. One volunteer was Timothy Mottl of Illinois. He said,

Helping Out These volunteers prepared food for rescue workers in New York City.

"The experience made me really look at . . . what being an American means to me.**"**

REVIEW In what ways do we show our shared culture?

Lesson Summary

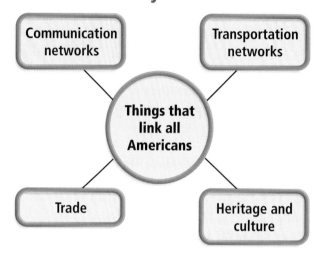

Communication networks

Transportation networks

Things that link all Americans

Trade

Heritage and culture

Why It Matters . . .

Although each region of the United States is different, we are connected in many ways.

Lesson Review

❶ **VOCABULARY** Write a paragraph that shows you know what **specialize** and **interdependence** mean.

❷ **READING SKILL** What can you **conclude** about the ways that government and private business help the economy?

❸ **MAIN IDEA: Geography** List three ways that people and businesses around the nation stay connected.

❹ **MAIN IDEA: Culture** In what ways does heritage connect people?

❺ **CRITICAL THINKING: Draw Conclusions** In an emergency, why do you think people volunteer to help each other?

HANDS ON

ART ACTIVITY What do you think it means to be an American? Create a poster with words and images that show our shared culture and heritage.

VOLUNTEERS at WORK

Why do volunteers work for free? Whether they teach students, help seniors, rescue animals, or clean up the environment, most volunteers feel that they get more than they give.

Volunteers are needed after a natural disaster, such as a flood or tornado. The Federal Emergency Management Agency does a lot to help after natural disasters, but volunteers often do much of the important rescue, relief, cleanup, and rebuilding work. They might work on their own, with church groups, or through organizations such as the American Red Cross. Volunteers contribute to the common good of the nation's communities.

Look Closely In September of 1999, Hurricane Floyd caused the Neuse River in North Carolina to flood.

RESCUE

Volunteers help rescue people, pets, and livestock stranded by the floodwaters.

RELIEF

Volunteers help in relief centers, handing out meals and supplies and talking with flood victims.

CLEANUP

After floodwaters go down, volunteers help with the huge cleanup job.

REBUILDING

Volunteers with building skills help repair or rebuild thousands of homes.

Activities

1. **DRAW IT** Volunteers show **civic virtue**, or the desire to do something for the common good. Draw a picture that shows an example of civic virtue.

2. **ACT IT OUT** Act out a skit of volunteers cleaning up a trail or a park.

Citizenship Skills

Skillbuilder

Resolve Conflicts

Sometimes, differences in opinions and beliefs can lead to a conflict. A **conflict** is a disagreement between groups of people or individuals. By working together, those involved in a conflict can sometimes overcome their disagreements and find a solution.

► **VOCABULARY**
conflict

Learn the Skill

Step 1: Identify the conflict.

> **Conflict:** The softball team and the school band want to use the auditorium after school on Tuesdays.

Step 2: Understand the reasons for the conflict. Have the people involved in the conflict state their goals.

> **Goal:** The softball team wants to hold meetings on Tuesdays.

> **Goal:** The school band wants to rehearse on Tuesdays.

Step 3: Think of all the possible ways to solve the conflict.

> **Possible Solution:** The softball team offers to hold meetings every other Tuesday.

> **Possible Solution:** The school band offers to practice at a later time.

Step 4: Choose the plan or compromise that is most acceptable to everyone involved. Each side may need to compromise on its goals. A compromise is when a person or group gives up something it wants in order to move closer to an agreement.

> **Solution:** The softball team will hold meetings every other Tuesday. The band will practice in the evening on the days that the softball team has meetings.

Michael and his sister Maya both need to use the telephone. Michael promised a friend he would call to talk because his friend was upset during school. Maya needs to call a classmate to discuss a group project. They both want to use the phone at the same time. Michael says that his phone call is important because his friend needs his help. Maya says that her phone call is important because she has to do her schoolwork.

Practice the Skill

Read the paragraph above. Then answer the questions.

1. Identify the conflict. What do Michael and Maya both need to do?
2. What are the goals of Michael and Maya?
3. Brainstorm possible solutions to resolve this conflict.

Apply the Skill

Find out about a conflict that exists in your community. Learn about ways that people have tried to compromise in order to find a solution.

Working Together

Build on What You Know When you and a friend
have a disagreement, how do you solve it? It is
important to have ways for settling disagreements.
Like people, countries need ways to do this.

Nations Work Together

Main Idea The United States and other nations have rules
for handling disagreements and facing challenges.

The United States works with many other nations
toward common goals. One of the most important
goals is greater peace around the world. Toward this
goal, countries formed an organization called the
United Nations. Through this organization, nations
can face challenges in peaceful ways. This helps
prevent nations from turning to war.

United Nations Flag The olive branches of the
United Nations flag stand for world peace.

The United Nations

The United Nations, or UN, was formed at the end of World War II. The United States helped create the UN. Today, more than 190 countries belong to this organization. One of its goals is to build peace and friendship among the countries of the world.

In 1948, the UN adopted the Universal Declaration of Human Rights. This document is intended to protect the basic rights of people in all countries. The World Bank, a UN agency, is supposed to help countries build their economies. The United Nations also helps improve health conditions through the World Health Organization. These and other UN programs help people all over the world.

International Law

In the United States, we have laws about how our citizens should behave. There are also rules of international law. **International law** is a set of basic rules to which the United States and many other countries have agreed. Treaties are examples of this kind of agreement. The United Nations helps nations work together to make agreements.

One area of international law has to do with war. Many countries have agreed to rules about what a country can and cannot do in war. The UN has helped organize trials for people accused of war crimes. Wars in the Balkans and Rwanda have led to trials for such crimes.

REVIEW When was the United Nations formed, and for what purposes?

Helping Out in Iraq UNICEF is a United Nations program that helps children around the world.

People Work Together

Main Idea Cooperation between countries takes many forms.

Many nongovernmental organizations work to build relationships across national borders. A **nongovernmental organization,** or NGO, is a group that is not part of a national government. Many NGOs work with the United Nations or with national governments to reach shared goals. These goals may include helping the poor and treating the sick.

You have probably heard of some NGOs. For example, the International Red Cross rushes to help people when disasters such as earthquakes strike. In the United States, the American Red Cross helps people give blood for others in need. Doctors Without Borders is another NGO. This group provides medical care to people who need help around the world. Other NGOs help spread useful farming techniques, protect people's rights, support democracies, and share business knowledge. There are thousands of NGOs around the world.

In general, NGOs exist for the purpose of helping people. They cross international borders in order to make the world a better place.

Help from Outside the Government Many NGOs help people all over the world.

Communicating Around the World

Today, technology helps people communicate more easily and quickly than ever before. Wireless phones, the Internet, and other communication tools allow people to get in touch with each other from nearly anywhere on the planet. Sounds, pictures, and other kinds of information take only seconds to travel around the world.

In the past, people were often unable to communicate with others during difficult times. For example, after World War II, the countries of Eastern Europe were shut off from the rest of the world. The governments of these countries prevented their people from communicating with anyone in the outside world. Today's technology makes it much more difficult for a government to control people's communication like this.

Some governments still try to control the information that their citizens receive, but wireless phones and the Internet can connect these people to the world and bring change.

REVIEW What are some goals of NGOs?

Lesson Summary

The UN works to build peace and improve living conditions.

International law helps countries work together peacefully.

NGOs help people with health, education, food, and other needs.

Technology keeps people around the world connected.

Why It Matters ...

The nations and people of the world must find ways to resolve conflicts to make the world a better place to live.

Lesson Review

❶ **VOCABULARY** Write a paragraph telling what a **nongovernmental organization** does.

❷ **READING SKILL** In what way has the United Nations tried to **solve the problem** of poor health conditions?

❸ **MAIN IDEA: Government** What role do national governments play in international law?

❹ **MAIN IDEA: Technology** In what ways has technology helped build links between the people of the world?

❺ **CRITICAL THINKING: Analyze** Why do you think countries agree to follow international law?

HANDS ON **ART ACTIVITY** Suppose you wanted to plan an Internet site for people to learn about life in the United States. Use words and pictures to tell about your life here.

Universal Human Rights

What rights should every person have? In a 1941 speech, President **Franklin D. Roosevelt** discussed four freedoms everyone should have. They were (1) freedom of speech and expression, (2) freedom of worship, (3) freedom from want, and (4) freedom from fear.

After World War II, the United Nations set up the Commission on Human Rights to protect the rights of all people in all nations. **Eleanor Roosevelt,** President Roosevelt's wife, was elected chairperson. The commission wrote the Universal Declaration of Human Rights. The declaration contains 30 articles, or brief statements, about specific human rights.

On December 10, 1948, the UN's member nations voted to adopt the declaration. It continues to guide international law today.

Human Rights Day December 10 is Human Rights Day. These children in India lit candles to mark the day.

Some Articles from the Declaration

> **"**All human beings are born free and equal in dignity and rights. . . .**"**
> — Article 1

> **"**Everyone has the right to freedom of opinion and expression. . . .**"**
> — Article 19

> **"**Everyone has the right to take part in the government of his country, directly or through freely chosen representatives.**"**
> — Article 21

THE UNIVERSAL DECLARATION OF Human Rights

Eleanor Roosevelt Eleanor Roosevelt said that respect for universal human rights begins in "small places, close to home."

Activities

1. **TALK ABOUT IT** Eleanor Roosevelt cared about **fairness** for all people. Discuss what each article above says about fairness.

2. **DRAW YOUR OWN** Draw pictures that show each of the four freedoms from President Roosevelt's speech.

Visual Summary

1 – 4.  Write a description of each item below.

Interdependence	Volunteers	United Nations	Technology

_____	_____	_____	_____
_____	_____	_____	_____
_____	_____	_____	_____
_____	_____	_____	_____

Facts and Main Ideas

✔ **TEST PREP** Answer each question below.

5. **Economics** In what ways does interdependence help people live better lives?

6. **Government** Name two things that the government has done to help people and businesses communicate.

7. **History** Why did many countries in the world form the United Nations?

8. **Government** Who makes international laws?

9. **Culture** Name two ways in which American citizens show their common heritage.

Vocabulary

✔ **TEST PREP** Choose the correct word from the list below to complete each sentence.

prosperity, p. 246
specialize, p. 245
nongovernmental organization, p. 254

10. Businesses _____ by making specific goods or providing specific services.

11. Doctors Without Borders is an example of a _____.

12. Active trade helps increase a nation's _____.

✔ **TEST PREP** **Resolve Conflicts** Read the newspaper article below. Then use what you have learned about resolving conflicts to answer each question.

Wetlands absorb floodwaters and restore underground water. They also help clean water by absorbing pollutants. Many animals depend on wetlands for survival. Some people think that the wetlands should be protected. Others want to drain wetlands to use the land for farming and building houses and roads.

13. What conflict might people have?

    A. Some want to protect animals, others do not.

    B. Some want to protect wetlands, others want to protect animals.

    C. Some want to protect wetlands, others want to drain wetlands.

    D. Some want to protect wetlands, others want to create more wetlands.

14. What is the second step to resolve a conflict?

    A. Understand the reasons for the conflict.

    B. Identify the conflict.

    C. Identify one solution.

    D. Choose the plan one person likes.

✔ **TEST PREP** Write a short paragraph to answer each question below.

15. **Draw Conclusions** Why do you think nations join the United Nations and develop international laws?

16. **Summarize** Explain the importance of nongovernmental organizations such as the International Red Cross.

Activities

Speaking Activity Learn more about three agencies within the United Nations. Explain to the class what each of the three agencies does.

Writing Activity Write a persuasive essay, explaining what rights you believe all children should have. Give reasons for your argument.

Technology
Writing Process Tips
Get help with your essay at
www.eduplace.com/kids/hmss/

Review and Test Prep

Vocabulary and Main Ideas

✔ **TEST PREP** Write a sentence to answer each question.

1. In what way do **consumers** affect the economy?

2. Why might people who live near a river build a **levee?**

3. What can cause **demand** for a product to rise?

4. What might cause the **supply** of a product to increase?

5. In what way does **international law** protect human rights?

6. What do **nongovernmental organizations** (NGOs) do to build relationships between nations?

Critical Thinking

✔ **TEST PREP** Write a short paragraph to answer each question.

7. **Infer** In what ways might wages and supply and demand affect what consumers choose to buy?

8. **Synthesize** In what ways have natural resources helped the economy of the Midwest?

Apply Skills

✔ **TEST PREP** Use a Special Purpose Map Read the Great Lakes States Industries map below to answer the questions that follow.

Great Lakes States Industries

9. Which states are major producers of paper and paper products?

   A. Michigan, Indiana, and Ohio
   B. Minnesota, Wisconsin, and Michigan
   C. Illinois, Wisconsin, and Indiana
   D. Minnesota, Ohio, and Illinois

10. Which state produces heavy machinery, cars and trucks, and paper products?

   A. Indiana
   B. Ohio
   C. Minnesota
   D. Michigan

Unit Activity

Create a "Dream Job" Comic Strip

- Think about a job you would like to have in the future.

- Write the answers to these questions: Where will you work? What will you do in your job? What skills will you need? What will you like the most about your job?

- Write a comic strip called "My Dream Job" in which you tell a friend all about your job. However, do not name the job!

- Have the class guess your dream job.

At the Library

Check out this book at your school or public library.

Eleanor Roosevelt: A Life of Discovery by Russell Freedman

This biography tells Eleanor Roosevelt's story from childhood to being First Lady.

Current Events Project

Create a display about how the United States works with other countries.

- Find articles about projects the United States has done with other nations.

- Pick one project and write a summary of it.

- Find or draw pictures that tell something about your project.

- Post your summary and pictures in a class display.

 Technology

Weekly Reader online offers social studies articles. Go to **www.eduplace.com/kids/hmss/**

References

Citizenship Handbook

Pledge of Allegiance R2
   English, Spanish, Tagalog, Russian, Arabic, Chinese

Character Traits R4

Illinois Counties R6

Illinois Databank R10

Illinois Governors R12

History Makers—Biographical Dictionary R14

Citizenship Handbook

Resources

Geographic Terms R18

Atlas R20

Gazetteer R34

Glossary R39

Index R44

Acknowledgments R50

Pledge of Allegiance

*I pledge allegiance to the flag
of the United States of America
and to the Republic for which it stands,
one Nation under God, indivisible,
with liberty and justice for all.*

Spanish

Prometo lealtad a la bandera
de los Estados Unidos de América,
y a la república que representa,
una nación bajo Dios, entera,
con libertad y justicia para todos.

Russian

Я даю клятву верности флагу
Соединённых Штатов Америки
и стране, символом которой
он является, народу, единому
перед Богом, свободному
и равноправному.

Tagalog

Ako ay nanunumpa ng katapatan
sa bandila ng Estados Unidos
ng Amerika, at sa Republikang
kanyang kinakatawan, isang
Bansang pumapailalim sa isang
Maykapal hindi nahahati, may
kalayaan at katarungan para
sa lahat.

Arabic

ادين بالولاء لعلم الولايات المتحده الامريكيه والى
الجمهوريه التي تمثلها دولة واحدة تؤمن باللة
متحدة تمنح الحرية والعدالة للجميع

Chinese

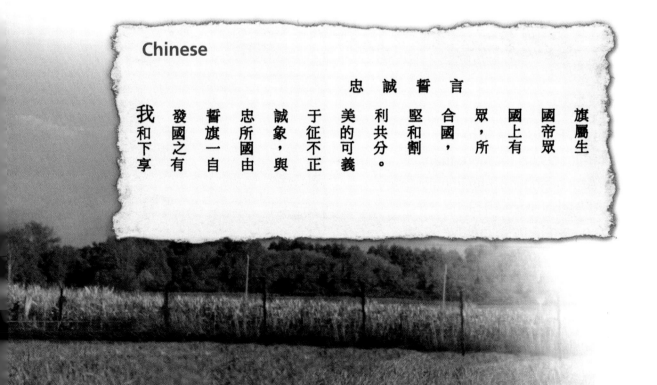

誓言

忠誠

旗屬生
國帝眾
國上有
眾，所

合國，
堅和割

利共分。
美的可義

于征不正
誠象，與

忠所國由
誓旗一自

發國之有
我和下享

Character Traits

Character includes feelings, thoughts, and behaviors. A character trait is something people show by the way they act. To act bravely shows courage, and courage is one of several character traits.

Positive character traits, such as honesty, caring, and courage, lead to positive actions. Character traits are also called "life skills." Life skills can help you do your best, and doing your best can help you reach your goals.

Bernie Wong

Caring Wong has spent her life helping people. She began the Chinese American Service League to provide education, career, and health services to people in Chicago.

Emil Jones Jr.

Civic Virtue Emil Jones Jr. has worked for Illinoisans for more than 30 years. As a member of the Illinois General Assembly since 1973, he has worked hard to help improve Illinois's public schools.

Courage means acting bravely. Doing what you believe to be good and right, and telling the truth, requires courage.

Responsibility is taking care of work that needs to be done. Responsible people are reliable and trustworthy, which means they can be counted on.

Fairness means working to make things fair for everyone. Often, one needs to try again and again to achieve fairness. This is diligence, or not giving up.

Caring means noticing what others need and helping them get what they need. Feeling concern or compassion is another way to define caring.

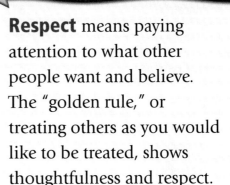

Patriotism means working for the goals of your country. When you show national pride, you are being patriotic.

Respect means paying attention to what other people want and believe. The "golden rule," or treating others as you would like to be treated, shows thoughtfulness and respect.

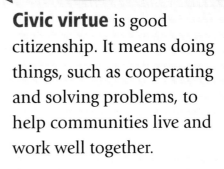

Civic virtue is good citizenship. It means doing things, such as cooperating and solving problems, to help communities live and work well together.

Illinois Counties

County	County Seat	Year Organized	Population*	Origin of Name
Adams	Quincy	1825	68,277	for President James Quincy Adams
Alexander	Cairo	1819	9,590	for William M. Alexander, early settler
Bond	Greenville	1817	17,633	for Governor Shadrach Bond
Boone	Belvidere	1837	41,786	for Daniel Boone, pioneer hunter and explorer
Brown	Mt. Sterling	1839	6,950	for General Jacob Brown
Bureau	Princeton	1837	35,503	for Pierre de Bureo, a French trader
Calhoun	Hardin	1825	5,084	for Vice President John C. Calhoun in the John Q. Adams administration
Carroll	Mt. Carroll	1839	16,674	for Charles Carroll, signer of the Declaration of Independence
Cass	Virginia	1837	13,695	for Lewis Cass, soldier and statesman
Champaign	Urbana	1833	179,669	for a county in Ohio
Christian	Taylorville	1839	35,372	for a county in Kentucky
Clark	Marshall	1819	17,008	for George Rogers Clark, American Revolutionary soldier
Clay	Louisville	1824	14,560	for Henry Clay, politician and author of "Missouri Compromise"
Clinton	Carlyle	1824	35,535	for DeWitt Clinton, chief promoter of the Erie Canal
Coles	Charleston	1830	53,196	for Governor Edward Coles
Cook	Chicago	1831	5,376,741	for first Illinois Attorney General Daniel P. Cook
Crawford	Robinson	1816	20,452	for Georgia Senator William H. Crawford
Cumberland	Toledo	1843	11,253	for Cumberland Road
DeKalb	Sycamore	1837	88,969	for German baron Johann DeKalb, soldier in American Revolution
DeWitt	Clinton	1839	16,798	for Dewitt Clinton, chief promoter of the Erie Canal; Clinton county named for him also
Douglas	Tuscola	1859	19,922	for U.S. Senator Stephen A. Douglas
DuPage	Wheaton	1839	904,161	for the DuPage River
Edgar	Paris	1823	19,704	for John Edgar, pioneer, merchant and politician
Edwards	Albion	1814	6,971	for Territory Governor Ninian Edwards
Effingham	Effingham	1831	34,264	for Lord Effingham, who resigned post rather than fight the colonies
Fayette	Vandalia	1821	21,802	for Marquis de Lafayette, French officer in the American Revolution

County	County Seat	Year Organized	Population	Origin of Name
Ford	Paxton	1859	14,241	for Governor Thomas Ford
Franklin	Benton	1818	39,018	for American leader Benjamin Franklin
Fulton	Lewiston	1823	38,250	for Robert Fulton, first successful steamboat builder on American waters
Gallatin	Shawneetown	1812	6,445	for statesman and financier Albert Gallatin
Greene	Carrollton	1821	14,761	for Major General Nathaniel Greene
Grundy	Morris	1841	37,535	for Tennessee Senator Felix Grundy
Hamilton	McLeansboro	1821	8,621	for American leader Alexander Hamilton
Hancock	Carthage	1825	20,121	for John Hancock, first signer of the Declaration of Independence
Hardin	Elizabethtown	1839	4,800	for a county in Kentucky
Henderson	Oquawka	1841	8,213	for a county in Kentucky
Henry	Cambridge	1825	51,020	for famous speaker Patrick Henry
Iroquois	Watseka	1833	31,334	for the Iroquois confederacy of six American Indian tribes
Jackson	Murphysboro	1816	59,612	for President Andrew Jackson
Jasper	Newton	1831	10,117	for American Revolution Sergeant William Jasper
Jefferson	Mount Vernon	1819	40,045	for President Thomas Jefferson
Jersey	Jerseyville	1839	21,668	for the state New Jersey
Jo Daviess	Galena	1827	22,289	for U.S. District Attorney Joseph Hamilton Daviess
Johnson	Vienna	1812	12,878	for Vice President Colonel Richard M. Johnson in Van Buren administration
Kane	Geneva	1836	404,119	for first Secretary of State for Illinois Elias Kent Kane
Kankakee	Kankakee	1853	103,833	for the Kankakee River
Kendall	Yorkville	1841	54,544	for Amos Kendall, Postmaster General in Jackson administration
Knox	Galesburg	1825	55,836	for American Revolution Major General Henry Knox
Lake	Waukegan	1839	644,356	for Lake Michigan
La Salle	Ottawa	1831	111,509	for Robert Cavelier, Sieur de La Salle, French explorer who started the first white settlement in Illinois
Lawrence	Lawrenceville	1821	15,452	for Chesapeake Commander Captain James Lawrence
Lee	Dixon	1839	36,062	for Virginia Senator Richard Henry Lee
Livingston	Pontiac	1837	39,678	for Edward Livingston, Secretary of State in Jackson administration
Logan	Lincoln	1839	31,183	for Dr. John Logan, pioneer physician, father of General John A. Logan

County	County Seat	Year Organized	Population	Origin of Name
McDonough	Macomb	1826	32,913	for Commodore Thomas McDonough
McHenry	Woodstock	1836	260,077	for William McHenry, pioneer of White County
McLean	Bloomington	1830	150,433	for John McClean, first Representative in Congress for Illinois
Macon	Decatur	1829	114,706	for American Revolution Colonel Nathaniel Macon
Macoupin	Carlinville	1829	49,019	for Macoupin Creek
Madison	Edwardsville	1812	258,941	for President James Madison
Marion	Salem	1823	41,691	for American Revolution soldier Francis Marion
Marshall	Lacon	1839	13,180	for Supreme Court Chief Justice John Marshall
Mason	Havana	1841	16,038	for a county in Kentucky
Massac	Metropolis	1843	15,161	for Fort Massac
Menard	Petersburg	1839	12,486	for Pierre Menard, first Lieutenant Governor of Illinois
Mercer	Aledo	1825	16,957	for American Revolution General Hugh Mercer
Monroe	Waterloo	1816	27,619	for President James Monroe
Montgomery	Hillsboro	1821	30,652	for American Revolution General Richard Montgomery
Morgan	Jacksonville	1823	36,616	for American Revolution General Daniel Morgan
Moultrie	Sullivan	1843	14,287	for American Revolution General William Moultrie, built Fort Moultrie
Ogle	Oregon	1836	51,032	for Joseph Ogle, Lieutenant of the Territorial militia
Peoria	Peoria	1825	183,433	for the Peoria American Indian Tribe of the Illinois Indians
Perry	Pinckneyville	1827	23,094	for Commodore Oliver Hazard Perry
Piatt	Monticello	1841	16,365	for John A. Piatt, early settler
Pike	Pittsfield	1821	17,384	for Louisiana Purchase explorer Zebulon Pike
Pope	Golconda	1816	4,413	for first Territorial Secretary of State Nathaniel Pope
Pulaski	Mound City	1843	7,348	for Polish exile Count Casimir Pulaski
Putnam	Hennepin	1825	6,086	for American Revolution Major General Israel Putnam
Randolph	Chester	1795	33,893	for Edmund Randolph, U.S. Attorney General in Washington administration
Richland	Olney	1841	16,149	for a county in Ohio
Rock Island	Rock Island	1831	149,374	for an island in the Mississippi River
St. Clair	Belleville	1790	256,082	for American Revolution Major General Arthur St. Clair

County	County Seat	Year Organized	Population	Origin of Name
Saline	Harrisburg	1847	26,733	for Saline Creek, also numerous salt springs in county
Sangamon	Springfield	1821	188,951	for the Sangamon River
Schuyler	Rushville	1825	7,189	for American Revolution Major General Phillip Schuyler
Scott	Winchester	1839	5,537	for a county in Kentucky
Shelby	Shelbyville	1827	22,893	for Kentucky Governor Isaac Shelby
Stark	Toulon	1839	6,332	for American Revolution Major General John Stark
Stephenson	Freeport	1837	48,979	for Benjamin Stephenson, Territory Adjutant General
Tazewell	Pekin	1827	128,485	for Virginia Senator Lyttleton W. Tazewell
Union	Jonesboro	1818	18,293	for the federal union of the American States
Vermilion	Danville	1826	83,919	for the Vermilion River
Wabash	Mt. Carmel	1824	12,937	for the Wabash River, from the American Indian word "oubache"
Warren	Monmouth	1825	18,735	for Joseph Warren, physician and soldier
Washington	Nashville	1818	15,148	for President George Washington
Wayne	Fairfield	1819	17,151	for American Revolution Major General Anthony Wayne
White	Carmi	1815	15,371	for territorial militia Major Leonard White
Whiteside	Morrison	1836	60,653	for Samuel Whiteside, Colonel of the territorial militia
Will	Joliet	1836	502,266	for Conrad Will, pioneer politician
Williamson	Marion	1839	61,296	for a county in Tennessee
Winnebago	Rockford	1836	278,418	for the Winnebago American Indian tribe, translates to "fish eater"
Woodford	Eureka	1841	35,469	for a county in Kentucky

*Source: Census 2000

Illinois Databank

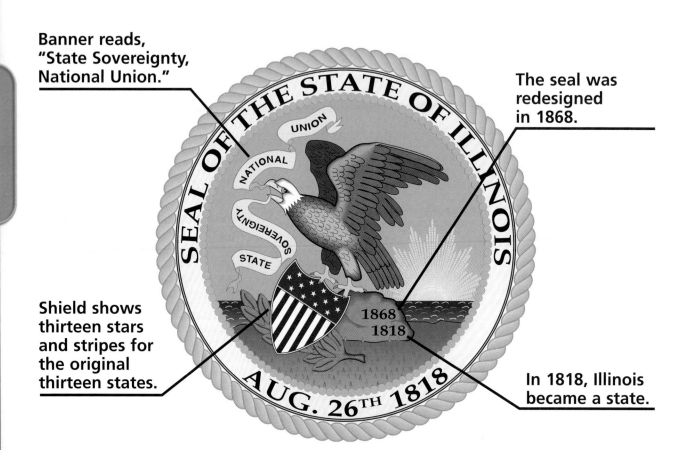

Banner reads, "State Sovereignty, National Union."

The seal was redesigned in 1868.

Shield shows thirteen stars and stripes for the original thirteen states.

In 1818, Illinois became a state.

Illinois Facts

Population, 2003	12,653,544
Land Area	56,400 square miles (146,075 square kilometers)
Economy	**Agriculture:** Corn, soybeans, hogs, cattle, dairy products, wheat **Industry:** Machinery, food processing, electrical equipment, chemical products, printing and publishing, metal products, transportation equpiment, petroleum, coal
Song	"Illinois" by Charles H. Chamberlin and Archibald Johnston
Motto	"State Sovereignty, National Union"
Slogan	"Land of Lincoln"
State Nickname	Prairie State

Illinois Databank

State Flower
Purple Violet

State Animal
White-Tailed Deer

State
Mineral
Fluorite

State Insect
Monarch
Butterfly

State Bird
Northern Cardinal

State Tree
White Oak

Illinois Governors

Illinois Governors

Territorial Governor

Ninian Edwards
Term: 1809–1818
Political Party: Democratic–Republican
Lifespan: (1775–1833)
Birthplace: Montgomery County, Maryland

State Governors

Shadrach Bond
Term: 1818–1822
Political Party: Democratic–Republican
Lifespan: (1773–1832)
Birthplace: Fredericktown, Maryland

Edward Coles
Term: 1822–1826
Political Party: Democratic–Republican
Lifespan: (1786–1868)
Birthplace: Albemarle County, Virginia

Ninian Edwards
Term: 1826–1830
Political Party: Democratic–Republican
Lifespan: (1775–1833)
Birthplace: Montgomery County, Maryland

John Reynolds
Term: 1830–1834
Political Party: Democratic
Lifespan: (1788–1865)
Birthplace: Montgomery County, Pennsylvania

William Lee Davidson Ewing
Term: 1834
Political Party: Democratic
Lifespan: (1795–1846)
Birthplace: Paris, Kentucky

Joseph Duncan
Term: 1834–1838
Political Party: Democratic
Lifespan: (1794–1844)
Birthplace: Paris, Kentucky

Thomas Carlin
Term: 1838–1842
Political Party: Democratic
Lifespan: (1789–1852)
Birthplace: Frankfort, Kentucky

Thomas Ford
Term: 1842–1846
Political Party: Democratic
Lifespan: (1800–1850)
Birthplace: Uniontown, Pennsylvania

Augustus C. French
Term: 1846–1853
Political Party: Democratic
Lifespan: (1808–1864)
Birthplace: Hill, New Hampshire

Joel Aldrich Matteson
Term: 1853–1857
Political Party: Democratic
Lifespan: (1808–1873)
Birthplace: Watertown, New York

William H. Bissell
Term: 1857–1860
Political Party: Republican
Lifespan: (1811–1860)
Birthplace: Hartwick, New York

John Wood
Term: 1860–1861
Political Party: Republican
Lifespan: (1789–1880)
Birthplace: Moravia, New York

Richard Yates
Term: 1861–1865
Political Party: Republican
Lifespan: (1818–1873)
Birthplace: Warsaw, Kentucky

Richard J. Oglesby
Term: 1865–1869, 1873, 1885–1889
Political Party: Republican
Lifespan: (1824–1899)
Birthplace: Floydsburg, Kentucky

John M. Palmer
Term: 1869–1873
Political Party: Republican
Lifespan: (1817–1900)
Birthplace: Eagle Creek, Kentucky

Richard J. Oglesby
Term: 1865–1869, 1873, 1885–1889
Political Party: Republican
Lifespan: (1824–1899)
Birthplace: Floydsburg, Kentucky

John L. Beveridge
Term: 1873–1877
Political Party: Republican
Lifespan: (1824–1910)
Birthplace: Greenwich, New York

Shelby M. Cullom
Term: 1877–1883
Political Party: Republican
Lifespan: (1829–1914)
Birthplace: Monticello, Kentucky

State Governors (cont.)

John M. Hamilton

Term: 1883–1885
Political Party: Republican
Lifespan: (1847–1905)
Birthplace: Ridgewood, Ohio

Frank O. Lowden

Term: 1917–1921
Political Party: Republican
Lifespan: (1861–1943)
Birthplace: Sunrise, Minnesota

Otto Kerner

Term: 1961–1968
Political Party: Democratic
Lifespan: (1908–1976)
Birthplace: Chicago, Illinois

Richard J. Oglesby

Term: 1865–1869, 1873, 1885–1889
Political Party: Republican
Lifespan: (1824–1899)
Birthplace: Floydsburg, Kentucky

Lennington Small

Term: 1921–1929
Political Party: Republican
Lifespan: (1862–1936)
Birthplace: Kankakee, Illinois

Samuel H. Shapiro

Term: 1968–1969
Political Party: Democratic
Lifespan: (1907–1987)
Birthplace: Estonia

Joseph W. Fifer

Term: 1889–1893
Political Party: Republican
Lifespan: (1840–1938)
Birthplace: Staunton, Virginia

Louis L. Emmerson

Term: 1929–1933
Political Party: Republican
Lifespan: (1883–1941)
Birthplace: Albion, Illinois

Richard B. Ogilvie

Term: 1969–1973
Political Party: Republican
Lifespan: (1923–1988)
Birthplace: Kansas City, Missouri

John P. Altgeld

Term: 1893–1897
Political Party: Democratic
Lifespan: (1847–1902)
Birthplace: Niedersellers, Germany

Henry Horner

Term: 1933–1940
Political Party: Democratic
Lifespan: (1879–1940)
Birthplace: Chicago, Illinois

Daniel Walker

Term: 1973–1977
Political Party: Democratic
Lifespan: 1922–
Birthplace: Washington, D.C.

John R. Tanner

Term: 1897–1901
Political Party: Republican
Lifespan: (1844–1901)
Birthplace: Booneville, Indiana

John H. Steele

Term: 1940–1941
Political Party: Democratic
Lifespan: (1891–1962)
Birthplace: McLeansboro, Illinois

James R. Thompson

Term: 1977–1991
Political Party: Republican
Lifespan: 1936–
Birthplace: Chicago, Illinois

Richard Yates, Jr.

Term: 1901–1905
Political Party: Republican
Lifespan: (1860–1936)
Birthplace: Jacksonville, Illinois

Dwight H. Green

Term: 1941–1949
Political Party: Republican
Lifespan: (1897–1958)
Birthplace: Ligonier, Indiana

James Edgar

Term: 1991–1999
Political Party: Republican
Lifespan: 1946–
Birthplace: Vinita, Oklahoma

Charles S. Deneen

Term: 1905–1913
Political Party: Republican
Lifespan: (1863–1940)
Birthplace: Edwardsville, Illinois

Adlai E. Stevenson

Term: 1949–1953
Political Party: Democratic
Lifespan: (1900–1965)
Birthplace: Los Angeles, California

George H. Ryan

Term: 1999–2003
Political Party: Republican
Lifespan: 1934–
Birthplace: Maquoketa, Iowa

Edward F. Dunne

Term: 1913–1917
Political Party: Democratic
Lifespan: (1853–1937)
Birthplace: Waterville, Connecticut

William G. Stratton

Term: 1953–1961
Political Party: Republican
Lifespan: (1914–2001)
Birthplace: Ingleside, Illinois

Rod R. Blagojevich

Term: 2003–
Political Party: Democratic
Lifespan: 1956–
Birthplace: Chicago, Illinois

Biographical Dictionary

The page number after each entry refers to the place where the person is first mentioned. For more complete references to people, see the Index.

A

Addams, Jane 1860–1935, opened Hull House in Chicago to help immigrants, 1889; worked to end child labor and improve public health (p. 160).

Aiken, Lizzie 1817–1906, civil war nurse (p. 129).

Altgeld, John P. 1847–1902, governor of Illinois, 1893–1897; worked to stop child labor and make workplaces safer (p. 160).

Anthony, Susan B. 1820–1906, led the national fight for women's suffrage (p. 161).

Arnold, Isaac 1815–1884, cofounder of the Chicago Historical Society; U.S. Congress representative from Illinois, 1861–1865 (p. 146).

Armstrong, Louis 1901?–1971, jazz musician (p. 174).

B

Bickerdyke, Mary 1817–1901, Union military nurse who worked to improve hospital conditions during the Civil War (p. 129).

Birkbeck, Morris 1764–1825, English farmer and Illinois settler (p. 74).

Blagojevich, Rod 1956–, governor of Illinois, 2003– (p. 194).

Bond, Shadrach 1773–1832, first governor of Illinois, 1818–1822 (p. 99).

Booth, John Wilkes 1838–1865, actor who killed Abraham Lincoln (p. 130).

Brooks, Gwendolyn 1917–2000, American poet who wrote about African American experiences (p. 169).

Bush, George W. 1946–, 43rd President of the United States, 2001– (p. 202).

Byrne, Jane 1934–, first female mayor of Chicago, 1979–1983 (p. 203).

C

Cavelier, René-Robert, Sieur de La Salle, 1643–1687, French explorer who was the first European to travel the length of the Mississippi River; built the first French fort in Illinois, 1680 (p. 40).

Chase, Andrew ? Boston engineer who improved the design of the refrigerated train car for Gustavus Swift in 1878 (p. 153).

Clark, George Rogers 1752–1818, led the war against Britain in present-day Illinois; helped win the lands that are now Ohio, Indiana, Michigan, and Illinois (p. 66).

Clark, William 1770–1838, with Meriwether Lewis, led an expedition to find a route to the Pacific Ocean; mapped the land west of the Mississippi River (p. 83).

Coles, Edward 1786–1868, governor of Illinois, 1822–1826 (p. 101).

Cook, Daniel Pope 1794–1827, nephew of Nathaniel Pope; newspaper editor for the *Illinois Intelligencer*; clerk in the Illinois House of Representatives (p. 98).

D

Daley, Richard 1902–1976, elected mayor of Chicago six times, 1955–1976 (p. 203).

Debs, Eugene V. 1855–1926, led the American Railroad Union, America's first industrial union, 1893 (p. 160).

Deere, John 1804–1886, inventor of the steel plow (p. 113).

de Priest, Oscar Stanton 1871–1951, first African American elected to Chicago's city council, 1915–1917; United States Congress representative from Illinois, 1929–1935 (p. 159).

Dirksen, Everett 1896–1969, United States senator from Illinois, 1951–1969 (p. 168).

Douglas, Stephen 1813–1861, United States senator from Illinois, 1847–1861 (p. 122).

du Sable, Jean Baptiste Point 1745?–1818, African American pioneer who began a settlement at the site of present-day Chicago (p. 81).

 E

Edgar, James 1946–, governor of Illinois, 1991–1999 (p. 194).

Edwards, Ninian 1775–1833, territorial governor of Illinois, 1809–1818; governor of Illinois, 1826–1830 (p. 82).

Ellwood, Isaac 1833–1910, worked with Joseph Glidden to begin manufacturing barbed wire in DeKalb, Illinois (p. 154).

 F

Ferris, George Washington Gale 1859–1896, Illinois inventor who created the Ferris Wheel for the World's Columbian Exposition, 1893 (p. 173).

Field, Marshall 1834–1906, Chicago department store owner (p. 155).

Franklin, Benjamin 1706–1790, inventor, writer, scientist, diplomat, and publisher; signer of the Declaration of Independence (p. 66).

 G

George III 1738–1820, king of England, 1760–1820; supported British policies that led to the American Revolution (p. 58).

Glidden, Joseph 1813–1906, invented and patented an improved barbed wire; worked with Isaac Ellwood to begin manufacturing barbed wire in DeKalb, Illinois (p. 154).

Grant, Ulysses S. 1822–1885, 18th President of the United States, 1869–1877; Union general in the Civil War (p. 130).

 H

Hastert, J. Dennis 1942–, United States Congress representative from Illinois, 1987–, Speaker of the House in the United States House of Representatives, 1999– (p. 202).

Harrison, William Henry 1773–1841, governor of the Indiana Territory, 1801–1813; won the Battle of Tippecanoe, 1811; ninth President of the United States, 1841 (p. 89).

Hodgers, Jennie 1844?–1915, dressed as a man and called herself "Albert D.J. Cashier" to serve in the Union army (p. 129).

Hook, Frances 1847–? dressed as a man and called herself "Frank Miller" to serve in the Union army (p. 129).

 J

Jackson, Jesse 1941–, American civil rights leader (p. 168).

Jarrett, Vernon 1918–2004, co-founded the National Association of Black Journalists, 1975; worked in Chicago newspapers, radio, and television (p. 169).

Jefferson, Thomas 1743–1826, third President of the United States, 1801–1809; writer of the Declaration of Independence (p. 65).

Jenney, William LeBaron 1832–1907, designed the first skyscraper for the Home Insurance Company, 1885 (p. 173).

Johnson, Andrew 1808–1875, 17th President of the United States, 1865–1869 (p. 130).

Jolliet, Louis 1645–1700, explorer, fur trader, and mapmaker who explored the Missisippi River with Jacques Marquette (p. 39).

Jones, John 1817?–1879, abolitionist who protected escaped slaves in his home in Chicago; Cook County Commissioner, 1872; husband of Mary Jones (p. 121).

Jones, Mary 1819–1910, abolitionist who protected escaped slaves in her house in Chicago; wife of John Jones (p. 121).

Jones, Mary Harris "Mother" 1830?–1930, worked with the United Mine Workers and worked for reforms in the mining industry (p. 160).

 K

Kane, Elias Kent 1794–1835, United States senator from Illinois, 1825–1835; helped write Illinois's first constitution (p. 99).

Biographical Dictionary

Kerner, Otto 1908–1976, governor of Illinois, 1961–1968; ended housing discrimination in Illinois, 1967 (p. 168).

King, Coretta Scott 1927–, civil rights leader (p. 212).

King, Dr. Martin Luther, Jr. 1929–1968, American civil rights leader who taught people to use nonviolent protest (p. 168).

Lazarus, Emma 1849–1887, poet who wrote "The New Colossus," which is inscribed on the Statue of Liberty (p. 188).

Lee, Robert E. 1807–1870, commander of the Confederate army (p. 130).

Leiter, Levi 1834–1904, partner of Marshall Field and Potter Palmer in Illinois's first department store (p. 155).

Lewis, Meriwether 1774–1809, with William Clark, led an expedition to find a route to the Pacific Ocean; mapped the land west of the Mississippi River (p. 83).

Lincoln, Abraham 1809–1865, 16th President of the United States, 1861–1865; issued the Emancipation Proclamation, 1863 (p. 122).

Livermore, Mary 1820–1905, collected money and supplies for Union army hospitals (p. 129).

Lovejoy, Elijah 1802–1837, brother of Owen Lovejoy; abolitionist who wrote and printed articles against slavery (p. 121).

Lovejoy, Owen 1811–1864, abolitionist and "conductor" on the Underground Railroad (p. 121).

Martin, Ellen 1847–1916 worked for suffrage, one of the first women to vote in Illinois, 1891 (p. 161).

Marquette, Jacques 1637–1675, French missionary and explorer who explored the Mississippi River with Louis Jolliet, 1673 (p. 39).

McCormick, Cyrus 1809–1884, inventor of the horse-drawn mechanical reaper (p. 113).

McCormick, Robert R. 1880–1955, editor and publisher who made the *Chicago Tribune* one of the most widely read newspapers in the country (p. 175).

Moseley Braun, Carol 1947–, first African American woman in the United States Senate, 1993–1999 (p. 202).

Obama, Barack 1961–, United States senator from Illinois, 2005– (p. 203).

Palmer, Potter 1826–1902, started Illinois's first department store (p. 155).

Pontiac 1720?–1769, Ottawa chief who united several American Indian nations to attack British forts (p. 57).

Pope, Nathaniel 1784–1850, uncle of Daniel Pope Cook; political leader who suggested Lake Michigan as Illinois border (p. 99).

Reagan, Ronald 1911–2004, 40th President of the United States, 1981–1989 (p. 202).

Roosevelt, Eleanor 1884–1962, wife of President Franklin D. Roosevelt; worked as an advocate for underprivileged people (p. 257).

Roosevelt, Franklin Delano 1882–1945, 32nd President of the United States, 1933–1945; started the New Deal Program; only President to be elected four times (p. 165).

Rumsfeld, Donald 1932–, Secretary of Defense, 2001– ; born in Illinois (p. 202).

Ryan, George 1934–, governor of Illinois, 1999–2003 (p. 194).

Sacagawea 1787?–1812?, American Indian guide for Lewis and Clark (p. 84).

St. Clair, Arthur 1736?–1818, first governor of the Northwest Territory, 1788–1802 (p. 82).

Sinclair, Upton 1878–1968, author of *The Jungle* (p. 160).

Starr, Ellen Gates 1859–1940, opened Hull House with Jane Addams (p. 160).

Biographical Dictionary

Stevenson, Adlai 1900–1965, governor of Illinois, 1949–1953 (p. 167).

Swift, Gustavus 1839–1903, founder of a meatpacking company in Chicago; promoter of the refrigerated railway car (p. 153).

Tecumseh 1768?–1813, Shawnee chief who formed confederation to protect American Indian land (p. 88).

Tenskwatawa 1775–1837?, Tecumseh's brother, also known as "the Prophet," helped to lead the Shawnee against westward settlement (p. 88).

Thompson, James 1936–, governor of Illinois, 1977–1991 (p. 203).

Trout, Grace Wilbur 1864–1955, women's suffrage leader and activist (p. 161).

Washington, George 1732–1799, first President of the United States, 1789–1797; commanded the colonial army during the American Revolution (p. 65).

Washington, Harold 1922–1987, United States Congress representative from Illinois, 1981–1983; first African American mayor of Chicago, 1983–1987 (p. 203).

Wells Barnett, Ida 1862–1931, journalist who started an organization to help African Americans who moved to Chicago (p. 159).

Willard, Francis 1839–1898, worked for women's suffrage (p. 161).

Williams, Daniel Hale 1858–1931, founder of Provident Hospital who hired and trained nurses and doctors of all races, 1891 (p. 159).

Wright, Richard 1908–1960, American author whose work focused on fair treatment for African Americans (p. 169).

Yates, Richard 1818–1873, governor of Illinois, 1861–1865; formed the 29th U.S. Colored Infantry (p. 129).

Geographic Terms

Geographic Terms

basin
a round area of land surrounded by higher land

bay
part of a lake or ocean that is partially enclosed by land

canyon
a valley with steep cliffs shaped by erosion

cape
a piece of land that points out into a body of water

coast
the land next to a sea or ocean

coastal plain
an area of flat land next to a coast

creek
a stream of water smaller than a river

delta
land that is formed by soil deposited near the mouth of a river

desert
a dry region with little vegetation

fault
a break or crack in the Earth's surface

floodplain
flat, low land around a river that often floods

▲ **glacier**
a large ice mass that pushes soil and rocks as it moves

gulf
a large area of sea or ocean partially enclosed by land

hill
a raised area of land

island
an area of land surrounded by water

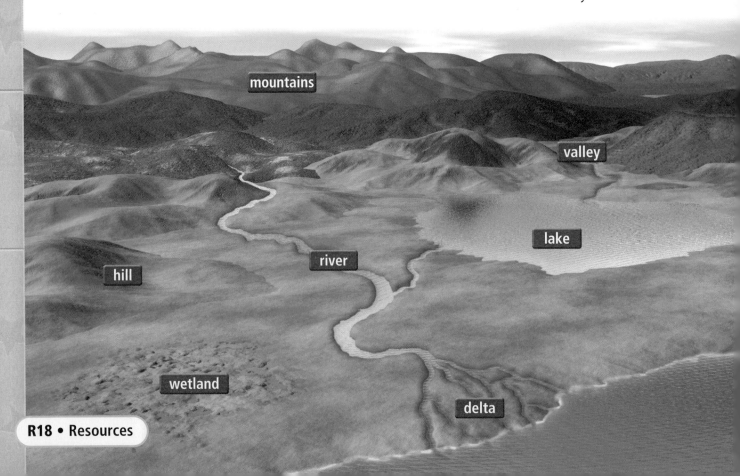

mountains

valley

lake

hill

river

wetland

delta

R18 • Resources

isthmus
a narrow piece of land connecting two larger land areas

lake
a large body of water surrounded by land

lowland
an area of low land surrounded by higher land

marsh
an area of soft wet grassland

mountain
a raised mass of land with steep slopes

ocean
a large body of salt water that covers much of Earth's surface

peninsula
a strip of land surrounded by water on three sides

plain
a large area of flat land

plateau
a high, flat area of land

pond
a body of water smaller than a lake

port
a sheltered part of a lake or ocean where ships can dock

prairie
a flat area of grassland with few trees

river
a body of water that flows from a high area to a lower area

river basin
an area that is drained by a river

swamp
a low area of wet land with trees and shrubs

tributary
a river or stream that flows into another river

upland
an area of land in a high elevation

valley
a low area of land between hills or mountains

wetland
an area that is soaked with water, such as a marsh or a swamp

Atlas

ALB. —Albania
AZER. —Azerbaijan
BOS. &
  HERZ. —Bosnia &
  Herzegovina
CEN. AFR. —Central African
  REP. Republic
DEM. REP. —Democratic Republic
  OF CONGO of Congo
FR. —France
IT. —Italy
LIECH. —Liechtenstein
LUX. —Luxembourg
NETH. —Netherlands
N.Z. —New Zealand
REP. OF —Republic of
  CONGO Congo
SERB. & —Serbia &
  MONT. Montenegro
SLOV. —Slovenia
SP. —Spain
SWITZ. —Switzerland
U.A.E. —United Arab Emirates
U.K. —United Kingdom
U.S. —United States

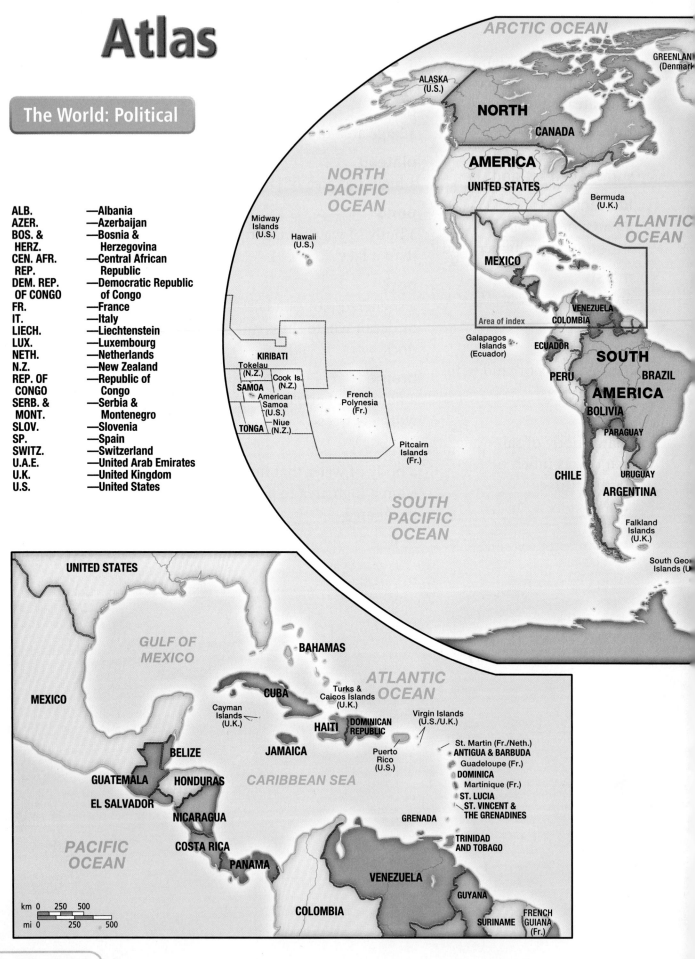

ARCTIC OCEAN
GREENLAND (Denmark)
ALASKA (U.S.)
NORTH
CANADA
AMERICA
UNITED STATES
Bermuda (U.K.)
ATLANTIC OCEAN
NORTH PACIFIC OCEAN
Midway Islands (U.S.)
Hawaii (U.S.)
MEXICO
Area of index
VENEZUELA
COLOMBIA
Galapagos Islands (Ecuador)
ECUADOR
SOUTH
KIRIBATI
Tokelau (N.Z.)
Cook Is. (N.Z.)
SAMOA
American Samoa (U.S.)
French Polynesia (Fr.)
PERU
BRAZIL
AMERICA
BOLIVIA
TONGA
Niue (N.Z.)
PARAGUAY
Pitcairn Islands (Fr.)
SOUTH PACIFIC OCEAN
CHILE
URUGUAY
ARGENTINA
Falkland Islands (U.K.)
South Geo. Islands (U

UNITED STATES
GULF OF MEXICO
BAHAMAS
ATLANTIC OCEAN
MEXICO
CUBA
Turks & Caicos Islands (U.K.)
Cayman Islands (U.K.)
HAITI
DOMINICAN REPUBLIC
Virgin Islands (U.S./U.K.)
St. Martin (Fr./Neth.)
ANTIGUA & BARBUDA
JAMAICA
Puerto Rico (U.S.)
Guadeloupe (Fr.)
BELIZE
DOMINICA
Martinique (Fr.)
GUATEMALA
HONDURAS
CARIBBEAN SEA
ST. LUCIA
ST. VINCENT & THE GRENADINES
EL SALVADOR
NICARAGUA
GRENADA
TRINIDAD AND TOBAGO
PACIFIC OCEAN
COSTA RICA
PANAMA
VENEZUELA
GUYANA
km 0   250   500
mi 0   250   500
COLOMBIA
SURINAME
FRENCH GUIANA (Fr.)

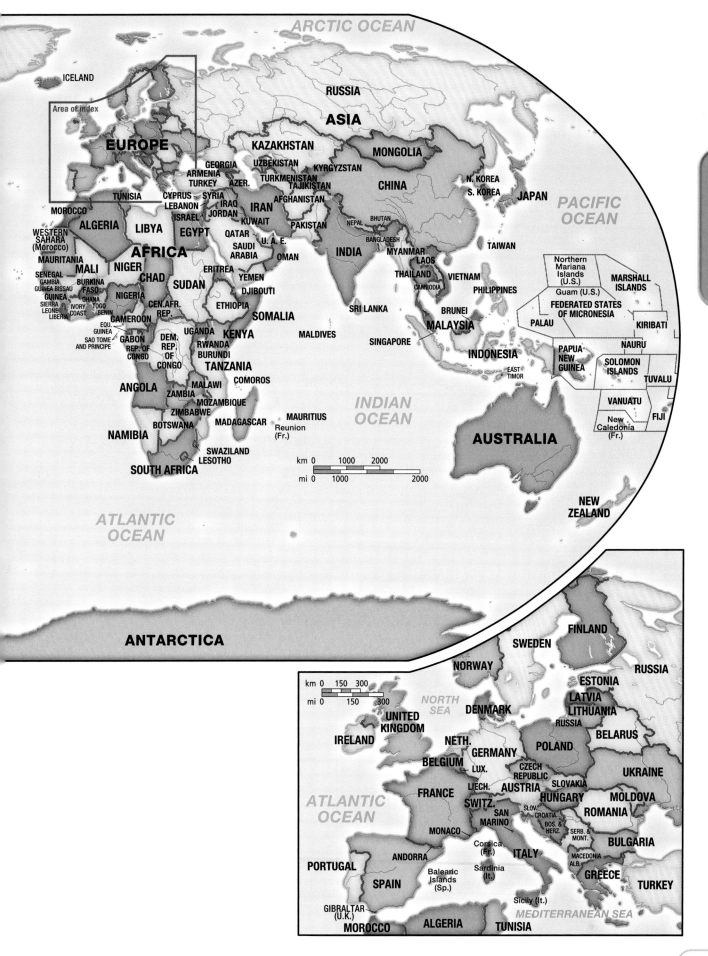

ARCTIC OCEAN

ICELAND

Area of index

EUROPE

RUSSIA

ASIA

KAZAKHSTAN

MONGOLIA

GEORGIA
UZBEKISTAN
KYRGYZSTAN
ARMENIA
TURKEY
AZER.
TURKMENISTAN
TAJIKISTAN
CYPRUS
SYRIA
IRAQ
AFGHANISTAN
LEBANON
JORDAN
IRAN
ISRAEL
KUWAIT
PAKISTAN

CHINA

N. KOREA
S. KOREA

JAPAN

PACIFIC
OCEAN

TUNISIA

MOROCCO
ALGERIA
LIBYA
EGYPT
QATAR
U. A. E.
SAUDI
ARABIA
OMAN

AFRICA

WESTERN
SAHARA
(Morocco)

MAURITANIA
MALI
NIGER
CHAD
SUDAN
ERITREA
YEMEN
DJIBOUTI

NEPAL
BHUTAN
BANGLADESH

INDIA

MYANMAR
LAOS

TAIWAN

Northern
Mariana
Islands
(U.S.)
Guam (U.S.)

MARSHALL
ISLANDS

SENEGAL
GAMBIA
GUINEA BISSAU
GUINEA
SIERRA
LEONE
LIBERIA
BURKINA
FASO
GHANA
IVORY
COAST
TOGO
BENIN
NIGERIA
CEN.AFR.
REP.
ETHIOPIA

SOMALIA

THAILAND
VIETNAM
CAMBODIA
PHILIPPINES
SRI LANKA
BRUNEI
MALAYSIA

FEDERATED STATES
OF MICRONESIA
PALAU
KIRIBATI

EQU.
GUINEA
SAO TOME
AND PRINCIPE
CAMEROON
GABON
REP. OF
CONGO
DEM.
REP.
OF
CONGO
UGANDA
RWANDA
BURUNDI
KENYA

MALDIVES

SINGAPORE

INDONESIA
EAST
TIMOR

NAURU

PAPUA
NEW
GUINEA
SOLOMON
ISLANDS

TUVALU

TANZANIA

INDIAN
OCEAN

ANGOLA
ZAMBIA
MALAWI
MOZAMBIQUE
ZIMBABWE
BOTSWANA
MADAGASCAR
COMOROS

MAURITIUS
Reunion
(Fr.)

VANUATU

New
Caledonia
(Fr.)

FIJI

NAMIBIA

km 0   1000   2000
mi 0   1000   2000

AUSTRALIA

SOUTH AFRICA
SWAZILAND
LESOTHO

ATLANTIC
OCEAN

NEW
ZEALAND

ANTARCTICA

FINLAND
SWEDEN
NORWAY
RUSSIA
ESTONIA
LATVIA
LITHUANIA
RUSSIA
BELARUS

km 0 150 300
mi 0   150   300

NORTH
SEA
DENMARK

UNITED
KINGDOM
IRELAND
NETH.
GERMANY
BELGIUM
LUX.
POLAND
CZECH
REPUBLIC
SLOVAKIA
UKRAINE
LIECH.
AUSTRIA
HUNGARY
MOLDOVA

ATLANTIC
OCEAN

FRANCE
SWITZ.
SAN
MARINO
SLOV.
CROATIA
BOS. &
HERZ.
ROMANIA

MONACO
SERB. &
MONT.
BULGARIA

Corsica
(Fr.)
MACEDONIA
ALB.

PORTUGAL
ANDORRA
Sardinia
(It.)
ITALY
GREECE
TURKEY

Balearic
Islands
(Sp.)

SPAIN

GIBRALTAR
(U.K.)

Sicily (It.)

MEDITERRANEAN SEA

MOROCCO
ALGERIA
TUNISIA

The World: Physical

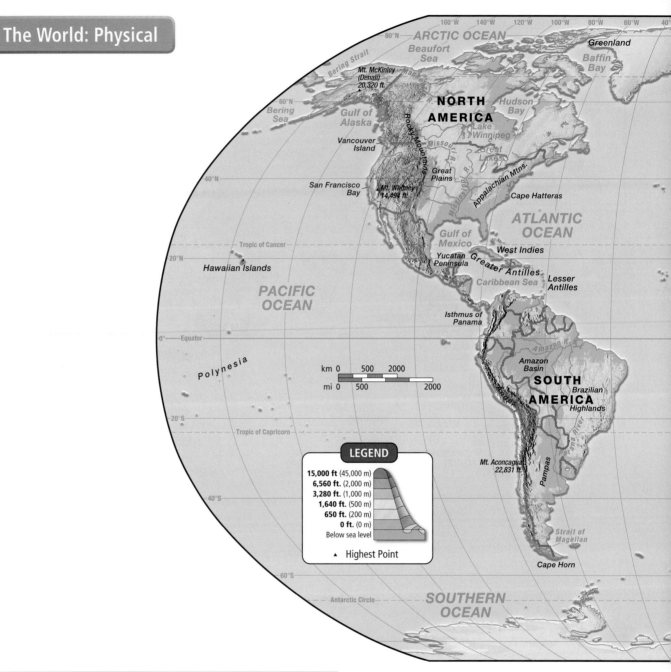

ARCTIC OCEAN
160°W 140°W 120°W 100°W 80°W 60°W 40°W
80°N
Beaufort Sea
Greenland
Bering Strait
Mt. McKinley (Denali) 20,320 ft.
NORTH AMERICA
Hudson Bay
Baffin Bay
60°N
Bering Sea
Gulf of Alaska
Rocky Mountains
Missouri R.
Lake Winnipeg
Great Lakes
Vancouver Island
San Francisco Bay
Mt. Whitney 14,494 ft.
Great Plains
Appalachian Mtns.
Cape Hatteras
40°N
ATLANTIC OCEAN
Tropic of Cancer
20°N
Gulf of Mexico
West Indies
Yucatan Peninsula
Greater Antilles
Caribbean Sea
Lesser Antilles
Hawaiian Islands
PACIFIC OCEAN
Isthmus of Panama
0° Equator
Polynesia
Amazon R.
Amazon Basin
SOUTH AMERICA
Brazilian Highlands

km 0 500 2000
mi 0 500 2000

20°S Tropic of Capricorn
Mt. Aconcagua 22,831 ft.
Pampas

LEGEND

15,000 ft. (45,000 m)
6,560 ft. (2,000 m)
3,280 ft. (1,000 m)
1,640 ft. (500 m)
650 ft. (200 m)
0 ft. (0 m)
Below sea level

▲ Highest Point

40°S
Strait of Magellan
Cape Horn
60°S
Antarctic Circle
SOUTHERN OCEAN

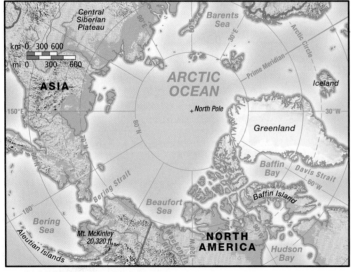

Central Siberian Plateau
Barents Sea
90°E
Arctic Circle
km 0 300 600
mi 0 300 600
ASIA
Prime Meridian
30°E
Iceland
ARCTIC OCEAN
150°E
60°N
+ North Pole
30°W
Greenland
180°
Bering Strait
Baffin Bay
Davis Strait
60°W
Bering Sea
Beaufort Sea
Baffin Island
Aleutian Islands
Mt. McKinley 20,320 ft.
NORTH AMERICA
Hudson Bay

ARCTIC OCEAN 80°N

Barents
Sea

Central
Siberian
Plateau

Iceland

EUROPE

ASIA

Sea of
Okhotsk

Kamchatka
Peninsula

60°N

Northern European Plain

Ural Mountains

Ob River

Volga River

Lake
Baikal

Amur River

Mt. Elbrus
18,510 ft.

Aral
Sea

Gobi Desert

40°N

Alps

Pyrenees

Caucasus
Mountains

Black Sea

Sea
of
Japan

Atlas Mtns.

Mediterranean Sea

Plateau
of Tibet

PACIFIC
OCEAN

SAHARA

Himalaya Mountains

Mt. Everest
29,035 ft.

East
China
Sea

Tropic of Cancer

SAHEL

Arabian
Sea

Bay of
Bengal

South
China
Sea

20°N

AFRICA

Philippine Islands

Micronesia

Nile River

Congo River

Lake
Victoria

Sumatra

Borneo

Equator 0°

Mt. Kilimanjaro
9,340 ft.

INDIAN
OCEAN

Strait of
Sunda

Java

New Guinea

Melanesia

Great
Rift
Valley

Madagascar

Coral
Sea

Prime Meridian

Kalahari
Desert

Great
Sandy
Desert

Tropic of Capricorn

20°S

ATLANTIC
OCEAN

AUSTRALIA

Nullarbor
Plain

Darling River

Tasman
Sea

Cape of
Good Hope

Mt. Kosciusko
7,310 ft.

North Island

South Island

60°S

Antarctic Circle

ANTARCTICA

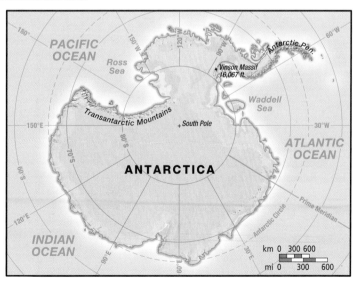

180°

PACIFIC
OCEAN

150°W

120°W

60°W

Ross
Sea

90°W

Antarctic Pen.

Vinson Massif
16,067 ft.

Transantarctic Mountains

South Pole

Waddell
Sea

150°E

80°S

30°W

ATLANTIC
OCEAN

60°E

70°S

ANTARCTICA

Prime Meridian

120°E

90°E

Antarctic Circle

30°E

INDIAN
OCEAN

60°E

km 0 300 600

mi 0   300   600

Western Hemisphere: Political

ARCTIC
OCEAN

Beaufort
Sea

140°W

GREENLAND
(DENMARK)

60°W

40°W

Alaska
(U.S.)

60°N

Hudson
Bay

Labrador
Sea

60°N

CANADA

Great
Lakes

Ottawa ⊛

40°N

Great
Salt
Lake

UNITED STATES

Washington, D.C. ⊛

40°N

ATLANTIC
OCEAN

Gulf of
Mexico

BAHAMAS

Tropic of Cancer

Havana

20°N

Hawaii (U.S.)

MEXICO

CUBA

HAITI

Mexico City ⊛

Kingston

DOMINICAN REPUBLIC

BELIZE

U.S. VIRGIN ISLANDS

GUATEMALA

Belmopan

Santo

ST. KITTS AND NEVIS

JAMAICA

Domingo

Guatemala City

ST. LUCIA

EL SALVADOR

Tegucigalpa

Port-Au-

BARBADOS

San Salvador

Managua

Prince

GRENADA

PACIFIC
OCEAN

HONDURAS

San José

Panama

Caracas

NICARAGUA

City

Georgetown

Paramaribo

COSTA RICA

VENEZUELA

Cayenne

PANAMA

Bogota

FRENCH GUIANA

COLOMBIA

SURINAME

(FRANCE)

0°

Equator

Galápagos Is.
(Ecuador)

ECUADOR

Quito ⊛

GUYANA

0°

BRAZIL

French Polynesia
(France)

Lima ⊛

PERU

Brasilia

La Paz ⊛

BOLIVIA

Sucre

20°S

PARAGUAY

Tropic of Capricorn

CHILE

Asunción ⊛

URUGUAY

Santiago ⊛

Buenos Aires ⊛

Montevideo

N

ARGENTINA

W   E

S

40°S

Falkland Islands
(U.K.)

LEGEND

⊛   National capital

South Georgia
(U.K.)

——   National border

km 0   500   1000

mi 0   500   1000

60°S

140°W   120°W   100°W   80°W   60°W   40°W

Western Hemisphere: Physical

160°W   140°W   40°W

80°N   80°N

ARCTIC
OCEAN   GREENLAND

Beaufort
Sea   Baffin
Bay

Bering
Strait

Yukon R.   Mackenzie R.   Davis
Strait

Mt. McKinley (Denali)
20,320 ft.
(6,194 m)   Hudson   Labrador
                                             Bay   Sea

60°N   60°N

Bering   Gulf of   CANADIAN SHIELD
Sea   Alaska

                ROCKY MOUNTAINS   NORTH AMERICA

                Coast Mountains   Great
                                             Lakes   APPALACHIAN MOUNTAINS

                Coast Ranges   Missouri R.

40°N   Range   GREAT   40°N
                and Basin   PLAINS   Coastal Plain
                Death Valley
                -282 ft.   Mississippi R.
                (-86 m)
Mt. Whitney   ATLANTIC
14,495 ft.   OCEAN
(4,418 m)   Rio Grande

                             Gulf of
                             Mexico   Bahamas
Tropic of Cancer   Cuba   Hispaniola
20°N   Hawaiian   20°N
            Islands   Puerto Rico

                             Caribbean
                             Sea
PACIFIC   Lake
OCEAN   Nicaragua   Lake
                                                     Maracaibo

Line
Islands   Galápagos
                             Islands
0°   Equator   AMAZON   Amazon R.   0°
                                                 BASIN

Marquesas
                                                      SOUTH
                                                      AMERICA
Society
Islands
Cook
Islands   Atacama
20°S   Tropic of Capricorn   Desert   20°S

                                          Mt. Aconcagua
                         N   22,834 ft.
                    W ⊕ E   (6,960 m)
                         S   Rio de la Plata

LEGEND
15,000 ft. (45,000 m)   + Valdés Peninsula
6,560 ft. (2,000 m)   -131 ft.
3,280 ft. (1,000 m)   (-40 m)
1,610 ft. (500 m)
650 ft. (200 m)   Falkland
0 ft. (0 m)   Islands
Below sea level
                                                              South
▲ Highest Point   Georgia

km 0   500 1000
mi 0   500 1000   Strait of
                          Magellan

40°S   40°S

60°S   60°S

160°W   140°W   120°W   100°W   80°W   60°W   40°W

R25

United States: Political

ARCTIC OCEAN

RUSSIA

ALASKA

CANADA

Yukon River

Fairbanks

Anchorage

Juneau

PACIFIC OCEAN

Aleutian Islands

km 0 250 500
mi 0 250 500

N
W E
S

WASHINGTON
Seattle
★ Olympia
Portland
Columbia R.
★ Salem

OREGON

IDAHO
★ Boise
Pocatello
Snake River

MONTANA
Helena ★
Billings

WYOMING
Casper
Cheyenne ★

Reno
★ Carson City
Sacramento ★
San Francisco

Salt Lake City ★
Provo
UTAH

Colorado River

COLORADO
Denver ★
Colorado Springs
Pueblo

NEVADA

CALIFORNIA
Las Vegas

Los Angeles

San Diego

PACIFIC OCEAN

ARIZONA
★ Phoenix

Santa Fe ★
Albuquerque

NEW MEXICO

Tucson

El Paso

Rio Grande

LEGEND
⊛ National capital
★ State capital
• Major city
— National boundary
— State boundary

Gulf of California

MEXICO

Kauai
Niihau
Oahu
Honolulu
Kailua
Molokai
Lanai
Kahoolawe
Maui
HAWAII

Hilo
Hawaii

PACIFIC OCEAN

km 0 50 100
mi 0 50 100

CANADA

St. Lawrence River

NEW HAMPSHIRE
VERMONT
MAINE

NORTH
DAKOTA
★ Bismarck   • Fargo

MINNESOTA

Lake Superior

SOUTH
DAKOTA
Pierre ★

• Sioux Falls

St. Paul ★
Minneapolis •

WISCONSIN

Madison ★

Lake Michigan

MICHIGAN
Grand
Rapids •

Lake Huron

• Detroit

Lake Erie

L. Ontario
• Rochester
• Buffalo

Augusta ★
Montpelier ★   • Portland
Burlington •   • Concord
                    • Manchester
NEW   ★ Boston
YORK   MASSACHUSETTS
Albany ★ • Providence
Hartford ★ RHODE ISLAND
New Haven • CONNECTICUT

IOWA

NEBRASKA

Missouri R.

Cedar Rapids •

Omaha •   • Des Moines
Lincoln ★

Milwaukee • Lansing ★

Chicago •

ILLINOIS
Springfield ★

Indianapolis
★

INDIANA

Cleveland •

OHIO
Columbus ★

Cincinnati •

PENNSYLVANIA Newark • • New York
Harrisburg ★   ★ Trenton
Pittsburgh •   • Philadelphia
                  NEW JERSEY
Baltimore • • Dover DELAWARE
⊛ Annapolis
  Washington, D.C.
              MARYLAND

KANSAS
Kansas City •
Topeka ★

Kansas City •
Jefferson City ★

MISSOURI

• St. Louis
Louisville •

WEST
VIRGINIA
Charleston ★

Richmond ★

Ohio R.

KENTUCKY
Frankfort ★

VIRGINIA
• Norfolk

OKLAHOMA
• Tulsa
Oklahoma ★
City

Fort Smith •

ARKANSAS
Little ★
Rock

Mississippi River

★ Nashville
• Memphis

TENNESSEE

Birmingham •

Greensboro •
• Raleigh ★

NORTH
CAROLINA

Columbia
★ SOUTH
CAROLINA

• Dallas

TEXAS

Austin ★
• Houston
• San Antonio

LOUISIANA

Jackson
★

MISSISSIPPI

Montgomery
★

• Atlanta

GEORGIA

Savannah •

• Charleston

ALABAMA

Baton Rouge ★
• New Orleans

• Mobile

Tallahassee ★

• Jacksonville

ATLANTIC
OCEAN

Gulf of Mexico

FLORIDA
• Tampa

• Miami

BAHAMAS

CUBA

km 0 100 200 300 400 500
mi 0   100   200   300   400   500

United States: Physical

ARCTIC OCEAN

RUSSIA

Brooks Range

CANADA

Bering Strait

Yukon River

Mt. McKinley
(Denali)
20,320 ft.

Alaska Range

Bering
Sea

Gulf of
Alaska

Aleutian
Islands

Kodiak Is.

km 0   250   500
mi 0   250   500

N
W   E
S

PACIFIC
OCEAN

San Francisco
Bay

Channel Islands

LEGEND

15,000 ft. (45,000 m)
6,560 ft. (2,000 m)
3,280 ft. (1,000 m)
1,640 ft. (500 m)
650 ft. (200 m)
0 ft. (0 m)
Below sea level

▲ Highest Point

Kauai
Niihau
Oahu
Molokai
Lanai   Maui
Kahoolawe
Hawaii
Mauna Kea
13,796 ft.
Mauna Loa
13,678 ft.

PACIFIC OCEAN

km 0   50   100
mi 0   50   100

Mt. Rainer
14,410 ft.

COAST RANGE

CASCADE RANGE

COLUMBIA PLATEAU

Mt. Hood
11,239 ft.

Columbia River

BITTERROOT RANGE

Snake River

Missouri River

Yellowstone River

ROCKY MOUNTAINS

BIGHORN MTNS.

GREAT

Black
Hills

Badlands

Mt. Shasta
14,162 ft.

Sacramento River

SIERRA NEVADA

CENTRAL VALLEY

San Joaquin River

BASIN
AND
RANGE

WASATCH RANGE

Mt. Whitney
14,494 ft.

Death Valley
282 ft. below sea level

Mojave
Desert

Grand
Canyon

Painted
Desert

Colorado
Plateau

Green River

Colorado River

Pikes Peak
14,110 ft.

PLAINS

SANGRE DE CRISTO MTNS.

Llano
Estacado

CONTINENTAL DIVIDE

Sonoran
Desert

Gila River

Gulf of California

MEXICO

Rio Grande

Pecos River

Edwards
Plateau

CANADA

Mesabi Range

Lake Superior

Lake Michigan

Lake Huron

St. Lawrence River

Mt. Washington 6,288 ft.

White Mtns.

Adirondack Mountains

L. Ontario

Connecticut River

Lake Erie

ALLEGHENY PLATEAU

APPALACHIAN MOUNTAINS

Catskill Mtns.

Hudson River

Nantucket

Martha's Vineyard

Long Island

Delaware River

Susquehanna River

Delaware Bay

Chesapeake Bay

Sand Hills

Missouri River

Des Moines River

Mississippi River

CENTRAL PLAINS

Platte River

Ohio R.

Wabash River

Mississippi River

Tennessee R.

Mt. Mitchell 6,684 ft.

Cumberland Plateau

BLUE RIDGE MOUNTAINS

FALL LINE

ATLANTIC COASTAL PLAIN

OZARK PLATEAU

Arkansas River

OUACHITA MOUNTAINS

Red River

Savannah River

Oconee R.

Altamaha R.

ATLANTIC OCEAN

Sabine River

Colorado River

Brazos River

Tombigbee R.

Pearl River

Alabama R.

Chattahoochee River

GULF COASTAL PLAIN

Mobile Bay

Pensacola Bay

Galveston Bay

Tampa Bay

Gulf of Mexico

Everglades

BAHAMAS

Florida Keys

| km | 0 | 100 | 200 | 300 | 400 | 500 |
| mi | 0 | | 100 | 200 | 300 | 400 | 500 |

CUBA

Illinois: Political

WISCONSIN

Lake Michigan

IOWA

IOWA

MISSOURI

INDIANA

KENTUCKY

Galena
JO DAVIESS
STEPHENSON
Freeport
WINNEBAGO
Rockford
BOONE
Belvidere
McHENRY
Woodstock
LAKE
Waukegan

Mt. Carroll
CARROLL
OGLE
Oregon
DE KALB
KANE
Sycamore
Geneva
DU PAGE
Wheaton
COOK
Chicago

Morrison
WHITESIDE
Dixon
LEE
KENDALL
Yorkville
WILL
Joliet
Morris
GRUNDY
KANKAKEE

Rock Island
ROCK ISLAND
HENRY
Cambridge
BUREAU
Princeton
LA SALLE
Ottawa
Hennepin
PUTNAM
Kankakee

MERCER
Aledo
STARK
Toulon
KNOX
MARSHALL
Lacon
LIVINGSTON
Pontiac
IROQUOIS
Watseka

Oquawka
HENDERSON
Galesburg
Monmouth
WARREN
PEORIA
Peoria
WOODFORD
Eureka
McLEAN
Bloomington
FORD
Paxton
VERMILION

McDONOUGH
FULTON
Lewistown
Pekin
TAZEWELL
CHAMPAIGN
Urbana
Danville

Carthage
HANCOCK
Macomb
MASON
Havana
LOGAN
Lincoln
DE WITT
Clinton
PIATT
Monticello

SCHUYLER
Rushville
ADAMS
CASS
MENARD
Petersburg
Virginia
MACON
Decatur
Tuscola
DOUGLAS
EDGAR
Paris

Quincy
Mt. Sterling
BROWN
Jacksonville
SCOTT
MORGAN
SANGAMON
Springfield
MOULTRIE
Sullivan
COLES
Charleston

PIKE
Pittsfield
Winchester
GREENE
Carrollton
MACOUPIN
Taylorville
CHRISTIAN
SHELBY
Shelbyville
CUMBERLAND
Toledo
CLARK
Marshall

CALHOUN
Hardin
Jerseyville
JERSEY
Carlinville
MONTGOMERY
Hillsboro
FAYETTE
Effingham
EFFINGHAM
JASPER
Newton
CRAWFORD
Robinson

MADISON
Edwardsville
BOND
Greenville
Vandalia
MARION
Salem
CLAY
Louisville
RICHLAND
Olney
LAWRENCE
Lawrenceville

Belleville
ST CLAIR
Carlyle
CLINTON
WAYNE
Fairfield
EDWARDS
Albion
WABASH
Mt. Carmel

Waterloo
MONROE
Nashville
WASHINGTON
JEFFERSON
Mt. Vernon
McLeansboro
WHITE
Carmi

RANDOLPH
Pinckneyville
PERRY
Benton
FRANKLIN
HAMILTON
SALINE
GALLATIN

Chester
JACKSON
Murphysboro
WILLIAMSON
Marion
Harrisburg
Shawneetown

UNION
Jonesboro
JOHNSON
Vienna
POPE
HARDIN
Golconda
Elizabethtown

PULASKI
ALEXANDER
MASSAC
Metropolis
Cairo
Mound City

LEGEND

★ State capital
◉ County seat
— State border
▨ County border
KNOX County name

km 0   25   50
mi 0   25   50

N W E S

Atlas

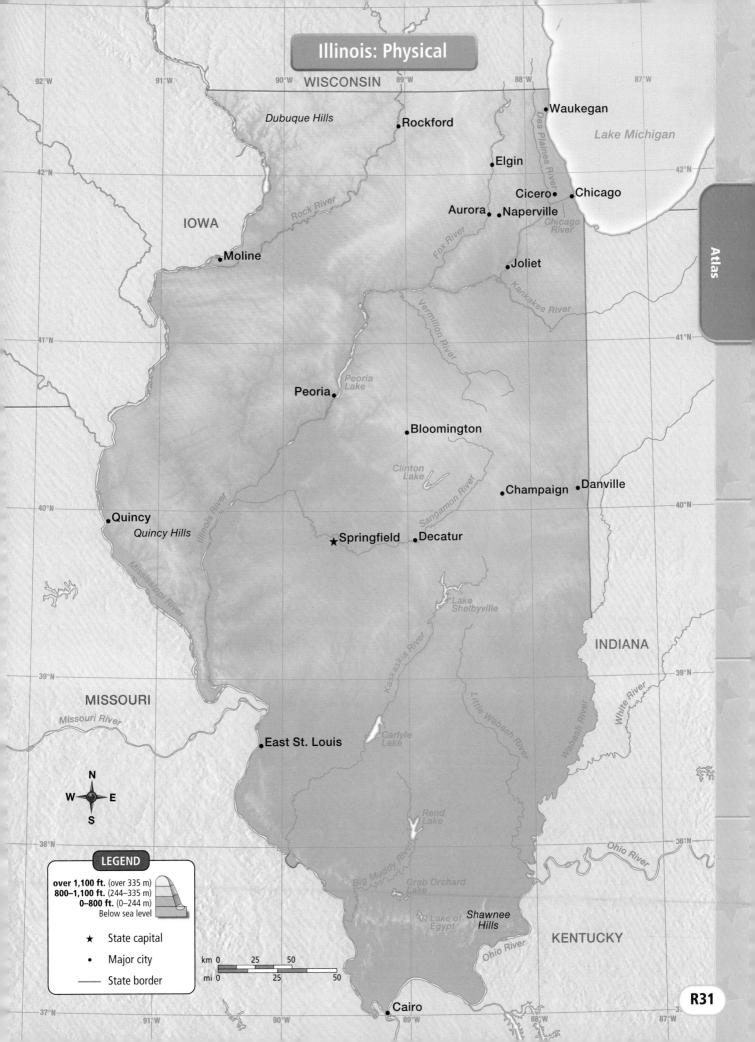

Illinois: Physical

WISCONSIN

Dubuque Hills

•Waukegan

Lake Michigan

•Rockford

•Elgin

Cicero• •Chicago

Aurora• •Naperville
Chicago River

•Joliet

IOWA

Rock River

Fox River

Des Plaines River

Kankakee River

•Moline

Vermilion River

•Peoria
Peoria Lake

•Bloomington

Clinton Lake

•Champaign •Danville

•Quincy
Quincy Hills

★Springfield •Decatur

Sangamon River

Illinois River

Lake Shelbyville

INDIANA

MISSOURI

Missouri River

Kaskaskia River

Little Wabash River

Wabash River

White River

•East St. Louis

Carlyle Lake

Rend Lake

Big Muddy River

Crab Orchard Lake

Lake of Egypt

Shawnee Hills

KENTUCKY

Ohio River

LEGEND

	over 1,100 ft. (over 335 m)
	800–1,100 ft. (244–335 m)
	0–800 ft. (0–244 m)
	Below sea level

★   State capital

•   Major city

—   State border

km 0   25   50
mi 0   25   50

•Cairo

Illinois: Precipitation

WISCONSIN
Lake Michigan
• Rockford
• Chicago
• Moline
• Joliet
ILLINOIS
IOWA
Peoria•
•Bloomington
Champaign
MISSOURI
★ Springfield
• East St. Louis
INDIANA
KENTUCKY
Cairo

LEGEND

Average Annual Precipitation
- More than 48 inches
- 44–48 inches
- 40–44 inches
- 36–40 inches
- Less than 36 inches

km 0 50 100
mi 0 50 100

Illinois: Temperature

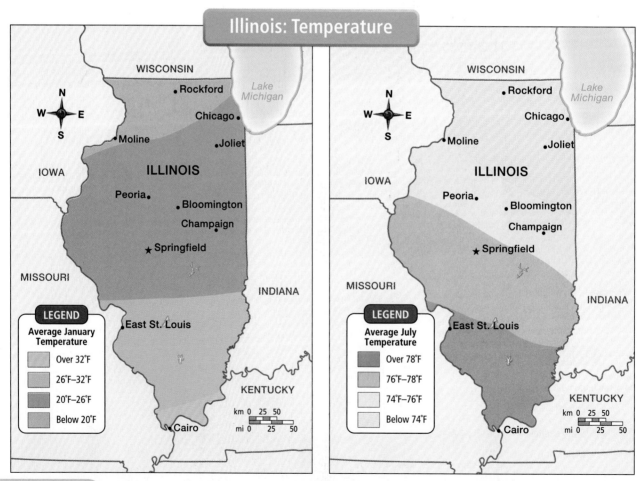

WISCONSIN
Lake Michigan
• Rockford
Chicago•
•Moline
•Joliet
ILLINOIS
IOWA
Peoria•
•Bloomington
Champaign
★ Springfield
MISSOURI
• East St. Louis
INDIANA
KENTUCKY
Cairo

LEGEND

Average January Temperature
- Over 32°F
- 26°F–32°F
- 20°F–26°F
- Below 20°F

km 0 25 50
mi 0 25 50

WISCONSIN
Lake Michigan
• Rockford
Chicago•
•Moline
•Joliet
ILLINOIS
IOWA
Peoria•
•Bloomington
Champaign
★ Springfield
MISSOURI
• East St. Louis
INDIANA
KENTUCKY
Cairo

LEGEND

Average July Temperature
- Over 78°F
- 76°F–78°F
- 74°F–76°F
- Below 74°F

km 0 25 50
mi 0 25 50

Atlas

Illinois: Resources and Products

WISCONSIN

Rockford

Lake Michigan

Chicago

Moline

Joliet

IOWA

ILLINOIS

Peoria

Bloomington

Champaign

Springfield

LEGEND

- Machinery
- Electronics
- Steel
- Sand, stone
- Fruit
- Grains
- Soybeans
- Beef
- Pork
- Poultry

East St. Louis

INDIANA

MISSOURI

KENTUCKY

Cairo

km 0 50 100
mi 0 50 100

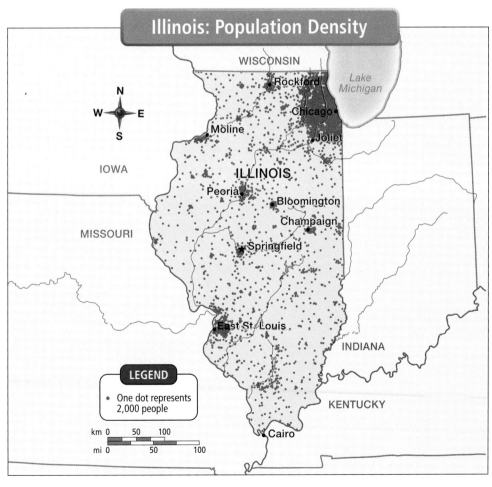

Illinois: Population Density

WISCONSIN

Rockford

Lake Michigan

Chicago

Moline

Joliet

IOWA

ILLINOIS

Peoria

Bloomington

Champaign

Springfield

MISSOURI

East St. Louis

INDIANA

LEGEND

- One dot represents 2,000 people

KENTUCKY

Cairo

km 0 50 100
mi 0 50 100

Gazetteer

 A

Africa 2nd largest continent (10°N, 22°E) p. R21

Algonquin City in Illinois (42°N, 88°W) page 1

Alton City in Illinois (39°N, 90°W) page 110

Antarctica Continent surrounding the South Pole, mostly covered in ice (90°S) pp. R20–R21

Appalachian Mountains Range stretching from Canada to Alabama (40°N, 78°W) page 54

Arkansas 25th state; capital: Little Rock (34°N, 92°W) page 39

Asia Largest continent in the world (50°N, 100°E) page 12

Atlantic Ocean Extends from the Arctic to Antarctic; east of the United States (5°S, 25°W) page 7

Australia Smallest continent (30°S, 151°E) p. R21

 B

Balkans Group of countries on the Balkan peninsula in southeast Europe (40°N, 23°E) page 253

Baltimore City in Maryland (39°N, 76°W) page 112

Belleville City in Illinois (38°N, 90°W) page 110

Big Muddy River River in southern Illinois (38°N, 89°W) page 7

Boston Capital of Massachusetts (42°N, 71°W) page 54

Boston Harbor Part of Massachusetts Bay; site of the Boston Tea Party (42°N, 71°W) page 65

 C

Cahokia Village in Illinois (38°N, 90°W) page 82

Cahokia Mounds Site of the largest Mississippian era city, Cahokia (38°N, 90°W) page 15

Cairo City in Illinois; Alexander county seat (37°N, 89°W) page 7

Camp Dubois Point of departure from Illinois by Lewis and Clark Expedition (39°N, 90°W) page 85

Camp Grant Training camp in Illinois; site where medical workers were trained during World War II, 1940–1945 (42°N, 89°W) page 166

Camp Robert Smalls Naval training station where African Americans were trained during World War II (42°W, 88°W) page 166

Canada Country bordering United States on north (50°N, 100°W) page 7

Carmi City in Illinois; White county seat (38°N, 88°W) page 110

Central Lowland Prairie region that covers most of Illinois, page 8

Chicago Large city in Illinois; founded by Jean Baptiste Point du Sable (42°N, 87°W) page 81

Chicago River River on the western shore of Lake Michigan along northeastern Illinois (42°N, 87°W) page 7

China Country in East Asia (37°N, 93°E) page 169

Cleveland City in Ohio (41°N, 81°W) page 219

Coastal Plain Flood plain caused by the meeting of the Mississippi River and the Ohio River (37°N, 89°W) page 8

Cumberland City in Maryland (39°N, 78°W) page 112

 D

Decatur Town in Illinois; Macon county seat (40°N, 89°W) page 137

DeKalb City in Illinois; site of Joseph Glidden and Isaac Ellwood's factory (42°N, 88°W) page 154

Des Plaines River River starts in Wisconsin and joins the Kankakee River in Illinois (42°N, 88°W) page 40

Detroit City in eastern Michigan, formerly Fort Detroit; Wayne county seat (42°N, 83°W) page 90

Dickson Mounds American Indian burial mounds in west-central Illinois (40°N, 90°W) page 19

East St. Louis City in Illinois (38°N, 90°W) page 153

Edwardsville City in Illinois; Madison county seat (38°N, 90°W) page 110

England Country in Western Europe; part of the United Kingdom (52°N, 2°W) page 38

Erie Canal Human-made waterway connecting Albany to Buffalo, New York, completed in 1825 (43°N, 76°W) page 109

Europe 6th largest continent, located between the Atlantic Ocean and Asia (50°N, 15°E) page 12

Floyd's Grave Encampment in Iowa on Lewis and Clark's Expedition; named for Sergeant Charles Floyd (42°N, 96°W) page 85

Fort Clatsop Winter encampment of the Lewis and Clark Expedition (46°N, 124°W) page 84

Fort Crevecoeur French fort in Illinois (40°N, 89°W) page 40

Fort Dearborn Illinois settlement (42°N, 87°W) page 90

Fort de Chartres French fort in Illinois along the Mississippi River (38°N, 90°W) page 32

Fort Detroit British fort in present-day Michigan (42°N, 83°W) page 57

Fort Mandan Encampment in North Dakota for Lewis and Clark Expedition (46°N, 101°W) page 85

Fort Massac Fort in Illinois (37°N, 88°W) page 87

Fort St. Louis Important trading center along the Illinois River, 1682–1683 (41°N, 89°W) page 40

France Country in Western Europe; origin of many Illinois settlers (47°N, 1°E) page 24

Galena Town in Illinois; site of lead mines which encouraged state growth; Jo Daviess county seat (42°N, 90°W) page 109

Germany Country in Western Europe; capital: Berlin (51°N, 10°E) page 167

Gettysburg Site in Pennsylvania of Civil War battle, 1863; site of the Gettysburg Address, 1863 (40°N, 77°W) page 130

Great Falls Five large waterfalls in Montana (47°N, 111°W) page 85

Great Lakes Five freshwater lakes between the United States and Canada (45°N, 83°W) page 7

Great Lakes Naval Training Base Base in Illinois where Navy soldiers are trained (42°N, 88°W) page 166

Greenville Location of the signing of the Treaty of Greenville, 1795; Darke county seat (40°N, 84°W) page 81

Gulf of Mexico Body of water off the southern coast of the United States (25°N, 94°W) page 7

Hodgenville Town in Kentucky near the birthplace of Abraham Lincoln (37°N, 85°W) page 136

Harlem Airport Airfield in Illinois where African American pilots trained in World War II (42°N, 88°W) page 166

Illinois 21st state; capital: Springfield; formerly Illinois Territory, 1809 (40°N, 91°W) page 1

Illinois and Michigan Canal Human-made waterway that connects the Mississippi River and the Great Lakes (41°N, 88°W) page 112

Illinois River River in Illinois that flows southwest across Illinois to the Mississippi River (39°N, 90°W) page 7

Illinois Territory Land separated from Indiana Territory, 1809 (40°N, 91°W) page 82

Indiana 19th state; capital: Indianapolis (40°N, 87°W) page 3

Indiana Territory Land separated from Northwest Territory, 1800 (40°N, 87°W) page 82

Indianapolis Capital of Indiana (39°N, 86°W) page 226

Iowa 29th state: capital: Des Moines (41°N, 93°W) page 20

Iran Country in southwestern Asia; capital: Tehran (32°N, 53°E) page 169

Ireland Island in North Atlantic Ocean, divided between Republic of Ireland and Northern Ireland (53°N, 6°W) page 129

Italy Country in southern Europe; capital: Rome (44°N, 11°E) page 158

Japan Island country off east coast of Asia; capital: Tokyo (37°N, 134°E) page 167

Joliet City in Illinois; Will county seat (41°N, 88°W) page 154

Kansas 34th state; capital: Topeka (38°N, 98°W) page 3

Kansas City City in Missouri (39°N, 94°W) page 226

Kaskaskia Second European settlement in Illinois; capital of the Illinois Territory, 1809–1818; capital of Illinois, 1818–1820 (38°N, 90°W) page 39

Kaskaskia Island Island in the Mississippi River (38°N, 90°W) page 7

Kaskaskia River River in Illinois; joins the Mississippi River (40°N, 88°W) page 7

Kentucky 15th state; capital: Frankfort (38°N, 88°W) page 92

Kickapoo Town in Illinois (40°N, 89°W) page 1

Kingston City in Illinois (40°N, 89°W) page 154

Korea Peninsula in east Asia; today divided between North Korea and South Korea (39°N, 128°E) page 168

Kyoto City in Japan (35°N, 135°E) page 259

Lake Erie Smallest of the Great Lakes (42°N, 79°W) page 43

Lake Huron 3rd largest of the Great Lakes (44°N, 83°W) page 43

Lake Michigan 2nd largest of the Great Lakes; forms part of the northeast border of Illinois (43°N, 86°W) page 7

Lake Ontario 4th largest of the Great Lakes (43°N, 77°W) page 43

Lake Shelbyville Lake formed by damming the Kaskaskia River (39°N, 88°W) page 7

Lake Superior Largest of the Great Lakes (47°N, 89°W) page 43

Lemhi Pass Passage through the Rocky Mountains between Idaho and Montana used by Lewis and Clark (45°N, 113°W) page 84

Lerna City in Illinois (39°N, 88°W) page 139

Louisiana 18th state; capital: Baton Rouge (31°N, 93°W) page 40

Maryland 7th state; capital: Annapolis (39°N, 76°W) page 245

Marietta City in Ohio; formerly the capital of the Northwest Territory (39°N, 81°W) page 82

Mascoutah Town in Illinois (38°N, 89°W) page 1

Massachusetts 6th state; capital: Boston (42°N, 73°W) page 65

Mexico Country bordering the United States to the South; capital: Mexico City (24°N, 104°W) page 169

Michigan 26th state; capital: Lansing (46°N, 87°W) page 20

Midwest Region of in United States composed of Illinois, Indiana, Iowa, Kansas, Michigan, Minnesota, Missouri, Nebraska, North Dakota, Ohio, South Dakota, Wisconsin, page 218

Milwaukee City in Wisconsin (43°N, 88°W) page 219

Minneapolis City in Minnesota (45°N, 93°W) page 219

Minnesota 32nd state; capital: St. Paul (45°N, 93°W) page 154

Mississippi River Principal river of the United States and North America; runs south connecting Illinois to the Gulf of Mexico; forms the western border of Illinois (32°N, 92°W) page 3

Missouri 24th state; capital: Jefferson City (38°N, 94°W) page 20

Missouri River Major river in the United States (41°N, 96°W) page 84

Moline City in Illinois; site of John Deere's factory (41°N, 90°W) page 154

Montreal city in Canada; province: Quebec (46°N, 74°W) page 47

Murphysboro City in Illinois; Jackson county seat (37°N, 89°W) page 154

Nebraska 37th state; capital: Lincoln (42°N, 102°W) page 219

Neuse River River in North Carolina (35°N, 77°W) page 248

New Jersey 3rd state; capital: Trenton (41°N, 75°W) page 245

New Orleans City in Louisiana (30°N, 90°W) page 137

New Salem Town in Illinois (40°N, 90°W) page 137

New York 11th state; capital: Albany (43°N, 78°W) page 109

New York City Large city in New York State (41°N, 74°W) page 247

North America Northern continent in the Western Hemisphere (45°N, 100°W) page 12

North Dakota 39th state; capital: Bismarck (46°N, 100°W) page 219

Northwest Territory Land extending from the Ohio and Mississippi rivers to the Great Lakes (41°N, 85°W) page 81

Ohio 17th state; capital: Columbus (41°N, 83°W) page 20

Ohio River River that flows from Pennsylvania to Cairo, Illinois, where it joins the Mississippi River; forms the southern border of Illinois (37°N, 88°W) page 7

Ohio Valley Farming region west of the Appalachian Mountains (37°N, 88°W) page 46

Oklahoma 46th state; capital: Oklahoma City (36°N, 98°W) page 3

Ottawa City in Illinois; La Salle county seat (41°N, 89°W) page 1

Pacific Ocean Largest ocean; west of the United States (0°N, 170°W) page 12

Paris Capital of France (49°N, 2°E) page 47

Pennsylvania 2nd state; capital: Harrisburg (41°N, 78°W) page 7

Peoria City in Illinois; Peoria county seat (40°N, 89°W) page 40

Peoria Lake Lake along the Illinois River (40°N, 89°W) page 7

Philadelphia Large port city in Pennsylvania (40°N, 75°W) page 189

Poland Country in Eastern Europe; capital: Warsaw (52°N, 21°E) page 158

Pontiac City in Illinois; Livingston county seat (41°N, 88°W) page 1

Prairie du Roche French town in Illinois; county: Randolph (38°N, 90°W) page 41

Prophetstown Village in Indiana Territory; Tecumseh and Tenskwatawa lived and fought here (41°N, 90°W) page 89

Quebec Province in Canada; capital: Quebec (47°N, 71°W) page 47

Quincy City in Illinois; Adams county seat (40°N, 91°W) page 154

Rend Lake Lake in southern Illinois (38°N, 89°W) page 7

Rockford City in Illinois; Winnebago county seat (42°N, 89°W) page 154

Rock Island City in Illinois; site of Weyerhauser's factory (37°N, 89°W) page 154

Rock River River in northern Illinois; beginning in Wisconsin, the river runs southwest toward the Mississippi River (42°N, 89°W) page 7

Rocky Mountains Mountain range in the western United States (50°N, 114°W) page 218

Rwanda Country in Africa; capital: Kigali (2°S, 30°E) page 253

St. Anthony Falls Waterfall in Minnesota (45°N, 93°W) page 219

St. Clair First county in Illinois; Illinois county; county seat: Belleville (38°N, 90°W) page 82

St. Louis City in Missouri (90°N, 90°W) page 85

Scott Field Area near Belleville, Illinois where pilots and air force workers trained for World War II (38°N, 90°W) page 166

Seneca Town in Illinois; known during World War II as the "Prairie Shipyard" (41°N, 88°W) page 166

Shawnee Hills Range of hills in southern Illinois (37°N, 88°W) page 8

Gazetteer

Shawnee National Forest Forest in southern Illinois (37°N, 88°W) page 1

Shawneetown First town in Illinois, Gallatin county seat (37°N, 88°W) page 110

Skokie City in Illinois (42°N, 87°W) page 167

South America Southern continent of western hemisphere (10°S, 60°W) p. R20

South Carolina 8th state; capital: Columbia (34°N, 81°W) page 123

South Dakota 40th state; capital: Pierre (44°N, 100°W) page 84

Spain Country in Western Europe; capital: Madrid (40°N, 5°W) page 38

Springfield Capital of Illinois (39°N, 89°W) page 159

Tamaroa Town in Illinois (38°N, 89°W) page 1

Tampico City in Illinois; birthplace of President Ronald Reagan (41°N, 89°W) page 202

Tennessee 16th state; capital: Nashville (36°N, 88°W) page 108

Texas 28th state; capital: Austin (31°N, 101°W) page 3

Three Forks Three rivers converge to create headwaters of the Missouri River; stop on Lewis and Clark's Expedition; city in Montana (46°N, 111°W) page 84

Tippecanoe Battle site of William Henry Harrison and Tenskwatawa (40°N, 87°W) page 89

Traveler's Rest Lewis and Clark Expedition campsite in Montana (46°N, 114°W) page 84

United States Country in central and northwest North America (38°N, 110°W) page 67

Vandalia City in Illinois; former Illinois state capital (39°N, 89°W) page 101

Vietnam Country in Southeast Asia (18°N, 107°E) page 168

Vicksburg Site of Mississippi Civil War battle, 1863 (32°N, 91°W) page 130

Vincennes City in Indiana; site of a British fort captured during the American Revolution by George Rogers Clark (38°N, 87°W) page 66

Virginia 10th state; capital: Richmond; once claimed Illinois as a county (37°N, 81°W) page 80

Wabash River River that forms part of the eastern border of Illinois; flows into the Ohio River (37°N, 88°W) page 7

Wisconsin 30th state; capital: Madison (43°N, 89°W) page 20

Glossary

abolitionist (ab uh LIH shuhn ihst) someone who wants to end slavery. (p. 121)

adapt (uh DAPT) to change in order to live in a new environment. (p. 13)

agriculture (AG rih kuhl chur) farming. (p. 14)

ally (AL ly) a person or group that joins another to work for the same goal. (p. 46)

amendment (uh MEHND muhnt) a change, as in a document, such as a constitution. (p. 101)

archaeologist (AHR kee ahl uh jihst) a scientist who studies past human life. (p. 13)

Archaic Indians (ahr KAY ihk IHN dee uhnz) a group of American Indians that lived in North America between 10,000 and 3,000 years ago. (p. 13)

architecture (AHR kih tehk chur) the method and style of constructing a building. (p. 173)

article (AHR tih kuhl) a part or section of a document, such as a constitution. (p. 100)

artifact (AHR tuh fakt) an object made by people long ago. (p. 13)

bill (bihl) a written idea for a law. (p. 194)

border (BOHR dur) a line that shows the edge of a region that has the same government (p. 7)

boycott (BOY kaht) the refusal to buy, sell, or use certain goods or services. (p. 65)

budget (BUHJ iht) a plan for spending money. (p. 193)

canal (kuh NAL) a human-made waterway. (p. 109)

capital (KAP ih tuhl) the city in which a state or national government is located. (p. 99)

cause (kawz) an event or action that makes something else happen. (p. 62)

checks and balances (chehks uhnd BAL uhns ehz) a system that lets each branch of government limit the power of the other branches. (p. 187)

circle graph (SUR kuhl graf) a circle that is divided into sections to show how information is related. (p. 86)

citizen (SIHT ih zuhn) someone who is born in a country or who promises to be loyal to a country. (p. 184)

civic virtue (SIHV ihk VUR choo) the desire to do something for the common good. (p. 249)

civil rights (SIHV uhl ryts) basic rights that are protected by the government. (p. 168)

climate (KLY miht) the usual weather of a place over time. (p. 13)

colony (KAHL uh nee) land ruled by another country. (p. 38)

common good (KAHM uhn gud) the best interests of the whole population. (p. 184)

compass rose (KUHM puhs rohz) a part of a map that shows the cardinal and intermediate directions. (p. 19)

compromise (KAHM pruh myz) to reach an agreement. (p. 122)

Confederacy (kuhn FEHD ur uh see) the name for South Carolina, Mississippi, Florida, Alabama, Georgia, Louisiana, and Texas and later Arkansas, North Carolina, Virginia, and Tennessee when these states seceded from the Union. (p. 123)

confederation (kuhn fehd ur AY shuhn) a group united for a purpose. (p. 89)

conflict (KAHN flihkt) a disagreement between individuals or groups of people. (p. 250)

consequence (KAHN sih kwehns) something that happens as a result of a decision or an action. (p. 206)

conservatory (kuhn SUR vuh tawr ee) a place for growing and protecting plants. (p. 174)

constitution

constitution (kahn stih TOO shuhn) a plan for setting up and running a government. (p. 67)

consumer (kuhn SOO mur) someone who buys goods and services. (p. 226)

county (KOWN tee) a part of a state with its own government. (p. 80)

culture (KUHL chur) the way of life of a group of people. (p. 20)

delegate (DEHL ih giht) a person chosen to speak and act for others. (p. 99)

demand (dih MAND) the amount of a product that consumers will buy at a certain price. (p. 227)

democracy (dih MAHK ruh see) a government in which the people hold the power. (p. 184)

depression (dih PREHSH uhn) a period of time when many businesses fail, prices drop, and jobs are hard to find. (p. 165)

discrimination (dih skrihm uh NAY shuhn) unjust treatment of a group of people. (p. 159)

diversity (dih VUR sih tee) variety. (p. 169)

economy (ih KAHN uh mee) the way people choose to use resources to produce goods and services. (p. 120)

effect (ih FEHKT) an event or action that is the result of a cause. (p. 62)

election (ih LEHK shuhn) a way of choosing someone by voting. (p. 122)

elevated train (EHL uh vayt uhd trayn) a railway that runs above the ground on raised tracks. (p. 231)

emancipation (ih man suh PAY shuhn) the freeing of enslaved people. (p. 130)

entrepreneur (ahn truh pruh NUR) a person who takes risks to start a business. (p. 175)

environment (ehn VY ruhn muhnt) the water, land, and air that surrounds living things. (p. 6)

erosion (ih ROH zhuhn) the wearing away of earth's surface by water and wind. (p. 8)

executive branch (ihg ZEHK yuh tihv branch) the branch of government that suggests laws and carries out the laws made by Congress. (p. 187)

expedition (ehk spih DIHSH uhn) a journey with a special purpose. (p. 83)

exposition (ehk spuh ZIHSH uhn) a public show. (p. 173)

flood plain (FLUHD playn) flat, low land around a river that often floods. (p. 8)

glacier (GLAY shur) a large, slow-moving sheet of ice. (p. 6)

government (GUHV ur muhnt) an organization that makes laws and keeps order. (p. 45)

governor (GUHV ur nur) an official who leads a state or territorial government. (p. 82)

grain elevator (grayn EHL uh vay tur) a tall building used to load and store grain. (p. 113)

grange (graynj) a group of farmers who came together during the late 1800s to work for change. (p. 160)

harvest (HAHR vihst) to gather a crop. (p. 23)

heritage (HEHR ih tihj) traditions that are passed down from earlier generations. (p. 246)

history (HIHS tuh ree) a record of the events of the past that led to the present. (p. 21)

hunter-gatherer (HUHN tur GATH ur ur) person who obtains food by hunting, fishing, and gathering nuts, berries, and plants. (p. 13)

immigrant (IHM ih gruhnt) someone who moves to another country. (p. 158)

income tax (IHN kuhm taks) the amount of money each person pays for government services, depending on how much that person earns in a year. (p. 193)

independence (ihn dih PEHN duhns) freedom from rule by another country. (p. 65)

Glossary

industry (IHN duh stree) a group of businesses that provide certain goods or services. (p. 113)

innovation (ihn uh VAY shuhn) a new idea or a new way of doing something. (p. 172)

interdependence (ihn tur dih PEHN duhns) a relationship in which people depend on one another. (p. 245)

international law (ihn tur NASH uh nuhl law) a set of basic rules to which the United States and many other countries have agreed. (p. 253)

judicial branch (joo DIHSH uhl branch) the branch of government that decides the meaning of laws and whether the laws have been followed. (p. 187)

jury (JUR ee) a group of citizens who decide a case in court. (p. 201)

labor union (LAY bur YOON yuhn) an organization of workers that tries to improve pay and working conditions for its members. (p. 160)

legend (LEHJ uhnd) the part of a map that explains what different symbols on the map mean. (p. 19)

legislative branch (LEHJ ih slay tihv branch) the branch of government that makes laws. (p. 187)

levee (LEHV ee) a high river bank that stops a river from overflowing. (p. 219)

liberty (LIHB ur tee) freedom from control by others. (p. 186)

livestock (LYV stahk) animals that people raise on farms, especially animals raised to sell. (p. 153)

lock (lahk) a part of a waterway that is closed off by gates. (p. 219)

longhouse (LAWNG hows) a large house made from wood poles and covered with bark or reed matting. (p. 22)

mail-order catalog (MAYL awr dur KAT l awg) a book that lists goods that customers can order and receive by mail. (p. 155)

manufacturing (man yuh FAK chur ihng) making goods by hand or by machine in a factory. (p. 152)

market (MAHR kiht) a place where goods and services are bought and sold. (p. 153)

mass media (mas MEE dee uh) the businesses that provide entertainment and information. (p. 175)

mining (MY ning) taking resources from underground. (p. 154)

mission (MIHSH uhn) a place for teaching a religion to local people. (p. 39)

missionary (MIHSH uh nehr ee) a person who goes to another country to teach a religion. (p. 39)

moccasin (MAHK uh sihn) a type of leather shoe or slipper. (p. 24)

mound (mownd) a hill made from earth, stones, and other natural materials. (p. 14)

natural resource (NACH ur uhl REE sawrs) a material from nature, such as soil or water. (p. 156)

nongovernmental organization (NGO) (nahn guhv urn MEHN tuhl awr guh nih ZAY shuhn) a group that is not part of a national government but focuses on political, social, and cultural issues. (p. 254)

ordinance (AWR dn uhns) a law made by a government. (p. 81)

Paleo-Indians (PAY lee oh IHN dee uhnz) a group of American Indians that lived in North America about 12,000 years ago. (p. 13)

point of view (point uhv vyoo) the way a person thinks about an issue, an event, or another person. (p. 126)

population (pahp yuh LAY shuhn) the people who live in an area. (p. 14)

pottery (PAHT uh ree) jars, bowls, and pots made from clay. (p. 14)

prairie (PRAYR ee) a flat or rolling grassland. (p. 8)

primary source (PRY mehr ee sawrs) an account of an event by a person who witnessed it. (p. 178)

proclamation (prahk luh MAY shuhn) an official public statement. (p. 58)

prosperity (prah SPEHR ih tee) wealth and success. (p. 246)

public service (PUHB lihk SUR vihs) something provided or done for the good of the community. (p. 193)

rebellion (rih BEHL yuhn) a fight against a government. (p. 57)

Reconstruction (ree kuhn STRUHK shuhn) the time when the former Confederate states rejoined the Union. (p. 131)

reform (rih FAWRM) a change that makes something better. (p. 160)

regiment (REHJ uh muhnt) a group of soldiers who train and serve together. (p. 129)

region (REE jehn) an area with features in common, such as landforms and bodies of water. (p. 8)

regulate (REHG yuh layt) to oversee. (p. 160)

resource (REE sawrs) something that can be used. (p. 24)

retail (REE tayl) the sale of goods to a customer. (p. 155)

rights (rytz) freedoms that are protected by a government's laws. (p. 161)

rodent (ROHD nt) a small mammal with special teeth for gnawing. (p. 221)

route (root) a way of going from one place to another. (p. 106)

rule of law (rool uhv law) the idea that laws should apply to everyone in the same way. (p. 186)

rural (ROOR uhl) in a country area with few people. (p. 154)

sales tax (SAYLZ taks) the extra money that people pay to the government when they buy certain things. (p. 193)

scale (skayl) a tool for measuring distances on a map. (p. 19)

scarcity (SKAYR sih tee) a situation that occurs when there are fewer resources available to produce the goods and services that people want. (p. 165)

scholarship (SKAHL ur shihp) money awarded to students to pay for school. (p. 176)

secede (sih SEED) to separate from a country and form a new nation. (p. 123)

secondary source (SEHK uhn dehr ee sawrs) an account of an event written by someone who did not witness it. (p. 178)

segregation (sehg rih GAY shuhn) the forced separation of people of different races. (p. 168)

service (SUR vihs) something that a person or a company provides for someone else. (p. 226)

siege (seej) the surrounding of a place that prevents people and supplies from entering or leaving. (p. 57)

skyscraper (SKY skray pur) a very tall building. (p. 173)

specialize (spehsh uh LYZ) a person or business makes a few goods or provides one service. (p. 245)

steel (steel) a strong metal made from iron ore. (p. 154)

strike (stryk) the refusal to work. (p. 160)

suburb (SUHB urb) a community near a city. (p. 167)

suffrage (SUHF rihj) the right to vote. (p. 161)

summarize (SUHM uh ryz) to tell the most important points of a piece of writing in your own words. (p. 190)

supply (suh PLY) the amount of a product businesses will make at different prices. (p. 227)

survive (sur VYV) to live. (p. 13)

tax (taks) money that people pay a government for services. (p. 64)

territory (TEHR ih tawr ee) a part of the United States that is not a state. (p. 81)

trade (trayd) the exchange of goods. (p. 24)

transportation (trans phr TAY shuhn) the way that people and goods move from one place to another. (p. 153)

treaty (TREE tee) an official agreement between nations or groups. (p. 47)

tribe (tryb) a group of people who share a culture, language, and history. (p. 160)

tributary (TRIHB yuh tehr ee) a river or stream that flows into another river. (p. 219)

Underground Railroad (UHN dur grownd RAYL rohd) a series of escape routes and hiding places to bring enslaved people out of the South. (p. 121)

unite (yoo NYT) to bring people together for a common purpose. (p. 89)

urban (UR buhn) of or relating to a city. (p. 154)

veto (VEE toh) to reject. (p. 187)

volunteer (vahl uhn TEER) a person who agrees to provide a service without pay. (p. 201)

voyageur (voy uh ZHUR) someone who moved furs and supplies for fur companies. (p. 44)

wages (WAY jihz) payments for work. (p. 231)

wigwam (WIHG wahm) a small house made from wood poles and covered with bark or reed matting. (p. 23)

Index

Page numbers with *m* after them refer to maps.

Abolitionists, 118, 121
**Abraham Lincoln Presidential Library
and Museum,** 142
Access Living, 177
Addams, Jane, 160, 162
African Americans, 158
civil rights movement of, 168
Civil War regiment of, 119, 129
discrimination against, 159
in leadership, 147, 169, 203
in politics, 159, 202
right to vote, 119, 131
slavery and, 120–122
World War I and, 164
World War II and, 166
Agriculture, 5, 8, 166, 167, 214, 222, 224
of Archaic Indians, 13
formation of granges, 160
Great Depression and, 165
in Great Lakes states, 230, 231
of Illinois Indians, 22, 23
in Midwest, 218, 225, 227
of Mississippian Indians, 15
new tools for, 97, 113, 114–115, 152,
154
specialization of, 245
of Woodland Indians, 14
of Mississippian Indians, 15
Aiken, Lizzie, 129
Air-traffic control system, 246
Algonquin, 2*m*
Allies
of British in War of 1812, 90
of the French, 37, 46
of Pontiac, 57
Almanac
American Indians in Illinois, 2*m*–3*m*
free and slave states in 1860, 76*m*–77*m*
immigration to Illinois, 148*m*–149*m*
North American land claims,
34*m*–35*m*
population density in US,
214*m*–215*m*
Altgeld, John P., 160
Alton, Illinois, 110, 111, 154, 158
Amendments, 101, 186
American heritage, 214, 246–247
American Indians, 3, 12, 32, 39, 41
Archaic Indians, 13, 15
Black Hawk War, 111
British land claims and, 56–57
confederation of, 79, 88–89
French and Indian War and, 46
growth of cities and, 109
Illinois Indians, 20–25
Mississippian Indians, 15
Paleo-Indians, 13, 15
Pontiac's Rebellion, 33, 54, 56–57
Proclamation of 1763 and, 35, 58, 60,
61*m*
settlers and, 110–111
Tecumseh, 74

trade of, 24, 26–27, 38, 44
Treaty of Greenville and, 81
War of 1812 and, 90–91
Woodland Indians, 14, 15
American Red Cross, 243, 248, 254
American Revolution, 64–67
Anthony, Susan B., 161
Archaeologists, 13
Archaic Indians, 4, 13, 15
Architecture, 173
Armour, Philip, 153
Armstrong, Louis, 174
Arnold, Isaac, 146
Art, 25
Artifacts, 4, 13
Art Institute of Chicago, 173
Automobile industry, 225, 226

Barnett, Ida Wells, 159
Battle of Bad Ax, 111
Battle of Fallen Timbers, 81, 89
Battle of Thames, 90
Battle of Tippecanoe, 89
Belleville, Illinois, 110, 154, 158
Bickerdyke, Mary Ann, 75, 129, 132
Bill, 183, 194
Bill of Rights, 100, 186, 193, 200
Birkbeck, Morris, 74
Black Hawk, 111
Black Hawk War, 111
Blagojevich, Rod, 194
Blagojevich, Rod, 194
Bond, Shadrach, 99, 100
Boone, Daniel, 60
Booth, John Wilkes, 130
Boston Tea Party, 54, 65
Boycott, 54, 65
Braun, Carol Moseley, 202
Bristo, Marca, 177
Brooks, Gwendolyn, 169
Buckingham Fountain, 174
Budget, 193, 195
Bush, George W., 202
Businesses, 110, 164, 165, 172, 232

Cahokia (people), 2*m*, 3, 21, 43*m*
Cahokia, Illinois, 15, 16, 17, 87
Cahokia Mounds, 2*m*, 16, 17, 18*m*
Cairo, Illinois, 128, 153, 168
Camp Grant, 166
Camp Robert Smalls, 166
Canals, 97, 109, 153, 173, 219
Capital, 99, 194
Kaskaskia, 100, 101, 110
Vandalia, 96, 101
Capitol, 193
Carmi, Illinois, 110
CCC, 165
Central Lowland, Illinois, 8
Character traits
caring, 234–237

citizenship, 162–163, 204–205
civic virtue, 248–249
courage, 84–85
fairness, 256–257
patriotism, 92–93, 132–133
responsibility, 124–125
Chase, Andrew, 153
Checks and balances system, 187
Cherokee, 3
Chicago, Illinois, 219
as a boom town, 173
civil rights movement in, 168
elevated train in, 217, 231
Great Fire in, 148, 158, 172, 178
growth of, 109, 110, 111
immigrants in, 158
museums in, 173, 174, 232
parks and recreation in, 174, 233
people in the news, 176–177
Sinclair's novel about, 160
steel industry in, 154
today, 174–175
as trade center, 81, 153, 226, 231
as transportation hub, 153, 156–157,
175, 231
World's Columbian Exposition, 151,
173
Chicago Public Library, 173
Chicago Symphony Orchestra, 174
Child labor laws, 160, 162
Chippewa, 3
Choctaw, 3
Citizens, 182, 184, 185, 186, 192,
200–201, 203
Citizenship skills
conflict resolution, 250–251
good decisions, 206–207
point of view, 126–127
reformers, 162–163
universal human rights, 256–257
volunteers, 248–249
voting rights, 204–205
City council, 195
Civic responsibilities, 193, 201, 203,
204–205
Civic rights, 186, 195, 200, 203
Civilian Conservation Corps (CCC),
165
Civil Rights Act, 168
Civil rights movement, 168
Civil War, 77, 119, 123, 128–131, 140
Clark, George Rogers, 66, 68, 69
Clark, William, 83
Climate, 13, 218, 220
Coastal Plain, Illinois, 8
Coles, Edward, 101
Colonies, 34*m*–35*m*, 38, 58*m*, 59, 61*m*,
64–67
Common good, 184, 193, 202
Communications systems, 244, 246,
255
Confederate States of America, 123,
128, 130, 131
Confederation, 79, 89
Conflict resolution, 250–251

Index

Congress of United States, 187
Consequences, 206
Conservatories, 174
Constitutional Convention, 96, 99, 102–105
Constitution of Illinois, 55, 67, 98
 amendment to, 101
 revisions of, 149, 192–193
 writing of, 99, 100
Constitution of the United States, 67, 100, 186–187, 192
Consumers, 226
Continental Army, 66
Cook, Daniel Pope, 98–99
Counties, 76m–77m
Courts, 187, 194
Cubs, 174
Culture, 20, 176–177, 246
 architecture, 173
 art, 25, 173
 diversity of, 169, 174
 of Illinois Indians, 22–25
 immigrant groups and, 150, 158
 museums, 173, 174, 232
 music, 25, 174
 traditions, 214, 246–247

 D

Daley, Richard J., 203
Dams, 219
Debs, Eugene V., 160
Decision making, 206–207
Declaration of Independence, 65
Deere, John, 113, 114, 154
DeKalb, Illinois, 154
Delegate, 96, 99
Demand, 217, 227, 228–229
Democracy, 182, 184–185, 204–205
Depression, 151, 165
Detroit, Michigan, 225, 233
Dickson Mounds, 2m, 18m
Dirksen, Everett, 168
Discrimination, 159, 168
Diversity, 174
Doctors Without Borders, 254
Dogstooth Bends Mounds, 2m, 18m
Douglas, Stephen, 122, 139

 E

East St. Louis, Illinois, 153, 168
Economics
 canoe traders, 26–27
 Chicago, economic center, 156–157
 consumers and, 226
 entrepreneurs, 175
 money, 246
 supply and demand and, 227, 228–229
 taxes, 64, 193, 195
 trade, 5, 24, 26, 27, 38, 40, 44, 46, 112, 246
Economy
 Great Depression and, 165
 industry, 113, 131, 150, 152, 153, 154, 155, 164, 165, 166, 175, 226, 231m
 jobs and, 158–159, 164, 165, 231
 of Midwest, 226–227
 slavery and, 120, 131
 supply and demand and, 227, 228–229

Edgar, James, 194
Edwards, Ninian, 78, 82, 90, 92, 93, 99
Edwardsville, Illinois, 110
Elections, 118, 122, 185, 187, 194, 204–205
 and Abraham Lincoln, 122, 138–139, 140
Elevated train, 217, 231
Ellwood, Isaac, 154
Emancipation Proclamation, 119, 130, 141
England
 American Revolution and, 54, 64–67, 68–69
 colonies of, 38, 61m
 control of Illinois, 56–57
 French and Indian War, 37, 46–47
 land claimed by, 46m, 58m
 War of 1812 and, 90–91
Entrepreneurs, 175
Environment, 6
 adaptations to, 13, 22–23, 221
 effect on humans, 10–11
 growth of suburbs and, 233
 and the Midwest, 218, 220
 pollution of, 233
 and settlers, 110
Erie Canal, 96, 109, 112
Ernst, Kathleen, 234–237
Erosion, 8, 9
Europeans
 American Revolution and, 54, 64–67, 68–69
 colonies of, 38, 61m
 control of Illinois, 56–57
 exploration of, 32, 33, 36, 37, 38–41
 French and Indian War, 37, 46–47
 as immigrants in Illinois, 148m–149m, 158, 159, 160, 162
 land claimed by, 34m, 46m, 56, 58m
 Proclamation of 1763, 54
 settlements of, 44–45, 48, 49
 trade with Indians, 24, 26–27
 War of 1812 and, 90–91
Executive branch, 187, 194
Expedition, 79, 83, 84–85
Exploration, 38
 of Jolliet and Marquette, 39
 of La Salle, 40
 of Lewis and Clark, 83

 F

Factories, 152–155, 160
 and African Americans, 158–159, 164
 and Civil War, 129
 and child labor, 160
 and Florence Kelley, 162
 and Great Depression, 165
 and immigrants, 158, 164
 in Midwest, 226
 and postwar growth, 167
 and railroads, 156–157
 and steel, 154
 and women, 164, 166
 and World War I, 164
 and World War II, 166
 See also Manufacturing.
Farming, 5, 8, 166, 167, 214, 222, 224
 of Archaic Indians, 13
 formation of granges, 160
 Great Depression and, 165

in Great Lakes states, 230, 231
 of Illinois Indians, 22, 23
 in Midwest, 218, 225, 227
 of Mississippian Indians, 15
 new tools for, 97, 113, 114–115, 152, 154
 post-war changes, 167
 specialization of, 245
 of Woodland Indians, 14
 World War II and, 166
Federal Emergency Management Agency (FEMA), 248
Federal government, 182, 184–187
Ferris, George Washington Gale, 173
Ferris Wheel, 151, 173
Field, Marshall, 146, 155
Flag of United States, 188
Flood plain, 8
Floods, 10, 219, 223, 248
Forests, 9, 224
Fort Crevecoeur, 40, 43m
Fort Dearborn, 90
Fort de Chartres, 34, 36, 40m, 41, 45, 48–49, 58–59
Fort Detroit, 57
Fort Massac, 43m, 87
Fort Sackville, 66m, 68
Fort St. Louis, 40, 43m
Fort Sumter, 123
Fox (people), 111
France
 colonies of, 38
 explorers of, 38–41
 forts of, 40–41, 48–49
 French and Indian War, 37, 46–47
 help during Revolutionary War, 66
 land claimed by, 34m, 42, 43m, 45, 46m, 58m
 sale of Louisiana Purchase, 83
 settlements of, 44–45
 voyageurs of, 36, 44
Franklin, Benjamin, 66
Free states, 100, 120–121, 122m
Freedoms, 186, 200
 of assembly, 186, 200
 of press, 186, 200
 of speech, 186, 200
 of religion, 186, 200
French and Indian War, 46–47
Fur trade, 26, 36, 38, 40, 44, 46

 G

Galena, Illinois, 110, 111, 124, 153, 158
Galena lead mines, 109
General Assembly, 99, 194
Geography
 Kaskaskia's disappearance, 10–11
 landforms, 6–7
 Mississippi River, 222–223
 regions of Illinois, 8–9
 westward expansion, 60
George III, 58
Gettysburg, Pennsylvania, 130
Glaciers, 4, 6, 7, 219
Gladwin, Henry, 57
Glidden, Joseph, 154
Government, 110
 capital of, 99
 citizens rights and responsibilities in, 200–201
 constitution and, 67, 100
 of counties and cities, 195

creation of links between regions, 245
of French settlements, 45
of Illinois state, 192–194
Northwest Ordinance, 81
reforms, 162–163
responsibilities of leaders, 202–203
trade and, 246
of United States, 182, 184–187
Governors, 78
Bond, Shadrach, 100
Coles, Edward, 101
Edwards, Ninian, 78, 82, 90, 92, 93
Harrison, William Henry, 89
responsibilities of, 193, 194
St. Clair, Arthur, 82
Stevenson, Adlai, 167
Grain elevator, 97, 113
Granges, 160
Grant, Ulysses S., 124–125, 130
Grant Park, 174
Graph and chart skills
circle graphs, 86–87
timelines, 50–51
Great Britain
American Revolution and, 54, 64–67, 68–69
colonies of, 38, 61*m*
control of Illinois, 56–57
French and Indian War, 37, 46–47
land claimed by, 34*m*, 36*m*, 46*m*, 56, 58*m*
Proclamation of 1763, 58–59, 60
War of 1812 and, 90–91
Great Depression, 165
Great Lakes, 7, 42, 109, 218, 219
effect on climate, 220
Illinois and Michigan Canal and, 112
as resource, 224
settlements near, 45
trade and, 24, 26, 43
transportation on, 153
Great Lakes Naval Training Base, 166
Great Lakes states, 219*m*, 226, 230–233
Great Plains, United States, 218

Hamilton, Alice, 163
Harlem Airport, 166
Harrison, William Henry, 89, 90
Hastert, J. Dennis, 202
Haudenosaunee, 3
Heritage, 246–247
History
Cahokia, 16–17
Fort de Chartres, 48–49
Lewis and Clark expedition, 84–85
surrender at Vincennes, 68, 69
Hodgers, Jennie, 129, 133
Hook, Frances, 129
House of Representatives, 187, 194
Hull House, 148, 160, 162
Human rights, 253, 256–257
Hunter-gatherers, 13
Hurricane Floyd, 248–249

Ice Age, 6, 12
Ice sheets, 6

Illinois, 2*m*
American Indians in, 12–15, 16, 20–25
Black Hawk War, 111
civil rights movement in, 168
in Civil War, 128–129
Constitutional Convention, 96, 99, 102–105
constitution of, 99, 100, 101, 149, 192–193
counties and population, 76*m*–77*m*
diversity in, 169
early people of, 12–15
as free state, 100, 101, 121
government of, 192–195
in Great Depression, 165
Illinois Indians in, 20–25
immigrants in, 158, 159, 160, 162
immigration to, 148*m*–149*m*
industry in, 152–155
land and water of, 6–7
natural resources of, 9
physical features, 6–9
post-war growth, 167
regions of, 8
resources of, 9
settlement of, 109–110, 112
social and labor reforms, 160–163
statehood, 96, 98–101
trade in, 26–27
World War I and, 164
World War II and, 166
Illinois and Michigan Canal, 112
Illinois Constitutional Convention, 96, 99,
"**Illinois Constitutional Convention,**" 102–105
Illinois Indians, 2*m*–3*m*, 5, 38, 39
art and music of, 25
groups and neighbors of, 20–21
life of, 22–23
trade of, 24, 26, 27
Illinois River, 2*m*, 7, 40, 109
Illinois Supreme Court, 194
Illinois Territory, 76, 79, 80–81, 82, 98
Immigrants, 148*m*–149*m*, 150, 152, 158, 159, 169, 172, 174
citizenship for, 182
Hull House and, 160, 162
World War I and, 164
Income tax, 193
Independence, 55, 65
Indiana Territory, 82, 89
Industry, 113, 231*m*
Civil War and, 131
Great Depression and, 165
lumber, 9, 154, 156–157, 224
manufacturing, 150, 152, 154, 157, 164, 165, 166, 167, 224, 226, 231
mass media, 175
meatpackers, 153, 160
in Midwest, 226
mining, 154, 160, 165, 166, 225
retail stores, 155, 174
steel, 154, 225
transportation, 153
World War I and, 164
World War II and, 166
See also Agriculture *and* Transportation.
Innovations, 151, 172
Interdependence of regions, 245

International law, 243, 253, 256
International Red Cross, 254
Internet, 244, 246, 255
Interstate Highway System, 245
Inventions, 97, 113, 114–115, 151, 152, 172, 173
Iroquois, 3

Jackson, Jesse, 168
Jarrett, Vernon, 169
Jefferson, Thomas, 65, 83, 84
Jemison, Mae, 177
Jenney, William LeBaron, 173
Jobs
African Americans and, 158–159
Great Depression and, 165
in Great Lakes states, 231
immigrants and, 158–159
World War I and, 164
World War II and, 166
Johnson, Andrew, 130
Joliet, Illinois, 111, 154, 158
Jolliet, Louis, xx, 33, 36, 39, 40*m*, 42, 43
Jones, John, 121
Jones, Mary, 121
Jones, Mary Harris "Mother," 160
Judicial branch, 187, 194
Jury duty, 201

Kane, Elias Kent, 96, 99
Kaskaskia (people), 2*m*, 3, 21
Kaskaskia, Illinois, 40*m*
British soldiers in, 59
as capital of Illinois state, 99, 100, 101, 110
as capital of Illinois Territory, 82
Clark's march on, 66
disappearance of, 10, 11
French mission at, 39
French settlements, 45
growth of, 45
population of, 87
Kaskaskia River, 2*m*, 10, 11
Kelley, Florence, 162
Kerner, Otto, 168
Kickapoo (people), 2*m*, 21
King, Coretta Scott, 212
King, Martin Luther, Jr., 151, 168
Kingston, Illinois, 154

Labor reforms, 160
Labor unions, 160
Lake Michigan, 7
Lake-effect snow, 220, *220*
Lakes, 7, 9, 219, 224
See also Great Lakes.
Land bridge, 12
Landforms, 6, 218
La Salle, Sieur de, 40
Lathrop, Julia, 162
Laws, 183, 187, 192, 193, 194
Lee, Robert E., 130
Legislative branch, 187, 194

Index

Leiter, Levi, 155
Levees, 219, 223
Lewis, Meriwether, 83
Lewis and Clark's expedition, 79, 83, 84–85
Liberty, 186
Liberty Bell, 189
Lincoln, Abraham
    Civil War and, 124
    early years, 136–137
    election of 1860, 122, 138–139
    Emancipation Proclamation and, 118, 130, 141
    legacy of, 142–143
    as politician, 122, 138–139
    as President, 123, 140–141, 202
Lincoln–Douglas debates, 139
Lincoln Memorial, 143
Lincoln Tomb, 142
Literature, 169
    "Trouble at Fort LaPointe," 234–237
    "Your Illinois," 170–171
Livermore, Mary, 129, 133
Local government, 195
Lockport, Illinois, 111
Locks, 219
Louisiana, 40, 58m
Louisiana Purchase, 83
Louisiana Territory, 84–85
Lovejoy, Elijah, 121
Lovejoy, Owen, 118, 121
Loyalists, 65
Lumber industry, 9, 154, 156–157, 224
Lyric Opera, 174

Magnificent Mile, 174
Manufacturing, 150, 152, 157, 224
    Great Depression and, 165
    in Great Lakes states, 231
    in Midwest, 226
    post-war growth, 167
    World War I and, 164
    World War II and, 166
    See also Factories.
Map and globe skills
    mapmaking, 106–107
    map skills review, 18–19
    special purpose maps, 238–239
Maps
    American Indians of Illinois, 2m–3m
    British colonies, 61m
    Clark's march through Illinois, 66m
    free and slave states in 1860, 76m–77m, 122m
    fur trade routes, 236m
    Great Lakes states industry, 231m
    Illinois and Michigan Canal, 112m
    Illinois Indians, 21m
    Illinois regions, 8m
    Illinois settlements, 45m
    Illinois Territory, 82m
    immigration to Illinois, 148m–149m
    Indiana Territory, 82m
    interstate highways in U.S., 245m
    Jolliet's of United States, 42m–43m
    Kaskaskia, 10m
    land rights in 1763, 58m
    LaPointe Island in 1732, 234m
    Lewis and Clark's expedition, 84m–85m
    of Lincoln's homes, 137m
    Midwest, United States, 219m
    Midwest farmbelts, 225m
    migration into Illinois, 109m
    mineral resources in Midwest, 238m
    mounds of Illinois, 18m
    North America in 1754, 46m
    North American land claims, 34m–35m
    Northwest Territory, 81m
    population density in U.S., 214m–215m
    railroads, 156m–157m
    routes of Jolliet, Marquette, and LaSalle, 40m
    trade routes, 24m
    transportation routes into Chicago, 156–157m
    Underground Railroad, 121m
Marietta, Ohio, 81
Market, 153
Marquette, Jacques, 32, 34, 36, 39, 40m, 42
Marshall Field and Company, 146, 155
Martin, Ellen, 161
Mascoutin (people), 21
Mass media industry, 175
Mayor, 195
McCormick, Cyrus, 115
McCormick, Robert R., 175
Meatpackers, 153, 160
Miami (people), 21
Michigamea (people), 2m, 3, 21
Michigan, 225
Midwest, United States, 219m
    agriculture in, 225
    climate, plants and animals of, 220–221
    economy of, 226–227
    land and waterways of, 218–219
    resources of, 224–225, 238m
Migration, 108–109
Military training, 166
Millennium Park, 174, 233
Mining, 154, 160, 165, 166, 225
Minnesota, 225
Missionaries, 36, 39
Missions, 39, 45
Mississippi River, 2m, 7, 8, 45, 48–49, 108, 222–223
    Civil War and, 128
    exploration of, 36, 39, 40, 42, 43m
    Illinois and Michigan Canal and, 112
    Kaskaskia's disappearance and, 10, 11
    trade and, 24, 26
    transportation on, 48
Mississippi River system, 219
Mississippian Indians, 5, 15, 16, 20
Missouri (people), 24m
Missouri River, 219
Moline, Illinois, 154
Money, 246
Morris, Nelson, 153
Mottl, Timothy, 247
Mound builders, 14–15
Mounds, 2m, 14–15, 16, 17, 18m
Mount Rushmore, 142
Murphysboro, Illinois, 154
Museum of Science and Industry, 174, 232
Museums, 173, 174, 232
Music, 25, 174

National Road, 96, 112
Native Americans, 3, 12, 32, 39, 41
    Archaic Indians, 13, 15
    Black Hawk War, 111
    British land claims and, 56–57
    confederation of, 79, 88–89
    French and Indian War and, 46
    growth of cities and, 109
    Illinois Indians, 20–25
    Mississippian Indians, 15
    Paleo-Indians, 13, 15
    Pontiac's Rebellion, 33, 54, 56–57
    Proclamation of 1763 and, 35, 58, 60, 61m
    settlers and, 110–111
    Tecumseh, 74
    trade of, 24, 26–27, 38, 44
    Treaty of Greenville and, 81
    War of 1812 and, 90–91
    Woodland Indians, 14, 15
Natural disasters, 10–11, 248–249
Natural resources, 9, 24, 154, 156, 224–225
New Deal, 165
Nongovernmental organizations (NGOs), 243, 248–249, 254
North American claims, 34m–35m
Northwest Ordinance, 81
Northwest Passage, 38, 39
Northwest Territory, 78, 81

Obama, Barack, 203
O'Hare International Airport, 175
Ohio River, 2m, 7, 8, 108, 219
O'Leary, Patrick and Catherine, 172
Ordinance, 81
Osage (people), 24m
Ottawa (people), 24m

Paleo-Indians, 2, 4, 13, 15
Palmer, Potter, 155
Parks and recreation, 174, 223, 232
Patriots, 65–67
Peoria (people), 2m, 3, 21
Peoria, Illinois, 87, 111, 154
Piankishaw (people), 21
Plains states, United States, 219m, 226
Plants, 221
Poets, 169, 170–171
Point of view, 126–127
Politicians and leaders, 124–125
    Black Hawk, 111
    Blagojevich, Rod, 194
    Bond, Shadrach, 99, 100
    Braun, Carol Moseley, 202
    Bush, George W., 202
    Coles, Edward, 101
    Cook, Daniel Pope, 98–99
    Daley, Richard J., 203
    Douglas, Stephen, 122, 139
    Edgar, James, 194
    Edwards, Ninian, 78, 82, 90, 92, 93, 99
    Franklin, Benjamin, 66
    Grant, Ulysses S., 124–125

Harrison, William Henry, 89, 90
Hastert, J. Dennis, 202
Jackson, Jesse, 168
Jefferson, Thomas, 65
Kane, Elias Kent, 99
Kerner, Otto, 168
King, Martin Luther, Jr., 168
Lincoln, Abraham, 122, 141, 202
Obama, Barack, 203
Pontiac, 33, 57
Pope, Nathaniel, 75
Reagan, Ronald, 202
responsibilities of, 202
Roosevelt, Franklin Delano, 165, 256
Rumsfeld, Donald, 202
Ryan, George, 194
St. Clair, Arthur, 82
Stevenson, Adlai, 167
Tecumseh, 74, 88–89, 90
Thompson, James, 203
Washington, George, 65
Washington, Harold, 147, 203
Yates, Richard, 129
Pontiac (Ottawa chief), 33, 57
Pontiac's Rebellion, 54, 56–57
Pope, Nathaniel, 75, 99
Population, 14
density, 214m–215m
growth of, 76m–77m, 98, 99,
108–109, 111, 112, 149
growth of cities, 110, 112
in Illinois settlements, 87
immigration and, 148m–149m, 158
Postal system, 244
Potawatomi (people), 24m
Prairie, 8, 218
Prairie du Rocher, 45, 87
Presidents, 187
Bush, George W., 202
Grant, Ulysses S., 124–125
Harrison, William Henry, 90
Jefferson, Thomas, 83, 84
Lincoln, Abraham, 122, 123, 124,
130, 131, 136–143, 202
Reagan, Ronald, 202
Roosevelt, Franklin Delano, 165, 256
Priest, Oscar Stanton de, 159
Primary sources, 178–179
account of Chicago fire, 178
Jolliet's map of North America, 42,
42m–43m
memoirs of Ulysses S. Grant,
124–125
national symbols, 188–189
Proclamation, 54, 58
Proclamation of 1763, 35, 58–59,
60–61, 90
Prophetstown, 89
Prosperity, 246
Public goods and services, 193, 195,
201
and Great Depression, 165

Quincy, Illinois, 111, 154

Railroads, 97, 112
Chicago as hub for, 156, 173, 175

Civil War and, 128
industry and, 153
reforms and, 160
refrigerated cars, 150, 153
Readers' theater
"Illinois Constitutional Convention,"
102–105
"Visit to the Capitol, A," 196–199
Reading and thinking skills
identification of cause and effect,
62–63
summarize, 190–191
Reading skills, See first page of each
lesson.
Reading strategies
monitor and clarify, 37, 97, 243
predict and infer, 5, 217
question, 79, 119, 183
summarize, 55, 151
Reagan, Ronald, 202
Reaper, mechanical, 113, 115, 152
Rebellion, 57
Reconstruction, 119, 131
Recreation, 174, 223, 224, 232
Reformers, 160–163
Reforms, 160–163
Regiment, 119, 129
Regions of Illinois, 8–9
Representative government, 185
Representatives, 185, 202–203
in federal government, 187, 202
in local government, 195, 203
in state government, 187, 203
Resources, 9
Illinois Indians use of, 24
in Midwest, 224–225
mining, 154
and national economy, 156–157
Retail stores, 155, 174
Revolutionary War, 64–67
Rights and responsibilities, 182, 184,
185, 186, 193, 200–201, 203
Rivers, 7, 9, 108, 109, 216, 219,
222–223, 224
See also Mississippi River and Ohio
River.
Roads, 244, 245
Rock Island, Illinois, 154
Roosevelt, Eleanor, 256
Roosevelt, Franklin Delano, 165, 256
Rule of law, 186
Rumsfeld, Donald, 202
Ryan, George, 194

Sable, Jean Baptiste Point du, 81
Sales tax, 193
Sauk (people), 111
Scales Mound, 2m, 18m
Schools, 110
Scott Field, 166
Sears Tower, 174
Secession, 123
Secondary sources, 178–179
Segregation, 168
Senate
of Illinois, 194
of United States, 187
Seneca, Illinois, 166
September 11, 2001 attacks, 247

Service industries, 226, 231
Settlers, 80, 81, 91, 98, 108–110, 112
and American Indians, 88, 89, 90, 111
British, 46, 56
French, 40–41, 44–45
and Illinois Territory, 82
and Proclamation of 1763, 58, 60–61
and Tecumseh, 88–89
Shawnee Hills, Illinois, 8
Shawneetown, Illinois, 110
Ship builders, 164, 166
Shipping, 112, 153, 156, 157m, 160
Siege, 57
Sinclair, Upton, 160
Sioux, 3
Skyscraper, 173
Slavery, 100, 118, 120–123
Emancipation Proclamation and, 119,
130, 141
end of, 131
Thirteenth Amendment to
Constitution and, 186
Slave states, 100, 120–121, 122m
Social reforms, 160–163
Soldiers
in Civil War, 124–125, 128–130,
132–133
in World War I, 164
in World War II, 166
South Dakota, 225
Spain, 34m, 38, 46m, 58m, 61m
Specialization, 245
Sports teams, 174, 232
Springfield, Illinois, 18m, 111, 194
Starr, Ellen Gates, 160
State government, 192–195
Statehood, 76, 81, 96, 98–101
Statue of Liberty, 188
St. Clair, Arthur, 82
Steamships, 153
Steel industry, 154, 225
Steel plow, 113, 114, 152
Stein, Kevin, 170–171
Stevenson, Adlai, 167
Stores, 155, 174
Strikes, 160
Study skills, 178–179
Suburbs, 167, 232
Suffrage, 119, 131, 147, 150, 161
Supply, 216, 227, 228–229
Supreme Court, 187
Swift, Gustavus, 153

Tamaroa (people), 2m, 3, 21
Taxes, 64, 193, 195
Technology
air-traffic control system, 246
communications systems, 244–246,
255
in farming, 114–115
and World's Columbian Exposition,
173
Tecumseh, 74, 88–89, 90
Telephone system, 244, 246, 255
Tenskwatawa, 88
Territory, 78, 81
Thompson, James, 203
Timelines, 50–51
See also first page of units and chapters,
and chapter reviews.

Tools, 5
    for farming, 113, 114–115, 152
    of Illinois Indians, 22
    of Woodland Indians, 14
Tornadoes, 220, 248
Towns and cities
    challenges to, 233
    government of, 195
    in Great Lakes states, 231*m*
    growth of, 109–110
    growth of industry and, 154
    along Mississippi River, 223
    suburbs of, 167, 232
    See also specific city by name.
Trade, 5
    Chicago as center of, 153, 156–157, 231
    European colonies and, 38
    for furs, 26, 38, 40, 44, 46
    of Illinois Indians, 24, 26, 27
    transportation and, 112, 246
    in United States, 246
Traditions, 214, 246–247
Transportation, 226
    Chicago as center of, 153, 156–157, 175, 231
    industry and, 153
    on land, 112
    as link between regions, 244
    suburban living and, 232, 233
    trade and, 112, 246
    on waterways, 112, 153, 219, 222, 224
Treaties, 37, 253
    with American Indians, 89, 111
    between British and Pontiac, 57
    at end of War of 1812, 91
    of Revolutionary War, 66
    Treaty of Chicago, 111
    Treaty of Greenville, 89
    Treaty of Greenville and, 81
    Treaty of Paris, 37, 47
Tributary, 216, 219
"Trouble at Fort LaPointe," 234–237
Trout, Grace Wilbur, 161

Underground Railroad, 121
Unemployment, 165

Union Army, 128, 129, 130
Unions, 160
United Nations, 215, 243, 252–253, 254, 256–257
United States
    Constitution of, 67, 186–187, 192
    government of, 182, 184–187
    Great Depression, 165
    growth of, 81*m*, 83
    links between regions of, 244–245
    population density in, 214*m*–215*m*
    responsibilities of leaders, 202–203
    rights and responsibilities of citizens of, 186, 193, 200–201, 203
    symbols of, 186
    trade and prosperity of, 246
    War of 1812 and, 90–91
    World War I, 164
    World War II, 166
    See also Great Lakes states; Midwest, United States; *and* Prairie states.
United States Children's Bureau, 160
United States Postal Service, 244
Universal Declaration of Human Rights, 253, 256–257
Universal human rights, 256–257

Vandalia, Illinois, 96, 99, 110
Vicksburg, Mississippi, 130
Vincennes, Indiana, 66, 68, 69
Virginia, 80
"Visit to the Capitol, A", 196–199
Volunteers, 183, 201, 247, 248–249
Voting rights, 131, 185, 186, 200, 204–205
    of African Americans, 131, 168
    of women, 147, 161
Voting Rights Act, 168
Voyageur, 36, 44

Wabash River, 2*m*, 7, 108
Wages, 231
War crimes trials, 253
War of 1812, 79, 90–91
War of Independence, 64–67

Washington, George, 60, 65, 66
Washington, Harold, 147, 203
Washington Monument, 189
Waterways, 219
Wea (people), 21
Westward expansion, 80, 108–110
    and Proclamation of 1763, 58, 60–61
    and Lewis and Clark, 83, 84–85
    and Louisiana Purchase, 83
    and Tecumseh, 88–89
    See also Settlers.
White Sox, 174
Wilderness Road, 60, 61*m*
Willard, Frances, 147, 161
Williams, Daniel Hale, 159
Winfrey, Oprah, 176
Wisconsin, 225
Women
    in Civil War, 129, 132–133
    in the news, 176–177
    in politics, 202
    suffrage for, 147, 150, 161
    World War I and, 164
    World War II and, 166
Woodland Indians, 2, 5, 14, 15
Works Progress Administration (WPA), 165
World Bank, 253
World Health Organization, 253
World's Columbian Exposition, 151, 173
World War I, 164
World War II, 151, 166
Wright, Richard, 169
Wrigley Field, 214, 232
Writers, 169

Yates, Richard, 129
Yorktown, Virginia, 66
"Your Illinois," 170–171

Acknowledgments

Permissioned Material

Excerpt from The American Girl History Mysteries Book *Trouble at Fort La Point*, by Kathleen Ernst. Copyright © 2000 by American Girl, LLC. Reprinted by permission of American Girl, LLC

Photography Credits

Authors page (b) Courtesy of the United States Mint. **v** (bkgd) PhotoDisc/Getty Images. (b) HMCo./Angela Coppola. **vi** (tl) David Muench/CORBIS. (b) Illinois State Museum. **vii** (tl) J.N. Marchand "detail"/Library and Archives Canada/C-008486. (bl) Courtesy of the Indiana State Museum. **viii** (tl) North Wind Picture Archives. (b) The Granger Collection, New York. **ix** National Portrait Gallery, Smithsonian Institute, Washington D.C., USA/Art Resource, NY. **x** (tl) Robertstock Retrofile. (b) Bettmann/CORBIS. **xi** (tl) Wilkinson Studio Photography. (b) AP/Wide World Photos. **xii** (tl) Al Fuch/NewSport/CORBIS. (b) AP/Wide World Photos. **xiii** (t) Larry Lefever/Grant Heilman Photography. (b) National Archives and Records Administration. **xvii** The Granger Collection, New York. **1** Willard Clay Photography, Inc. **2** (bl) Courtesy of the Illinois State Museum: Artsit Andy Buttram. (bc) Bettmann/CORBIS. **3** (tl) Marilyn "Angel" Wynn/Native Stock. (tr) Roger Stewart/KJA Artists **4** (cl) Theo Allofs/CORBIS. (cr) Ohio Historical Society. **5** (cl) Bettmann/CORBIS. (cr) Marilyn "Angel" Wynn/Native Stock. (b) The Historical Shop. **6** Theo Allofs/CORBIS. **7** (t) Illinois State Water Survey, 2204 Griffith Dr.,Champaign, IL 61820. (c) James P. Rowan Photography. **8** (br) Larry Lefever/Grant Heilman Photography. **9** (t) David Muench/CORBIS. **10-1** (tc) Illinois Historic Preservation Agency. **11** Lake County Discovery Museum. **12** (br) Courtesy of The Illinois State Museum, Painting by Robert Larson. **13** (t) Courtesy of the Illinois State Museum: Artist Andy Buttram. (cr) Ohio Historical Society. **14** (t) Courtesy of The Illinois State Museum. (cr) Bettmann/CORBIS. **16-7** Cahokia Mounds State Historic Site, illustration by William R. Iseninger. **19** Ray Boudreau. **20** Smithsonian American Art Museum, Washington, DC/Art Resource, NY. **21** George Catlin A'h-tee-wat-o-mee, a woman 1830 oil on canvas 29x24 inches Smithsonian American Art Museum Gift of Mrs. Joseph Harrison, Jr. ©2005 Smithsonian Institute. **22** (b) Chuck Eckert/Alamy. (bl) Marilyn "Angel" Wynn/Native Stock. (b) Bruce Leighty/Index Stock Imagery. **23** James P. Rowan Photography. **25** Courtesy of the Illinois State Museum: Drawings by Robert E. Warren and Jason Arnold, based on specimens at the Musee de l' Homme, Paris, France. **26** (br) Courtesy of Lysa Oeters/Mazer Photography. (bl) Lowell Georgia/CORBIS. **26-7** (c) Roger Stewart/KJA Artists27 (bl) Marilyn "Angel" Wynn/Native Stock. (bc) The Historical Shop. **32** (tr) John Nielson/Patrick and Beatrice Haggerty Museum of Art, Marquette University. (br) The Western Jesuit Missions Collection of The Jesuits of the Missouri Province, Saint Louis University. **33** (tl) Courtesy of the Abraham Lincoln Presidential Library, Springfield, IL. (tr) The Granger Collection, New York. (bl) Newberry

Library/SuperStock. (br) The Granger Collection, New York. **34** (bl) Richard Cummings/CORBIS. (br) Raymond Bial. **35** Canadian Institute for Historical Microreproductions. **36** (cr) Peabody Essex Museum, Salem, Massachusetts, USA/Bridgeman Art Library. (cl) Richard Cummings/CORBIS. **37** (cl) The Granger Collection, New York. (cr) Gerald Coke Handel Collection, Foundling Museum, London/Bridgeman Art Library. **38** (br) North Wind Picture Archives/North Wind Pictures Archives. **39** (tr) J.N. Marchand "detail"/Library and Archives Canada/C-008486. **41** Raymond Bial. **42-3** Newberry Library/SuperStock. **44-5** Photo by MPI/Stringer/Hulton Archive/Getty Images. **48-9** (c) Roger Stewart/KJA Artists. **51** Ray Boudreau. **54** (cl) Canadian Institute for Historical Microreproductions. (cr) Bettmann/CORBIS. **55** (cl) Pete Saloutos/CORBIS. (cr) The Granger Collection, New York. **56** Portsmouth Murals, Inc. **57** The New York Public Library/Art Resource, NY. **60** The Granger Collection, New York. **61** SuperStock, Inc./SuperStock. **63** (br) Ray Boudreau. **64** North Wind Picture Archives. **65** Bettmann/CORBIS. **66** Réunion des Musées Nationaux/Art Resource, NY. **67** National Archives and Records Administration. **68** (bl) C & D Jarnagin, Corinth, Mississippi. (br) Courtesy National Park Service, Museum Management Program and Morristown National Historical Par. (bc) American Memory Collection, Library of Congress. **68-9** Indiana Historical Bureau, State of Indiana. **70** (tc) Roger Stewart/KJA Artists. **74** (br) Lisa Podgur Cuscuna/Index Stock Imagery. (tr) The Field Museum, A114223d, Photographer John Weinstein. **75** (bl) The Granger Collection, New York. (br) National Library of Medicine. (tl) Courtesy of the Abraham Lincoln Presidential Library, Springfield, IL. (tr) Library of Congress. **76** (br) Illinois Trails History and Genealogy. (bl) Courtesy of the Abraham Lincoln Presidential Library, Springfield, IL. **77** Scala/Art Resource, NY. **78** (cr) Library of Congress. (cr) Archives and Special Collections, Dickinson College, Carlisle, PA. **79** (cl) Lewis and Clark at Three Forks, E.S. Paxson, Oil on Canvas, 1912 Courtesy of the Montana Historical Society, Don Beatty photographer 10/1999. (cr) Courtesy of the Woodland Cultural Center. **80** Bettmann/CORBIS. **83** New York Historical Society, New York, USA/Bridgeman Art Library. **84** (c) North Wind Picture Archives. (cr) North Wind Picture Archives. **85** Courtesy of the United States Mint. **87** Ray Boudreau. **88** (National Portrait Gallery, Smithsonian Institution/Art Resource, NY. **89** (tr) Delaware Art Museum, Wilmington, USA/Bridgeman Art Library. (tl) Pandamerica Corp. **90** (b) North Wind/North Wind Productions. (tr) National Portrait Gallery, Smithsonian Institution/Art Resource, NY. **92** (bc) Library of Congress, Geography and Map Divition. (br) Archives and Special Collections, Dickinson College, Carlisle, PA. (bl) North Wind Picture Archives. **92-3** Library of Congress, Washington D.C., USA/Bridgeman Art Library. **93** (all) Courtesy of the Abraham Lincoln Presidential Library, Springfield, IL. **96** (cl) Courtesy U.S. Senate Historical Office. (cr) Andre Jenny/Alamy. **97** (cl) James P. Rowan Photography. (cr) CORBIS.

98 Bettmann/CORBIS. **99** Courtesy of the Abraham Lincoln Presidential Library, Springfield, IL. **100** Courtesy of the Abraham Lincoln Presidential Library, Springfield, IL. **101** Andre Jenny/Alamy. **102** Joel W. Benjamin. **102-3** (bkgd) Roger Stewart/KJA Artists. **104** Joel W. Benjamin. **104-5** (bkgd) Roger Stewart/KJA Artists **107** Ray Boudreau. **108** (br) The Granger Collection, New York. (bl) Courtesy Conner Prairie Collection. **110** Lake County Discovery Museum. **111** The Granger Collection, New York. **112** (b) Courtesy Buck County Historical Society. **113** CORBIS. **114** (all) Deere & Company Archives. **114-5** (ZF) G. Rossenbach/Masterfile. **115** (c) The Granger Collection, New York. (tr) Image Select/Art Resource, NY. **118** (cl) 2003 History LLC, All Rights reserved. (cr) Bettmann/CORBIS. **119** Scala/Art Resource. **120** Private Collection/Bridgeman Art Library. **121** 2003 Picture History LLC, All Rights reserved. **123** Scala/Art Resource. **124** Bettmann/CORBIS. **126** Ray Boudreau. **128** CORBIS. **129** Chicago Historical Society, ICHi-22051. **130** (t) CORBIS. (br) The Strobridge Lith. Co. Cincinnati. "Abraham Lincoln and the Emancipation Proclamation." c1888. Prints and Photographs Division, Library of Congress. **132-3** (b) Wilkinson Studio Photography. (br) The Granger Collection, New York. (tl) Courtesy of the Abraham Lincoln Presidential Library, Springfield, IL. **136** (bl) Bettmann/CORBIS. (br) Library of Congress. **136-7** Bettmann/CORBIS. **137** Lloyd Ostendorf. **138** (t) Bettmann/CORBIS. (bc) James P. Rowan. (br) The Granger Collection, New York. **138-9** State Historical Society of Illinois, Chicago, IL, USA/Bridgeman Art Library. **139** (br) Stanley King Collection. (bc) Bettmann/CORBIS. **140** (cr) Abraham Lincoln: Last sitting four days before his assassination at Ford's Theater on April 14, 1865, Library of Congress. (br) Bettmann/CORBIS. (bl) Library of Congress. **141** (br) Andre Jenny/Alamy. (bl) Library of Congress. (t) Bettmann/CORBIS. **142** (b) Blain Harrington III/CORBIS. (bc) AP/Wide World Photo. **143** (c) Getty Images/Staff. (b) Gary Randall/Getty Images. **146** (cr) Bettmann/CORBIS. (br) Angelo Hornak/CORBIS. **147** (br) Mazer Photography. (cl) Print and Photographs Division, Library of Congress. (cr) Chicago Public Library, Special Collections and Preservation Division. (bl) National Council of Women, Great Britain. **148** (bl) Chicago Historical Society. (br) Courtesy of Mary Ann Johnson Private Collection. **149** Andre Jenny/Alamy. **150** (cl) CORBIS. (cr) Courtesy of the Abraham Lincoln Presidential Library, Springfield, IL. **151** (cl) PN2/Popperfoto Robertstock/Retrofile All Rights Reserved. (cr) The Granger Collection, New York. **152** Courtesy of the Wisconsin Historical Society. **154** (b) CORBIS. (tr) Library of Congress. **155** Angelo Hornak/CORBIS. **156** (br) CORBIS. (bl) Steve Terrill/CORBIS. **157** (bl) Victoria and Albert Museum, London/Art Resource, NY. **158** Courtesy of the Abraham Lincoln Presidential Library, Springfield, IL. **159** (tr) Chicago Historical Society. (bl) Courtesy of the Provident Foundation. (bl) Bettmann/CORBIS. **160** (all) Brown Brothers Sterling, PA 18463. **161** Bettmann/CORBIS.

162 (tr) Bettmann/CORBIS. (br) Brown Brothers Sterling, PA 18463. (bl) Brown Brothers Sterling, PA 18463. 162-3 Courtesy of Mary Ann Johnson Private Collection. 163 Visual Images Presentations (VIP). 164 Courtesy of the McLean County Museum of History. 165 (tl) PN2/ Popperfoto Robertstock/Retrofile. (br) Library of Congress. 166 (tc) Great Lakes Naval Museum. (tl) K.J. Historical/ CORBIS. 167 (bl) Bettmann/CORBIS. (tl) Robertstock/ Retrofile. 168 Bettmann/CORBIS. 168-9 Bettmann/ CORBIS. 170-1 Ray Mathis/EcoStock. 172 Chicago Historical Society. 173 (tl) The Granger Collection, New York. (tr) CORBIS. 174-5 Joseph Sohm/Visions of America, LLC. 175 (tl) Vito Palmisano/Getty Images. Inc. 176 Louis Gubb/CORBIS. 177 (br) Access Living, (tl) NASA. 179 Ray Boudreau. 182 (all) AP/World Wide Photos. 183 (cl) Doris De Witt/Getty Images. (cr) Photo by Craig Chamberlain, Habitat for Humanity of Champaign and Piatt Counties. 184 AP/Wide World Photos. 185 AP/Wide World Photos. 188 Artbase Inc. 189 (cl) Lee Snider/CORBIS. (tr) Artbase Inc. 191 Ray Boudreau. 192 Courtesy Illinois Trails History and Genealogy. 192-3 Doris De Witt/Getty Images.com. 193 Richard Cummings/CORBIS. 194 (tl) One Mile Up, Inc. (tc) Stock Connection Distribution/Alamy. (tr) Ingram Publishing/Alamy. 195 Gabe Palmer/CORBIS.

196-7 (bkgd) Roger Stewart/KJA Artists. 198-9 (bkgd) Roger Stewart/KJA Artists. 200 Wilkinson Studio Photography. 201 (tl) Photo by Craig Chamberlain, Habitat for Humanity of Champaign and Piatt Counties. (tr) David Young-Wolff/Photo Edit. 202 (tr) Photo by Michael Evens/The White House/Getty Images. (bl) Zack Seckler/CORBIS. 203 Ron Sachs/CORBIS. 207 Ray Boudreau. 212-3 AGEfotostock/Superstock. 214 (bl) Garry Black/Masterfile. (bc) Andre Jenny/Alamy. (br) Bernd Obermann/CORBIS. 215 Digital Vision/Getty Images. 216 (cr) Amy Etra/Photo Edit. (cl) Myrleen Ferguson Cate/PhotoEdit. 217 (cr) Artbase, Inc. (cl) David Young-Wolff/Photo Edit. 218 Garry Black/Masterfile. 221 Steve Harper/Grant Heilman Photography, Inc. 224 Al Fuchs/NewSport/CORBIS. 226 David Young-Wolff/Photo Edit. 230 Mark Segal/Getty Images. 232 Andre Jenny/Alamy. 233 Peter Christopher/Masterfile. 242 (cl) Geoff Scheerer/Pioneer Press. (cr) J. Palton/Robertstock. 243 (cl) Peter Morgan/CORBIS. (cr) Photo by Jim and Mary Whitmer. 244 (bl) Michael Macor/San Francisco Chronicle/CORBIS. 246 (cr) Jack Hollingsworth/Getty Images. (b) Artbase, Inc. 247 (cl) Bemd Obermann/ CORBIS. 248-9 (b) Reuters NewMedia Inc./CORBIS. 249 (tl) Chris Todd/Getty Images. (tr) Reuters NewMedia Inc./CORBIS. (bl) Dave Gatley/FEMA News Photo. (br)

AP/Wide World Photos. 251 Ray Boudreau. 252 Digital Vision/Getty Images. 253 AP/Wide World Photos. 254 (cl) Grothe/D.M.N./CORBIS Sygma. (bc) Photo by Jim and Mary Whitmer. (bl) Reuters, 2001. 256-7 (c) FDR Library. R0 Howard Buffet/Heilmanphoto. R0-1 Panoramic Images/Getty Images. R4 (cl) Illinois State Senate. (br) Photo by Roy Vesely, courtesy of the Chinese American Service League. R10 One Mile Up, Inc. R11 (tl) Photodisc Blue/Getty Images. (bl) Gary W. Carter/CORBIS. (tr) Tom Brakenfield/CORBIS. (br) Richard Hamilton Smith/CORBIS. (cl) Jose Manuel Sanchis Calvete/CORBIS. (cr) Photodisc Blue/Getty Images.

Map Credits

All maps created by Maps.com